LAW AND PRACTICE
OF CREDIT FACTORING

by

PETER M. BISCOE, LL.B.(HONS.), LL.M.

Barrister and Solicitor of the Supreme Court of Tasmania;
Solicitor of the Supreme Court of New South Wales

LONDON
BUTTERWORTHS
1975

ENGLAND: Butterworth & Co. (Publishers) Ltd.
           London: 88 Kingsway, WC2B 6AB

AUSTRALIA: Butterworths Pty. Ltd.
           Sydney: 586 Pacific Highway, Chatswood, NSW 2067
           Melbourne: 343 Little Collins Street, 3000
           Brisbane: 240 Queen Street, 4000

CANADA: Butterworth & Co. (Canada) Ltd.
           Toronto: 2265 Midland Avenue, Scarborough M1P 4S1

NEW ZEALAND: Butterworths of New Zealand Ltd.
           Wellington: 26/28 Waring Taylor Street, 1

SOUTH AFRICA: Butterworth & Co. (South Africa) (Pty.) Ltd.
           Durban: 152/154 Gale Street

© BUTTERWORTH & CO. (PUBLISHERS) LTD.
1975

ISBN 0 406 11850 7

CREDIT FACTORING

TO MY PARENTS

Preface

Credit factoring (or "factoring" as it is more commonly but somewhat confusingly called) is steadily becoming an integral part of English commercial life. Probably about one thousand manufacturers and distributors, and even some service companies, are factoring trade debts owed to them or have done so since credit factoring was introduced into England from America in 1960. They have sent notices of assignment to tens of thousands of other business concerns, their customers, instructing them and thereby legally binding them to pay their debts to a third party, a credit factor. The trend is towards an even greater involvement of credit factoring in commerce: the volume of factored debts continues to increase annually in value as well as in relation to the Gross National Product and the industry is gaining in acceptability as a result of its vastly improved standards and the entry of banks into the field.

My object has been to fill a literary gap: there is no other book on the law and practice of credit factoring. My hope is that it will cater adequately for the varying reference requirements of a wide range of readers: credit factors, their clients and the clients' customers; their lawyers, accountants, financial consultants, and bankers who are increasingly being required to analyse, advise on and take other action in respect of credit factoring relationships; and students who conduct research into the subject or encounter it in their courses. I base that hope on the fact that I have striven to deal with all aspects of the subject—whether commercial or legal, theoretical or practical—in roughly equal and reasonable depth. It is, of course, unwise if not foolish to regard the commercial and the legal aspects of any subject as divorced. Subject to that principle, readers concerned with commercial aspects should refer primarily to Chapters One to Four, those with legal aspects primarily to Chapters Five to Eight.

I wish to record my sincere appreciation to the following for reviewing the manuscript or proofs of the book and for offering many helpful suggestions for improvement: Roy M. Goode, Professor of Laws, Queen Mary College, London; a solicitor in the City of London with considerable professional experience of credit factoring who has had to remain anonymous; Jane R. Levine, Senior Lecturer in Law, the University of New South Wales; Roger A. Pilcher, Managing Director, Credit Factoring Limited; Frederick J. Salinger, Director, Griffin Factors Limited; and my cousin, Piers Butler, an articled law clerk. Whilst the book has benefited from their comments, I alone am responsible for any errors in fact, law or opinion. I would also like to thank Credit Factoring Limited and Griffin Factors Limited for permission to use some of their standard form documentation in the Appendices.

Law and practice are stated as at 1st February, 1975.

1st May, 1975   PETER M. BISCOE
Sydney, Australia.

Table of Contents

APPENDICES

Table of Statutes

References in this Table to "*Statutes*" are to Halsbury's Statutes of England (Third Edition) showing the volume and page at which the annotated text of the Act will be found.

List of Cases

Selected Bibliography

1 Practice

A BOOKS

Classon, Bruce D., *Commercial Credit and Collection Guide*, New Jersey, U.S.A., Prentice Hall Inc., 1968.
Credit Research Foundation Inc. (N.Y.):—
    Accountant's Report—Its Significance and Meaning to Credit Granters (1970).
    Case History of an EDP Credit Management Information System (1968).
    Cash Flow Projection—A Tool of Credit Management (1961).
    Credit Control and Administration (1971).
    Credit Department Operations: A Guide to Profits (1972).
    Credit Department Profile (1965).
    Credit Limits Established by Formula and Computer (1970).
    Handling Deductions and Disputes in Accounts Receivable (1971).
    The Implicit Cost of Trade Credit and Theory of Optimal Terms of Sale (1969).
    Marginal Accounts: Their Characteristics, Cost and Profitability (1970).
    Microfilm Systems for Credit Departments (1971).
    Practical Credit-Sales Relationships (1962).
    The Role of Trade Credit in the Flow of Funds through Manufacturing Corporations (1969).
    Trends in Cash Application and Control of Accounts Receivable (1969).
Foulke, Roy A., *The Sinews of American Commerce*, N.Y., Dun & Bradstreet, 1941.
Foulke, Roy A., *The Story of the Factor*, N.Y., Dun & Bradstreet, 1953.
Helfert, Erich A., *Techniques of Financial Analysis*, Homewood, Illinois, U.S.A., Richard D. Irwin, 3rd Edition, 1972.
Hillyer, William H., *James Talcott, Merchant*, N.Y., Charles Scribner's Sons, 1937.
Hutson, T. B., and Butterworth J., *Management of Trade Credit*, London, Gower Press, 1969.
Jones, F. H., *Guide to Company Balance Sheets and Profit and Loss Accounts*, Cambridge, England, W. Heffer & Sons Ltd., 7th Edition, 1970.
Lazere, Monroe R., *Commercial Financing*, N.Y., The Ronald Press Co., 1968.
Naitove, Irwin, *Modern Factoring*, N.Y., American Management Association, 1969.
National Association of Credit Management, *Credit Management Handbook*, Homewood, Illinois, U.S.A., Richard D. Irwin, 2nd Edition, 1965.
National Association of Credit Management, *Mathematical Approaches to Credit Management*, N.Y., 1971.
Phelps, Clyde William, *The Role of Factoring in Modern Business Finance*, Baltimore, U.S.A., Commercial Credit Co., 1956.
Phelps, Clyde William, *Accounts Receivable Financing as a Method of Securing Business Loans*, Baltimore, U.S.A., Commercial Credit Co., 2nd Edition, 1961.
Saulnier, Raymond J., and Jacoby, Neil H., *Accounts Receivable Financing*, N.Y., National Bureau of Economic Research, 1943.
Siedman, Walter S., *Finance Companies and Factors*, N.Y., National Conference of Commercial Receivable Companies, 1948.
Seidman, Walter S., *Accounts Receivable and Inventory Financing*, Ann Arbor, Michigan, Masterco Press, 1957.
Silverman, Herbert R., *From Cloth Cap Factor to the New Force in Finance*, N.Y., Neeomen Society, 1962.

B GOVERNMENT PUBLICATIONS

Report of The Committee on Consumer Credit, March 1971, Cmnd. 4596 ("The Crowther Report").

C ARTICLES

Greenberg, Robert H., "Inventory and Accounts Receivable Financing", University of Illinois Law Forum, Winter 1956.

Hillyer, William H., "Four Centuries of Factoring", The Quarterly Journal of Economics, vol. LIII, No. 2, February 1939, p. 305.

Jones, Owen T., "Factoring", Harvard Business Review, vol. XIV, No. 2, Winter 1936.

Moore, Carroll G., "Factoring—A Unique and Important Form of Financing and Service", (1959) 14 Business Lawyer, p. 703.

Shay, Robert P., and Greer, Carl C., "Banks move into High-risk Commercial Financing", 1968 Harvard Business Review, November.

Silbert, Theodore H., "Financing and Factoring Accounts Receivable", Harvard Business Review, January–February, 1952.

Silverman, Herbert R., "Factoring: Its Legal Aspects and Economic Justification", (1948), 13 Law and Contemporary Problems, p. 593.

Silverman, Herbert R., "Factoring as a Financing Device", Harvard Business Review, vol. XXVII, No. 5, September, 1949.

Steffen and Danziger, "The Rebirth of the Commercial Factor" (1936), 36 Columbia Law Review, p. 745.

Walker, Ernst W., "Factoring: Its Function and Techniques", Texas Business Review, vol. XXXIV, No. 1, January 1960.

National Commercial Finance Conference Inc. (N.Y.):—

"Accounts Receivable Division Field Audit Program" (1963).

"Auditing Procedures and Control—External and Internal" (1968).

"Automatic Data Processing Equipment for Commercial Finance Companies" (1962).

"Bulk Handling of Receivables" (1963).

"Employees' Manual on Methods and Operations" (1963).

"Fraud Prevention" (1956).

"Imaginative Solutions to Unusual Financing Situations—Case Histories" (1970).

"Methods Employed and Areas Considered in Accepting a New Account" (1965).

"Losses—The Whys and Wherefores" (1967).

"Modern Techniques for Analysing Collateral and Client Trends" (1970).

"The Ultimate Credit Decision" (1961).

Factors Chain International (Secretariat: Amsterdam, Holland):—

Speeches delivered to, by:

Bobroff, Alan H., "Internal Security", February 1971.

Dwek, Solo M., "Specific Credit Assessment and Collection Problems in Italy", December 1970.

Gunnerud, Oivind, "Sales Tools in Factoring", June 1970:—

Hohmann, Hans, "Special Problems in Germany", December 1970.

Livijn, Claes-Olof, "Advantages and Disadvantages of Factoring", June 1970.

Naitove, Irwin, "Suitable and Unsuitable Clients for Factoring", June 1970.

Pilcher, Roger A., "New Business", June 1969.

Salinger, F., "Credit Information and Credit Assessment", December 1970.

Suhl, Merrold, "Credit Information and Assessment", June 1969.

Svirsky, Rolf, "The Present Position of Factoring in Different Countries", June 1971.

Tiihonen, Jorma, "The Organization of Export–Import Factoring in a FCI Member Country", November 1970.

Vertessen, Herman, "Dunning Procedures in a FCI Member Country", December 1970.

Wessel, Hans R. V., "Organizational Structure of a Factoring Company", November 1970.

Wessel, Hans R. V., "How to Lose Less Money", February 1971.

Yates, Charles P., "Fraud Prevention", June 1969.

D ACADEMIC THESES (unpublished)

Becker, Frederick, *Factors, Their Development Practices and Financing by Banks,* 1951, Rutgers University, N.Y.
Rowley, Jean F., *A Banker's Guide to An Old-Line Factoring Service,* 1967, Rutgers University, N.Y.

2 Law

A BOOKS

Marshall, O. R., *The Assignment of Choses in Action,* London, Pitman, 1950.
Meston, M., *The Law Relating to Moneylenders,* London, Oyez Publications, 1968, 5th Edition.
Starke, J. G., Assignments of Choses in Action in Australia, Sydney, Butterworths, 1972.
Warren, W. R., *The Law Relating to Choses in Action*, London, Sweet & Maxwell, 1899.
Ziegel, Jacob S., and Foster, William F., *Aspects of Commercial Law,* N.Y., Oceana Publications, 1969; Ch. 22, "Is Article 9 of the Uniform Commercial Code Exportable: an English Reaction", by Goode, R. M., and Gower, L. C. B.

B ARTICLES

Bailey, S. J., "Assignment of Debts in England", (1931) 47 L.Q.R. 516–535, (1932) 48 L.Q.R. 248–271, 547–582.
Firth, E. C. C., "The Rule in *Dearle* v. *Hall* (1895)" 11 L.Q.R. 337.
Glenn, Garrard, "Assignments of Choses in Action; Rights of Bona Fide Purchaser", 20 Virginia Law Review 621 (1933–34).
Pisar, Samuel, "Legal Aspects of International Factoring, An American Concept Goes Abroad", 25 The Business Lawyer 1505 (July 1970).

Part One: Practice

CHAPTER ONE

What is Credit Factoring?

"Another subsidiary of the second defendants are (X) Ltd., who carry on the business nowadays somewhat confusingly called factoring . . .": Hamilton Finance Co., Ltd. v. Coverley, Westray, Walbaum and Tosetti, Ltd. and Portland Finance Co., Ltd.[1] *per* Mocatta, J.

"Particularly in the social sciences, we must watch out for the tyranny of words. The world is complicated enough without causing further confusions and ambiguities because . . . the same one word is being applied to two quite different phenomena": Samuelson, *Economics*.[2]

1 Definition

Credit factoring may be defined as a continuing legal relationship between a financial institution (the "factor"), and a business concern (the "client") selling goods or providing services to trade customers (the "customers") whereby the factor purchases the client's book debts either without or with recourse to the client, and in relation thereto controls the credit extended to customers and administers the sales ledger.

It is apparent from this definition that credit factoring is concerned with debts due from traders as opposed to consumers[3], and has four functions:

(*a*) Sales ledger administration
(*b*) Credit control, including collections
(*c*) Credit protection (when without recourse to the client)
(*d*) Finance

The primary collection device is notice of assignment endorsed on invoices directing customers to pay the factor.

Common adjunctive activities are sales analyses services to, and supplementary financing of, clients, usually to meet seasonal or temporary requirements.

The general rule is that all debts are sold to one factor, but it is not uncommon (i) for a client who sells domestically and abroad to factor only domestic or only export debts because one or the other is the only

---

[1] [1969] 1 Lloyds Rep. 53, at p. 58.
[2] 1967, McGraw-Hill, N.Y., 7th Edn., p. 8.
[3] See p. 29, *post.*

category either acceptable to the factor or which the client wishes to factor; and (ii) for certain debts which are unsuitable for factoring to be excluded at the factor's insistence. Other exceptions to the general rule are very rare because they tend to diminish the benefits of factoring, but they could occur in the following circumstances. First, specified debts may be excluded at the client's insistence on the ground that they are so safe, easy to control and administer that there is no inducement to factor them. Secondly, in America, although not yet in England, debts are occasionally divided between two or more factors, probably on an alphabetical basis, where either (i) the client insists in order to keep the factors on their toes competitively; or (ii) the client is so big that the purchase of all its debts represents an unacceptably large exposure for one factor. Obviously, when exceptions are made, the debts factored, when viewed in isolation from the debts excluded, have to represent an attractive proposition for the factor.

While it is quite usual and probably more convenient in loose discussion to talk of the factor providing "services" this is legally inaccurate. The typical factoring agreement does not purport to be an agreement for the provision of services but an agreement for the purchase of debts. Conceptually, the factor is servicing his own debts for his own benefit. This, of course, has the same effect as providing services because the client by selling the debts is relieved of the necessity of servicing them or obtaining services in respect of them. But, strictly, factoring does not provide services but, rather, has certain effects or functions. Only its adjunctive activities can accurately be described as services.

2   Credit Factoring Distinguished from other Kinds of Factoring

"Credit factoring" is usually described simply as "factoring", and, for the sake of brevity, the shorter expression "factoring" will be used, context permitting, throughout this work to describe credit factoring, except where otherwise indicated. The object of using the term "credit factoring" at all is to avoid confusion by giving the activity a label by which it can be readily distinguished from the strict legal and many popular meanings of "factoring".[4] In strict legal parlance, a "factor" is a mercantile agent who in the ordinary course of business is entrusted with the possession of goods or the documents of title thereto for the purpose of sale.[5] In this legal sense, a "factor" is one of the two main classes of mercantile agent, the other being the broker who performs

---

[4] Irwin Naitove may have attempted to do the same thing in entitling his book on credit factoring *Modern Factoring* (1969, American Management Association, New York).

[5] See 1 Halsbury's Laws of England (3rd Edn.), para. 362 (not reproduced in fourth edition); but note pp. 143–144, *post*.

the same functions but without being put in possession of the goods or documents of title.[6]

As we shall see in Chapter Two, the factor in this strict legal sense is the direct forebear of the credit factor: it is, therefore, for historical reasons that the expresson "factor" is also commonly used to describe a credit factor. However, it is unfortunate that a totally different description has not evolved because, as Mocatta, J. perceived and Professor Samuelson explained in the respective quotations at the commencement of this Chapter, confusion is inevitable when the same word is used to describe different phenomena.

The confusion will be compounded if "factor", in the sense of credit factor, is not also carefully distinguished from the many popular usages of the term. These were canvassed by Lord Stowell 150 years ago in *The Matchless*[7]

> 'The word 'factor' is not a term of the Civil Law; it is not to be found in the language in which that system of laws is written. I believe it has a French origin in the word "facteur' and, in common parlance, it continues in a sense of great latitude to signify any agent whatever. In the northern district of this island, it is very generally applied to land-stewards, bailiffs, and managers of estates. . . . In seaport towns, where there are great manufactories, besides the great manufacturers themselves, there may be factors to export upon commission: a very great part of the commerce of this great town is conducted on foreign goods imported, and our own manufactures to be exported. But I take the real and established distinction in our statutes to be that a merchant buys and sells for his own direct mercantile profit, and the factor only buys or sells upon commission. . . . To be a factor, he must be empowered to sell by commission; and if not so empowered, he is not a factor, whatever else he may do."

It does seem that there is a less obvious Latin root in the verb *"facere"*, meaning "to do" (hence "factor", one who does things on behalf of another) which precedes the French origin which his Lordship gave to the word. Perhaps the many popular uses of the term arose from a confusion with the word *"factotum"* (Latin *facere totum,* to do everything required), one who does all sorts of services for his employer.

Even the meaning of "credit factoring" has not always been constant. Until 1960 credit factoring did not exist outside North America. In the United States, the prevailing view until 1960 was that assumption of the credit risk by the factor and notice of assignment to customers were both essential elements.[8] However, credit factoring with recourse to

[6] See *Baring* v. *Corrie* (1818), 2 B. Ald. 137, *per* Holroyd, J.; *Re Henley, Ex parte Dixon* (1876), 4 Ch.D. 133 (C.A.), *per* Brett, J. A., at p. 137.
[7] (1822) 1 Hag. Adm. 97, at p. 101.
[8] See, for example, Phelps, *The Role of Factoring in Modern Business Finance* (1956, Commercial Credit Co., Baltimore), pp. 9, 14; Moore, "Factoring—A Unique and Important Form of Financing and Service", (1959) 14 Bus. Law 703.

the client has existed in Canada since 1951, and in England and other countries since the early 1960s. Further, in America itself, confidential non-recourse factoring has been practised since the early 1960s. In this facility, notice of assignment is not given to customers and the factor's function is limited to credit advice and assumption of the credit risk. This facility must not be confused with the species of receivables (i.e. trade debt) financing commonly called "invoice discounting", which, in recent years, has often, wrongly, been called confidential factoring.[9]

3   The Credit Factoring Family Tree

A   SPECIES: NON-RECOURSE (OLD-LINE) AND RECOURSE

Factoring may be divided into two species:

> non-recourse (or old-line)
> recourse

A synonym for non-recourse factoring is "old-line" factoring. This curious expression was originally coined in America some decades ago to distinguish true factors from receivables financiers who were causing confusion by describing themselves as factors. The expression's intrinsic defect is that it is not self-explanatory, but, on the other hand, there is less of a tendency to stutter if the expressions "old-line" and "recourse" are used, rather than "non-recourse" and "recourse".

In non-recourse, or "old-line", factoring, the factor assumes the credit risk on debts which it approves. The "credit risk" means the risk that the customer will be financially unable to pay. If the customer fails to pay for any reason other than financial inability, the old-line factor has recourse to the client. In recourse factoring, although the debt is assigned to the factor, the credit risk remains with the client, to whom the factor has recourse if the customer fails to pay for any reason.

Each species of factoring may be applied to domestic and/or international trade.

Recourse factoring is a hybrid between old-line factoring and invoice discounting. Which one it bears a closer resemblance to is a moot point. Recourse factoring resembles old-line factoring in that, with the exception of assumption of the credit risk, it has the same functions. However, its non-financial functions—credit control (including collections) and sales ledger administration—distinguish it from invoice discounting as it has traditionally been conducted, that is, as a purely financial facility without any non-financial element. On the other hand, the fact that the credit risk remains with the client makes recourse factoring comparable with invoice discounting. If the view is taken, as it generally is in America, that the cardinal ingredient of "factoring"

[9] For the distinction between factoring and invoice discounting, see pp. 24–27, *post.*

is assumption of the credit risk by the factor, the inevitable conclusion is that "recourse factoring" is a misnomer and that it should be re-classified as "invoice discounting with services", or the like. Recourse factoring does not exist in the United States: there, only old-line factoring and invoice discounting (or "receivables financing" as they call it) are practised. It is entrenched in Canada and in a number of European countries and the general view outside America is to accept it as a species of factoring. One sympathises with the purist's objection to the classification of recourse factoring as factoring, but there comes a time when it is impractical to try and turn back the clock and expunge words from the (non-American) vocabulary. Consequently, in this book, recourse factoring is accepted, with some misgivings, as a species of factoring. Provided it is clearly understood that recourse factoring differs in a crucial respect from old-line factoring in that it does not pass the credit risk to the factor, no confusion should arise and those encountering the word "factoring" being used without qualification will be careful to ascertain precisely whether it refers to the old-line or recourse species.

B   SUB-SPECIES: ADVANCE AND MATURITY

Old-line and recourse factoring may each be divided into two sub-categories, commonly called:

>   maturity factoring
>   advance factoring

Old-line maturity factoring means that the purchase price for pur-chased debts is paid either on what is usually called their maturity date, or on collection, depending on the arrangement; or, sometimes, on the earlier insolvency of the customer. Recourse maturity factoring means that the purchase price is paid on collection. The "maturity date" does not mean the due date but the estimated actual collection date which in most industries is considerably later than the due date. This is calcu-lated at the outset of factoring by reference to the client's historical sales ledger experience and periodically adjusted thereafter to reflect any change in the average collection period—which is likely since factoring tends to accelerate cash flow. Often, for administrative convenience, the maturity dates of all debts purchased in a month are averaged and the resultant date is called the "average maturity date".

In both old-line and recourse advance factoring, the factor pays for debts in advance of their average maturity date or collection, as required by the client. Very often the payments are made upon assignment. Normally, such advance payments are limited to about 80 per cent of the value of the debts, although a higher percentage may be paid to meet seasonal or other temporary needs. Some factors contract to pay a specified percentage in advance while others follow the American practice of reserving an absolute discretion as to the amount, if any, of advance payments. The object, in either case, is to provide the factor with security for any claims or defences which customers may raise against the client in respect of approved debts and for any risk of non-payment in respect of unapproved debts. The balance of the purchase price is known as the client's equity or the factor's reserve and should appear in the client's balance sheet as "amount due from factor", as should the unpaid purchase price in maturity factoring.

It should be clear from the foregoing that the term "advance" is not used here to describe a loan for this would run foul of the Moneylenders Acts 1900–1927, which factors are anxious to avoid,[10] but, rather simply to describe the fact that a portion of the purchase consideration is paid in "advance" of the average maturity date or collection. An obscurity in some agreements is that they are silent as to when the balance of the purchase price of a particular debt is paid but instead stipulate that the purchase consideration will be credited to the client's current account and that the factor will make advance payments against the credit balance in the account subject to the aforesaid discretion or the aforesaid maximum percentage. From the accounting viewpoint, this is convenient because advance payments can be viewed globally against total debts purchased and outstanding less debits, but conceptually it seems to detract from the purchase concept and hints of a revolving loan against the security of an assignment of debts which would be subject to the restrictive provisions of the Moneylenders Acts 1900–1927, which, however, are shortly to be repealed by the Consumer Credit Act 1974.

Maturity factoring is designed for clients with substantial equity capital who have the financial strength to satisfy their financing requirements on an unsecured basis from banks or other financial institutions but require the non-financial aspects of factoring. At present, a minor but nevertheless significant and increasing portion of old-line factoring is being conducted on a maturity basis. Recourse maturity factoring, on the other hand, is very rare.

C   REFINEMENTS: BANK PARTICIPATION, SUPPLIER GUARANTY (DROP SHIPMENT), CONFIDENTIAL

Old-line factoring may be refined in three ways and the resultant facilities may be called:

> bank participation factoring
> supplier guaranty (or drop shipment) factoring
> confidential factoring

---

[10] The present situation with regard to the Moneylenders Acts is discussed in Chapter 8, *post*.

(*i*) Bank participation factoring

The object of bank participation factoring is to enable the client's bank to lend more to the client than it would otherwise be able to based on the client's balance sheet and profits. The arrangement is that the bank takes a floating charge over the client's equity, that is, the amount due from factor to client for purchased debts; the factor, with the client's agreement, undertakes to pay all sums into the client's bank account and to inform the bank periodically, perhaps daily, of the current client's equity; and the bank lends to the client against this equity. Factoring is on a maturity basis where the bank is to provide all the financing. However, the financing may be shared by the factor: for example, the factor makes advance purchase payments of 50 per cent. of the value of purchased debts, and the bank lends against the security of the client's 50 per cent. equity. In either case, the amount of the bank's loan is normally expressed as a specified amount rather than as a percentage of the client's equity.

The amount of a bank loan under such an arrangement is greater than it could otherwise be, because the bank is lending on the basis of (*a*) the fact that the factor is policing the debts through sales ledger and credit control including collections, and (*b*) the factor's credit strength since the varying credit responsibility of a host of customers is replaced by that of the factor, normally a debtor of undoubted credit strength.

The attractions of bank participation factoring (*a*) for the bank are that it enables the bank to increase its lending business and to forge a closer relationship with small and medium businesses which may well grow into important banking customers; (*b*) for the factor are that it enables him to eliminate or reduce the risk of loss inherent in advance factoring and to increase his overall return on funds employed, while having little effect on net income since factoring profits are derived largely from the factoring charge which is not directly related to financing; (*c*) for the client are that the security of the arrangement may enable the bank to lend to it at a higher level and possibly at a cheaper interest rate than it would otherwise command and/or than the factor's discount equivalent under advance factoring, and the arrangement enables it to continue its banking relationship on a closer basis which may stand it in good stead in the future.

Assuming the factor's credit strength is undoubted, the bank's security for its loan is very attractive. Nevertheless, the client's equity can be diluted, even, in extreme circumstances, to the point where it disappears. The astute bank lending officer should therefore regularly (perhaps once a month) check the following dilution matters with the factor:

Debts at the client's risk. These represent deliveries or shipments made without the factor's credit approval. In other words, the factor's opinion, based on investigation, is that the credit risk is unduly high and deliveries or shipments should not have been made. If the risk should eventuate, the client must absorb the loss; the bank's security is diminished; and, if the amount is significant relative to its financial strength, the client's solvency may be prejudiced.

Dilutions to debts, that is, occurences which reduce their value. In this category fall disputes, credits, discounts taken, allowances and returns.

Fraud. If the client commits a fraud, such as phony debts or deliberately delaying reporting credits and disputes, the value of debts will be overstated in the factor's books. The factor's policing procedures are designed to minimise the fraud risk, but occasionally a fraud is not discovered until after an advance is made.

Factor's efficiency. An inefficient factor may not have current information concerning the status of factored debts due to delay in posting or recording items. The bank lending officer's best method of obtaining an impression of efficiency is to meet and assess the ability of the factor's management and to visit the factor's premises to study procedures and controls at first hand.

(ii)   *Supplier guarantee (or drop shipment) factoring*

Supplier guarantee factoring (also called drop-shipment factoring) may be used where the client's suppliers deliver goods sold to the client direct to the client's customers, that is, where the client is a distributor who buys and sells as principal but has no warehouse facilities. The factor guarantees that he will pay the supplier the amount due from client to supplier in respect of each such sale out of the amount due from factor to client. The object of the guarantee is to facilitate the client's lines of credit from its suppliers. The factor therefore receives a copy of the supplier's invoice as well as the client's invoice plus proof of delivery. The difference in the selling prices on the two invoices is the client's gross profit on the transaction and is paid by factor to client less the factor's charges.

Supplier guaranty factoring is conducted on a maturity basis where supplier's terms are at least as long as the customer's historical payment period, as, for example ,where a supplier sells on terms of net 90 days, the clients sells on terms of net 60 days, and customers pay in 30 days or less. It has to be conducted on an advance basis where this is not the case. For example, if the supplier's terms are net 90 days, the client's terms are net 60 days and customers generally pay 45 days slow, the factor would make an advance purchase payment in the amount of the supplier's receivable on the date it matured for payment, charge the client factor's discount on the advance from the date it was made to the agreed maturity date of the customer's receivable, and remit the balance of the purchase price to the client on the latter date. Supplier guaranty factoring has rarely been used outside North America.

(*iii*) *Confidential factoring*

When notice of assignment is not given to customers so that the client collects the receivables but the factor carries out the credit advisory function and assumes the credit risk, the facility is termed confidential factoring. This is a new and still rare American development which, reportedly, has been used in England on isolated occasions but not recently. Generally, it is conducted on a maturity basis with the client administering the sales ledger and advising the factor of prior ledger experience with the customer when submitting orders for approval. Where it is conducted on an advance basis, it is prudent for the factor to administer the sales ledger and to require the client to collect the receivables as the factor's agent and to remit them *in specie* to the factor as they are collected.

4 Benefits

The benefits of factoring lie in its ability to overcome certain problems which are typically encountered by medium and small businesses: restricted expansion due to limited financial resources, credit expertise and efficiency, and vulnerability to bad debt losses. If none of these problems exist, it is doubtful that factoring has much to offer. Where they do exist there is an advantage in factoring provided the factor is efficient and responsible and the benefits outweigh the cost.

A   NON-FINANCIAL FUNCTIONS

Four benefits flow from factoring's non-financial functions:

      (i) credit security
      (ii) improved efficiency (including accelerated cash flow)
      (iii) more management time for production, sales and planning
      (iv) higher credit standing

(*i*) *Credit security*

The ugly cloud of bad-debt losses hovers over every business trading on credit, threatening a deluge in which it may either drown or emerge severely sodden. Many would say that herein lies the most important benefit of factoring: it is a dam guarding a client from the flood through effective credit control, and, in the case, of old-line factoring where the factor assumes the credit risk, it is a lifeboat carrying the client to safety should the dam of preventative measures burst. Recourse factoring, by contrast, has no lifeboat, an important omission in rough seas.

The 100 per cent. credit protection flowing from the factor's approval of a debt means that the client's profit margin is fully protected in contrast to conventional credit insurance where 80–90 per cent. cover is the usual maximum. At one time, it was popular to think that the old-line factor had little to offer in the way of security to the firm with blue-chip customers, but the fairly recent demise by liquidation of some notable "blue-chip" companies has cast doubt on this premise.

Credit security also has a psychological impact on management since the elimination of worry over bad debts changes the complexion of doing business and is generally conducive to a good night's sleep.

(ii)   Improved efficiency (including accelerated cash flow)

Efficiency paves the way to profits. It is for this reason that as firms become large enough, they invariably develop specialised credit, collection and sales ledger departments in order to avoid or minimize bad debt losses, accelerate cash flow, ensure the availability of current information and analyses, and eliminate delays and wastage of man hours. Such large firms do not usually need a factor because they have resources and economies of scale to develop such specialization internally at a reasonable cost.

The resources of medium and small sized firms, on the other hand, are usually much more limited and priority has to be given to production and sales with the result that other areas can be and often are neglected. Further, managers of these firms are typically entrepreneural types: technicians and salesmen, often with imaginative ideas, good products and plenty of energy, but not otherwise noted for their business ability. This is not so much a criticism as a comment on the fact that every business has several facets, each requiring expertise if the business is to be a success. As a factor lacks the technical expertise to be a successful widget manufacturer, a small or medium sized widget manufacturer lacks the factor's expertise in the credit control and sales ledger areas. The combination of lack of resources and of skill in these areas means inefficiency is usually present and often rife.

Factoring is designed to put such firms on the same level of efficiency in the credit control and sales ledger areas as the most sophisticated large company. It can do this, at a reasonable cost, because a well established factor is like a gigantic credit, collection and sales ledger department serving many firms, with a high degree of specialization and economies of scale and using a basically standardized system for all clients. Ideally, factoring personnel are skilled in their field; sophisticated computers and business machines are used; comprehensive current credit information is maintained; and streamlined work flow systems are operative. Thus, intelligent, informed credit decisions can be made; statements and reminders dispatched in a timely manner;

efficient collection efforts generated; and current, clear sales ledger records and analyses maintained. Constant availability of the factor's management for consultation, on an informal basis, with respect to business problems generally means that business decisions are likely to be sounder. Finally, budgeting is more reliable, because the cost of running credit, collection and sales ledger departments crystallises into a fixed percentage of sales turnover, since this is the way that the factoring charge is always expressed. The cost can therefore be forecast exactly, unlike a non-factoring situation where these costs can be difficult to predict.

(iii)   More management time for production, sales and planning

Despite delegation of responsibility, it is inevitable that a certain proportion of management time is diverted from production, sales and planning into sales ledger credit and collection work. Large companies, can, of course, afford specialized managers, whose whole time is spent in these areas, but small businesses usually cannot so their management take time off from production and sales to tend to these matters. Factoring releases management from these chores and channels their time and energy back into production, selling and planning. Since, in the absence of adverse economic conditions, lack of resources or poor management, time and energy bear a direct correlation to results, this should produce a larger sales volume. Net profit should not only be larger than before but also greater as a percentage of sales, following the principle that once fixed costs have been covered by break-even sales, the net profit rise is proportionately higher than an increase in sales volume.

(iv)   Higher credit standing

A higher credit standing assures a more reliable flow of merchandise from suppliers, facilitates bank and other financing, and lowers interest rates on borrowed funds. There are four reasons why a client's credit standing should improve, although only two of these apply to recourse factoring.

First, in the case of old-line factoring, the factor's undoubted credit responsibility (we speak here of factors with impeccable ownership, as is the case with most factors) is substituted, by virtue of assumption of the credit risk, for that of customers of varying degrees of credit strength. Naturally, the more cash standing to the client's credit with the factor (i.e. the larger the client's equity in factored receivables) the better as far as the client's trade and other creditors are concerned; hence, they find maturity factoring more attractive than advance factoring.

Secondly, the astute credit analyst will know that the depth of analysis which the responsible factor conducts before accepting a client makes it reasonably certain that the client is a viable concern, and that this viability has been bolstered as a result of the support rendered by factoring. The lingering notion held by some people that factoring is a rescue operation for firms in distress stems from the early days, before the takeover of the industry by the banks, when factoring was certainly sometimes conducted along these lines, but today it is a mistake to think that any responsible factor acts in this fashion.

Thirdly, in the case of old-line factoring, the bad debt reserve may be eliminated, improving the balance sheet value of receivables, and, consequently, the current and liquid ratios.

Finally, if the client's profits increase as a result of factoring, its tangible net worth will increase directly if they are retained, and indirectly by a likely rise in the price/earnings ratio of its equity enabling equity to be sold at a higher price.

B FINANCE

Accounts receivable may be "liquid" or "quick" assets, but until such time as they are paid they are effectively frozen. Advance factoring provides a thaw. Under this arrangement, the client receives up to an agreed percentage of the value of receivables, usually about 80 per cent., at any time after they are assigned to the factor. The profitable uses to which the accelerated cash flow may be put include reduction of costs and expenses, acceleration of expansion and financing acquisitions. Raising finance in this manner also has the advantages of avoidance of dilution of equity, avoidance of increased debt, increased credit strength, and increased return on capital.

(i) *Reduction of costs and expenses*

Opportunities to cut costs and expenses—such as taking suppliers' prompt payment and quantity discounts, and purchasing more efficient machinery and cut-price stock and equipment—can be tantalisingly obvious yet remote because finance is not available to utilise them. In many cases, the saving which utilisation of these opportunities will produce outweighs the costs of factoring.

An example which often startlingly proves the point is the taking of prompt payment discounts. The offering of prompt discounts is a well-established practice in many manufacturing and wholesaling industries. A prompt payment discount is an optional premium which the seller offers the buyer in return for payment within a shorter period of time. The rates offered vary between industries, which seems to be the result of historical accident, but they are nearly always so far in excess of current interest rates that their economic justification must rest solely on the advantages accruing to the seller from the benefits derived from acceleration of working capital turnover. The following table shows the interest rate equivalent (decimal points excluded) of prompt payment discounts, i.e. the effective interest which a buyer is paying on the value of purchases by not taking the prompt payment discount:

1%	10 days, net 30 days	–	18% per annum
2%	10 days, net 60 days	–	14% per annum
2%	30 days, net 60 days	–	24% per annum
2%	10 days, net 30 days	–	36% per annum

The formula is:

$$\frac{365}{\text{number of days between cash discount period and net credit period}} \times \frac{\text{prompt payment discount}}{1}$$

If base rate is 10 per cent. and factoring finance costs 3 per cent. over, i.e. 13 per cent. the saving to a client whose suppliers' discounts fall within the above range, is from 5 per cent to 23 per cent. per annum.

(ii) *Accelerating expansion*

The firm whose capital, either alone or as a basis for obtaining unsecured credit, is inadequate to support its potential rate of expansion, needs, but cannot finance, more plant, machinery, equipment, space, staff and perhaps, product development and diversification. Consequently, despite a brimming actual or potential order book its sales and profits are curtailed. Factoring finance can release this brake on expansion.

(iii) *Financing acquisitions*

Financing takeovers and mergers through factoring is not an area which has been much explored to date in England, but it is not an uncommon practice in America. Particularly attractive benefits flow to the prospective client, because, before the factor will agree to this course, he will assess *pro-forma* financial statements of the merged firms to test whether the resultant balance sheet and profit ratios are adequate to support factoring and will generally provide counsel on the intended acquisition. This will be done at no cost to the prospective client but is part of the assessment of the suitability of the factoring proposition and the only reward to the factor is the obtaining of a new client in the event that the factor satisfies himself as to the merits of the case. Such financing would probably have to be confined to the purchaser's debts because factoring the acquiree's debts for such a purpose may be prohibited by section 54 of the Companies Act 1948.

(*iv*) *Avoidance of dilution of equity*

One way of raising finance is to sell shares. However, access to the capital markets is often a problem to the small and medium-sized firm, and even if new shareholders can be found, there are significant disadvantages in the sacrifice of a portion of future profits and reduction or even loss of control. For the medium and small company, which is typically closely held and often a family concern, these consequences are likely to be particularly unattractive, and factoring finance can be an appealing alternative.

(*v*) *Avoidance of increased debt*

Unsecured loans equivalent in amount to 80 per cent. of debts outstanding, the typical factoring advance payment, are usually unavailable to a client from other sources on the basis of the balance sheet and profit criteria on which such loans are normally made. Even if loans of comparable levels and at comparable rates are available, they have three inherent deficiencies compared to factoring finance:

> they weaken the client's balance sheet whereas factoring finance, being consideration for the sale of an asset, and not a loan, has the opposite effect (as is explained in the next section), despite the fact that the debtors asset on the balance sheet is reduced. However, in the case of recourse factoring a contingent liability should be noted in the balance-sheet footnotes;

> repayment schedules must be planned for and met whereas factoring finance is self-liquidating;

> long-term debt agreements, in particular, usually contain inconvenient and restrictive covenants, such as maintenance of liquidity ratios at certain levels, and commitment fees on available funds regardless of usage. Clauses such as these are not found in factoring agreements currently in use.

(*vi*) *Improved credit standing*

Credit strength can improve in two ways. First, where the accelerated cash flow is used to pay trade suppliers on a prompt or discount basis, credit standing will improve because the customer's payment record is one of the most important criteria of credit responsibility investigated by trade suppliers when extending credit.

Secondly, utilisation of the funds released can improve the balance sheet position by raising the current ratio, as the following example illustrates:

CLIENT'S BALANCE SHEET

Before Factoring Current Assets	£	*After Factoring* Current Assets	£
Cash	10,000	Cash	10,000
Debtors	150,000	Due from factor	30,000
Stocks	90,000	Stocks	100,000
	£250,000		£140,000
Current Liabilities		*Current Liabilities*	
Bank loan	10,000	Bank loan	10,000
Creditors	170,000	Creditors	80,000
Taxes	10,000	Taxes	–
Other	10,000	Other	–
	£200,000		£90,000

Current ratio: 1·25:1   1·55:1

The change in the balance sheet shows that the client received £120,000 in cash from the factor and used it to more than halve creditors in order to improve credit standing with suppliers and to take advantage of prompt payment discounts; to halve other current liabilities; and to add to stocks in order to meet increasing orders. The current ratio improved from 1·25 to a more acceptable 1·55. It is true that at the same time the liquid ratio declined from 0·8 to 0·44, but, in view of the markedly lower level of current liabilities and the protection afforded by the high current ratio, this should be no cause for concern.

Advance factoring will not, however, improve the client's balance sheet strength as much as maturity factoring where debts of varying quality, according to the financial strength of customers who owe them are replaced *in toto* by one debt due from the factor, normally a debtor of undoubted credit strength. Provided current liabilities are being retired satisfactorily, the larger the client's equity, that is the credit balance due from factor, the more advantageous the position of unsecured creditors because this is evidence that the client's liquidity is adequate without the need to draw down available funds from the factor, and that there are substantial quick assets available in the event of the client's liquidation.

(vii) *Increased return on Capital*

If a client offers credit terms of net 30 days and his customers pay on average 30 days slow, his trade debts are turning over six times per year. In other words, every pound of working capital tied up in debts is available for reuse through conversion to cash only six times per year.

With factoring finance on the basis of 80% of the value of the debts, 80% of the debts therefore take no days to turn over and are equivalent to sales for cash. Taking into account the 20% which is not paid over immediately, the debts on average take only 12 days to turn over, i.e. they turn over more than 30 times per year. This results in improved profitability through a better return on capital, either because of a greater volume of business on the same amount of capital, or the same amount of business on a smaller amount of capital.

(*viii*)   *Flexibility*

Factoring provides a remarkably flexible form of financing. In the first place, availability is directly geared to sales, normally up to about 80 per cent. thereof, without any ceiling as to amounts, so that as sales increase so does availability without the inconvenience and delay of negotiating new limits, as with most other types of financing. Indeed, by this formula, the amount of funds available can be well in excess of net worth whereas bank lending is invariably limited to a conservative percentage of net worth. Secondly, the extent to which the availability is utilised is entirely up to the client. As stated earlier, there is no commitment fee on unused available funds. This flexibility is particularly useful to meet occasional but healthy problems such as financing extra machinery, storage facilities, or stock to meet a big order, for the client need not draw down any funds ordinarily yet knows that the funds are always available to meet these special situations.

5   International Credit Factoring

For the United Kingdom, foreign trade is a life-line. The nation's high level of industrialization and standard of living necessitate major imports of resources which it lacks—raw material, food and luxury items—while exports are essential to maintain the balance of payments and to contribute to the growth of the Gross National Product. In fact, international trade is relatively more important to the United Kingdom than it is for many other industrialized countries.

International factoring is designed to eliminate the risks and the credit control, sales ledger and financial problems of international trade. It is convenient to consider international factoring under two headings: export factoring and import factoring.

A   EXPORT FACTORING

The credit control, sales ledger and financing problems which are faced in domestic trading are usually magnified in exporting and new problems are encountered. Credits and collections are difficult because of the hurdles of foreign languages, unfamiliar commercial customs and laws, long-distance communications, and absence of knowledge of sources and reliability of credit information and of the accounting principles upon which financial information is based. On the sales ledger side, the problem arises, where sales are in foreign currency, of multi-currency sales ledger administration including the difficulty of finding staff who are experienced in foreign currency transactions. Credit is typically for longer periods than in domestic selling and perhaps twice or three times as much working capital is frozen in book debts. There is also an increasing trend away from selling against bills of exchange and towards selling on open account terms, which reduces or eliminates the ability to raise finance by the traditional method of discounting bills. Finally, the exporter incurs a political risk, and, where sales are in foreign currency, the risk of adverse exchange fluctuation.

Export factoring has the capacity to eliminate these problems. However, they can only be effectively overcome if the exporter's factor ("the export factor") has the assistance of other factors or his own overseas branches ("import factors") located in the countries to which the exporter is selling, for otherwise the problems outlined above will prove as formidable for the factor as for the exporter. Since the early 1960s, four international groups or associations have been formed for just this purpose and this has enabled export factoring to be conducted efficiently for the first time. The members of two of these groups are affiliated through equity links. They are: the International Factors group (First National Bank of Boston) and the Heller Group (Walter E. Heller Inc. Chicago). Members of the Credit Factoring Group (Credit Factoring International Ltd., London) are branches. The fourth group, whose members are unaffiliated, is Factors Chain International which has a permanent secretariat in Amsterdam. Between them, the four groups have over eighty members in all West European countries except Greece, and in North America, Japan, Australia, South Africa, Israel, the Philippines, Hong Kong and Singapore. In the rest of the world, such two-factor export factoring is impossible, and some but not all factors avoid export factoring to those countries. Those that do usually obtain credit protection through their own credit insurance policy or as co-insured under the client's credit insurance policy, with the Export Credit Guaranty Department.

The export factor agrees or arranges with the import factor for the latter to assume responsibility for credit control and protection. Where export factor and import factor are separate corporate entities, there are two contracts involved: a contract between client and export factor, and a contract between export factor and import factor. The responsibilities of the export factor to the client are similar to those of the import factor to the export factor. Legally, the exporter is insulated from the import factor. The export factor approves whatever orders the import factor is prepared to approve. The client assigns the debts to the export factor without notice of assignment and the export factor reassigns the debts to the import factor with notice of assignment endorsed on the invoices thereby enabling the import factor to collect the debts and affording the customer a local payment facility which eliminates the need to obtain central bank permission to remit payments out of the country.

Where export factor and import factor are unaffiliated, potential disadvantages of the two-factor system are that the export factor depends on the efficiency of the import factor and does not have full control of the situation, whereas centralised control is possible where the factors are affiliated and this may result in greater efficiency; and duplicate sales ledger records have to be kept by export factor and import factor, whereas with affiliated groups it is possible to centralise sales ledger administration—and, indeed, in one such group this has already been done.

B IMPORT FACTORING

Import factoring has three different meanings. First, it simply describes the function of the import factor in the two-factor export factoring system described above.

Secondly, it describes the situation where the factor (the "import factor") is located in the country to which his foreign exporter client is selling. For such an exporter, the facility is an alternative to export factoring, and has enabled exporters in countries where factoring does not exist to utilise factoring. Historically, this type of import factoring is older than export factoring, but it is rare, mainly because marketing the facility abroad is expensive, and the distance between factor and client poses communication problems.

The third type of import factoring, also rare, is simply supplier guarantee (that is, drop-ship) factoring, described earlier, applied to a client who is an importer. The factor either guarantees payment to the foreign supplier or to the client's bank to enable the bank to issue a letter of credit. The arrangement may embrace temporary loans to the client to cover (a) freight and import duty; and (b) any period between when the foreign supplier has to be paid and the time that the goods are resold and the resultant debts factored.

C COMPARISON WITH ECGD

A substantial number of exporters utilise the facility of the Export Credit Guaranty Department ("ECGD"), a Government department. The ECGD facility is less comprehensive, except in geographical application, than factoring. The following specific points of comparison may be made. First, factoring provides 100 per cent. credit protection compared with ECGD's maximum 90 per cent. Secondly, although not all factors offer political risk protection, those that do provide 100 per cent. protection compared with ECGD's maximum 95 per cent. Thirdly, although not all factors offer foreign exchange risk protection, those that do provide 100 per cent. protection whereas ECGD does not insure this risk. Fourthly, payment from a factor is administratively simpler than payment from ECGD because a factor pays the debt automatically upon assignment, collection or maturity, depending on the arrangement, whereas a detailed and substantiated claim for payment has to be made to ECGD and the time for payment by ECGD varies according to the circumstances. Fifthly, factors collect the debts and institute legal proceeding, at their own expense where debts are approved, whereas ECGD leaves the burden and expense of collection to the exporter although it will make a retrospective contribution (and may in special circumstances make a prospective contribution) to the expnse of litigation in proportion to its insurance liabilities. Sixthly, in advance factoring 80 per cent. of the value of debts is obtainable upon assignment whereas, pursuant to an arrangement between ECGD and the British banks, 90 per cent. of the value of open account debts is obtainable from British banks on the basis of the ECGD's guarantee of the loan. However, only exporters who have held an ECGD policy for at least a year qualify for such finance. Finally, ECGD credit protection extends to the contract, whereas a factor's credit protection only commences when a debt arises.

Whether export factoring or an ECGD policy is better for an exporter depends upon his needs. ECGD operates in respect of sales to many countries, mainly underdeveloped countries, where factoring is unavailable. On the other hand, factoring is a significantly more comprehensive facility. For the latter reason, it is invalid to compare ECGD's premium rate, which averaged 0·245 per cent. of turnover in 1969–70, with the factoring charge, which is discussed in the next section.

6 Cost

The cost of factoring is divisible into two distinct parts: the factoring charge (sometimes called the service charge or the factoring commission), and the factor's discount, relating, respectively, to the cost of non-financial functions and to the cost of finance. An error sometimes made is to confuse factoring with invoice discounting, that is to consider it as a purely financial facility; to therefore add the factoring charge and factor's discount; and to express the total as an alarmingly high cost of finance.

The factoring charge is expressed as a percentage of the value of debts factored, and usually ranges from 0·5 per cent. to 2·5 per cent, depending on turnover, the work load involved and the bad debt risk although individual cases may fall outside these parameters. The work load is determined by the number of invoices and credit notes the number and nature of disputes, the number of customers, the number of repeat orders and any special operational difficulties which may be anticipated. One practice is to deduct the factoring charge from the first advance made: if, for example, the advance is 80 per cent. the factoring charge 1·5 per cent. and £10,000 of receivables are assigned to the factor on a particular occasion, the client will receive £7,850 and not £8,000. Other factors advance the full 80 per cent. and debit the client's account monthly with the factoring charge for the preceding month's assignments.

Factor's discount currently ranges from 1·5 per cent (domestic) or 1 per cent (export) to 4 per cent. above bank base rate, calculated on either an investment or maturity basis. The investment basis is a day-to-day calculation on the net amount of the factor's investment which usually consists of advances, charges, credits and disputes less collections or matured debts. The maturity basis means that the factor's discount is calculated from the date of the advance to the maturity date of the receivable, as defined in the factoring agreement on which the factor warrants that he will pay the client if the customer fails to pay for credit reasons. Old-line advance factoring may be conducted on one or other of these bases but recourse factoring is always conducted on an investment basis since the factor does not assume the credit risk.

Some recourse factors also have a refactoring charge, commonly 0·5 per cent. per month of the value of receivables more than two months past due. The supposed justification is that the factoring charge is insufficient to cover the collection costs on such receivables and the client must therefore pay more. It would be inconsistent with the assumption of the credit risk for old-line factors to make this charge in respect of approved receivables, but it is notable that they do not make it even in respect of unapproved receivables, and the competitive situation is therefore likely to cause the eventual disappearance of the refactoring charge concept in recourse factoring.

Recourse factors also usually charge the client for all legal collection costs, whereas the old-line factors only reserve this right in respect of unapproved receivables, since it would be illogical to charge in respect of approved receivables where the old-line factor has assumed the credit risk and therefore must swallow the losses, including collection costs.

The client may be provided with a monthly aged analysis of debts at no extra cost, but there may be a relatively small additional charge for other sales analyses, or this may be built into the factoring charge. Often, an old-line client may receive an ageing only of debts at the client's credit risk, if any, rather than of all debts. In support of this practice, it can be argued that the old-line client has no further interest in debts which have been sold to the factor on a non recourse basis. On the other hand, it may be contended that the client is entitled to review the status of all debts because it bears the merchandise risk and in order to gauge the factor's collection performance. Perhaps the best practice for a factor is to let each client decide which argument it prefers. Under this practice the policy might be to provide a client with an ageing of debts at its own risk only, unless the client stipulates otherwise.

7　Weighing the Benefits against the Cost

In order to assess whether there is an advantage in factoring, it is sensible for a company which is considering factoring to quantify the benefits as far as possible and to compare then with the cost. Certain benefits cannot, of course, be quantified because they are indirect or intangible: for example, improved credit standing and the complete protection of profit margins which cannot be achieved through credit insurance.

PROSPECT 'A': MATURITY FACTORING

Reduction in Expenses	£
Staff wages, pensions, benefits and expenses	3,000
Bad debt losses or credit insurance at 0·20%	1,000
Credit information	200
Collection agency or legal costs	150
Telephone	250
Postage	300
Stationery	100
Miscellaneous (equipment, furniture, maintenance, power, rent)	100
	5,100
Plus: Increase in net profit	5,000
	10,000
Less: Factoring charge, 1·2% of £500,000	6,000
Net direct benefit	4,100

PROSPECT 'B': ADVANCE FACTORING

Finance utilised to take 2% prompt payment discount on purchases (£300,000 per annum)	6,000
Less: factor's discount, 10% of £50,000	5,000
Additional net direct benefit	1,000

The two cost/benefits analyses above concern two old-line factoring prospective clients, A and B. In the first, Prospect A has a turnover of £450,000 at the stage of factoring negotiations, 300 customers and £100 average invoices. It is considering maturity factoring. It is realistically estimated that turnover will increase to £500,000 in the first year of factoring as a direct result of increased efficiency and more management time for production, sales and planning, and that the net profit on the additional sales will be 10 per cent or £5,000. This example supposes that Prospect A has no need of finance and is therefore considering a maturity factoring arrangement. The second example hypothesises Prospect B which is in the same circumstances as Prospect A, except that, in addition, it needs finance of £50,000 to utilize profitable opportunities, in this case mainly to take 2 per cent. prompt payment discounts on all purchases. In both cases, the factoring charge is 1·3 per cent. and is calculated on the projected turnover of £500,000. In the case of Prospect B, the factor's discount is calculated at 10 per cent. on an investment basis on the advance.

In the examples above the direct tangible benefit of factoring's non-financial functions for both firms was £4,100. Prospect B realised an additional £1,000, total £5,100, through profitable utilization of finance.

8   Credit Factoring Distinguished from Invoice Discounting

Factoring should be carefully distinguished from invoice discounting, which is purely a financial facility without the non-financial elements of factoring. Regrettably, the distinction is blurred and confusion caused by the practice, in some quarters, of calling invoice discounting "confidential factoring" which, as stated earlier, is the form of non-recourse factoring which bears no relation to invoice discounting apart from the common element of non-disclosure of assignment to customers. In invoice discounting the financier takes an assignment of debts with recourse to the client, and pays the client an advance purchase payment up to about 80 per cent. of the value thereof, normally with a credit limit of a specified amount. The common expression "invoice discounting" is actually a misnomer in that an invoice is only a piece of paper evidencing a debt. The activity should, more logically, be called receivables discounting or debt discounting. Many factors also offer invoice discounting.

In form, an invoice discounting agreement resembles a factoring agreement in that the financier purchases the debts and the client makes much the same warranties concerning their validity and enforceability. However, the similarity goes little further. The main differences are: (*a*) the purchase is always with recourse to the client; (*b*) notice of assignment is not given to customers, although the financier reserves the right to give notice if he feels that his security is imperilled; (*c*) the client collects the debts as the financier's agent and remits collections *in specie* to the financier; (*d*) the client usually has a discretion as to the frequency of assignments, unlike factoring where the client is normally obliged to assign all debts—consequently, the discounting client can use the facility whenever he chooses, turning it on and off like a tap; (*e*) the financier provides no non-financial services to the client whatsoever—the arrangment is purely financial.

It is part of the security of the arrangement for the financier to exercise some control over the debts. He cannot do this as effectively as a factor because he does not exercise credit or sales ledger control, customers do not receive notice of assignment and payments are made directly to the client. Nevertheless, a reasonable amount of dominion and control may be affected as follows:

(*a*) The client annexes original and/or copy invoices to assignment schedules. The financier can then reconcile the details on the schedule with those on the invoices, before mailing originals to the customers. It is also important for the financier to have copy invoices on hand in order to be able to particularise debts and to be able to provide customers with copy invoices, if requested, in the event of exercise of the emergency power to give notice of assignment to customers. It is usually not mandatory for the client to remit original invoices. To do so is a deterrent to fraud since the fraudulent client runs a greater risk if customers become involved in the fraud, as they will if they receive fictitious invoices.

(*b*) The client forwards to the financier all collections relating to assigned debts, *in specie,* as they are received. This requirement constitutes a check that debts assigned actually exist. There is scope for fraud if the client is allowed to bank collected cheques, and to forward its own cheque in substitution, for its own cheque may purport to represent collections in respect of debts which are in fact fictitious. Further, if the client's bankruptcy or liquidation intervenes, the commingled collections may belong to his general creditors whose ranks the financier will then join. Nevertheless, where particularly strong confidence exists between financier and client, it is not uncommon for this requirement to be relaxed, and for an "account and pay weekly arrangement" to be entered into, whereby for the sake of the client's administrative convenience, he is permitted to bank collections and forward his own cheque weekly in substitution, accompanied by details of the collections which it represents. Where a customer pays by credit transfer to the client's bank account, arrangements can be made with the bank for onwards transmission to the factor. Often, however, such debts are specifically excluded from the invoice discounting arrangement.

The requirement that *all* collections be remitted to the financier is a safeguard against another type of fraud: fictitious debts, in a batch of genuine debts, representing the difference between the supposed full value of the batch and the advance. If the client was allowed to keep any collections once the financier had recovered his advance, this would facilitate such a fraud. For example, if the client is receiving an 80 per cent advance and knows that he does not have to account to the financier for collections in excess of 80 per cent. he could fraudulently produce 20 per cent in value dummy invoices, and the financier might never realise it, and wrongly think there was a 20 per cent margin of security between his advance and the value of the debts purchased. On the other hand, if the client has to remit all collections to the financier, this fraudulent course is denied him. The financier, in effect, reimburses the client the value of collections in excess of the advance, although the legal nature of the "reimbursement" is payment of the balance of the purchase price.

(*c*) Auditing of the client's books and records usually every six weeks to three months, in order to verify the existence of debts purchased, the receipt of goods by customers, and the proper forwarding to the factor of collections relating to the receivables purchased; and to ascertain the nature and level of credits, disputes, returns, allowances, contra-accounts, and conditional sales, all of which affect the value of purchased debts. The American practice of assessing the client's current financial condition by taking off a trial b lance also has merit. These audits are considered to be of prime importance in the policing process.

(*d*) Direct debt verification. This is done either on the client's headed letter-paper with a box number return address controlled by the factor, or it is done in the name of the client's auditor or an anonymous audit company. In any case, the object is to preserve the confidentiality of the invoice discounting arrangement. A reasonable target under this scheme would be to verify 10 per cent. of debts assigned in a month.

(*e*) A credit rating check is made of larger exposures, say over £5,000. The client warrants that by an agreed date, commonly called the "settlement date", or the "due date", all debts sold to the financier will be paid. This date corresponds with the date on which it is anticipated that all debts will have been collected. If this date has been calculated accurately, there is no problem. But if it has been miscalculated, perhaps due to unusually slow collections, collections received by the financier may be less than the advance, and the client has to account to the financier for the difference, pursuant to its warranty. At the same time, a warranty by the financier to pay the balance of the purchase price to the client becomes effective. Respective warranties of the parties operate by book entry setoffs. Thus, on an 80 per cent advance, if only 78 per cent. has been received by settlement date, the financier credits the client with the 20 per cent. balance of the purchase price and debits the client with 22 per cent: the net result is that the client owes the financier 2 per cent. In discounting jargon this amount is sometimes called a "short-fall". At the same time, the financier reassigns the unpaid debts to the client which allows the client to retain the collections relating to them without the necessity of accounting to the financier since the financier has divested himself of any further interest in them. Where discounting is being done on a continuing basis, the usual arrangement is to assign fresh debts to the financier on the settlement date of the previous assignment and for any short-fall to be deducted from their purchase price.[11]

The cost of invoice discounting is a discount calculated either on the daily balance of purchase payments paid for outstanding debts; or on the period from the date of assignment to the settlement date with a rebate, usually at a lower rate, on the excess of any collections received by the factor before the settlement date for the period from the date of receipt to the settlement date. The cost usually works out at about 5 per cent. to 8 per cent above base rate.

9   Credit Factoring and the Economy

There are two considerations when considering factoring and the economy: the effect of factoring on the economy and the effect of the economy on factoring.

The economic sign ficance of factoring lies in the stabilising influence on industry of authoritative and judicious credit control; the promotion of the efficiency and profitability of the medium and small firm; and facilitation of expansion of such firms thereby promoting employment and the growth of the Gross National Product.

Government recognition of some of these economic benefits is contained in the American Federal Reserve System's report entitled *"Financing Small Business"*:[12]

---

[11] See Chapter 3, *post.*

[12] U.S. Congress Report to the Committees on Banking and Currency and the Select Committees on Small Business, Washington, D.C., Government Printing Office, 1958, 1958, pp. 449–450. See also Report of the Committee on Consumer Credit (The Crowther Report) (1971), Cmnd. 4596, Vol. 1, para. 2.6.13.

"Commercial Finance Companies and Factors are specialised financing institutions whose operations are particularly adapted to the needs of small businesses in manufacturing and wholesale trade. These financing institutions have developed operating techniques for supplying credit to businesses that cannot qualify for ordinary bank loans. They provide a continuing supply of credit as needed, based on receivables, as well as additional credit to meet seasonal needs and special opportunities for expansion. They also give managerial guidance and budgeting and financial management.

"Commercial financing and factoring are particularly significant in a study of small business financing because credit is made available to small businesses that do not have access to bank credit or to the markets for equity and long-term debt funds."

An analysis of the effect of the economy on English factoring is subject to certain difficulties: the newness of the industry in England (it was founded here in 1960); the high degree of reorganization within the English industry during its short life, viz. entry of the banks, take-overs, mergers and reorganizations; and the tendency of factors not to disclose many operating results.

Macro-economic variables appear to have little influence on factoring. The relative smallness of most clients means that they are less affected by broad movements in the economy than, say, a Marks and Spencer. They are unaffected by the major components of economic activity such as Total Consumer Spending or Manufacturing Investment whereas Marks and Spencer are vitally affected. The smaller firm can expand its sales rapidly when the economy is stagnant; it is very difficult for large firms to do so otherwise than by acquisitions or overseas sales.

This conclusion is borne out by figures on the American factoring industry which has grown at a rate steadily approximating 1 per cent of the Gross National Product over the last thirty years, even during recessionary and post-recessionary periods (such as 1970–1971):

Year	Gross National Product ($ billion)	Factoring Volume ($ billion)	(% of GNP)
1944	210·0	1·50	0·71
1947	231·3	2·43	1·05
1950	284·8	2·70	0·95
1953	364·6	3·10	0·85
1956	418·2	4·30	1·03
1959	483·6	4·68	0·97
1962	560·3	5·40	0·96
1965	681·2	6·66	0·98
1967	785·0	7·80	0·99
1968	865·0	8·80	1·02

Year	Gross National Product ($ billion)	Factoring Volume	
		($ billion)	(% of ONP)
1969	929·1	9·50	1·01
1970	976·1	10·10	1·03
1971	1,050·4	11·90	1·13
1972	1,155·0	13·50	1·17

Annual Compound Growth Rates

1967–72	10·6%
1962–72	10·3%

Source: National Commercial Finance Conference Inc., N.Y

There appears to be no reason why the English factoring industry's volume should not also reach one per cent of the U.K. Gross National Product. This will probably occur within the next ten to twenty years: to be more precise is to become highly speculative. There are no official figures on English factored volume, but the following are considered to be fairly accurate estimates:

Year	Gross National Product (£ billion)	Factoring Volume	
		(£ million)	(% of GNP)
1968	43·16	130	0·30
1969	46·32	150	0·32
1970	50·67	175	0·35
1971	55·99	200	0·36
1972	57·95	220	0·38
1973		260	

10 Why Consumer Debts are not Factored

It will be recalled that the definition of "credit factoring" on page 1 stated that it was concerned with "trade debts", i.e. with debts due from traders as opposed to consumers. There are two commercial reasons for this tradition. First, the invoice value of a consumer debt is generally less than the minimum which enables factors to administer the sales ledger and discharge the credit control function at a reasonable cost to the client.[13] Secondly, obtaining adequate current credit information on which to base credit decisions and assume credit risks is much more difficult with respect to a consumer than a trader for a party such as a factor who has no contractual relationship with either.[14]

A tradition may die if the circumstances which gave rise to it change. It is conceivable that advancements in computer science will significantly reduce the unit cost of sales ledger administration, and that adequate consumer credit information will become more readily available. In such a future world, it should be possible to factor consumer debts.

[13] See p. 65, *post.*
[14] See pp. 68–70, *post.*

CHAPTER TWO

The History of Credit Factoring

"What is all knowledge too but recorded experience and the product of history":
Thomas Carlyle, *On History, Critical & Miscellaneous Essays,* Vol. I.

The credit factor is the offspring of the "factor" in the strict legal sense
of the term; that is, the mercantile agent who in the ordinary course of
business is entrusted with goods, or the documents of title to goods,
for sale, and who together with other types of mercantile agents, is
subject to the Factors Act 1889. The birth of the credit factor took
place in America and has been traced to the year 1889. During the 1930s
it spread to Canada; and since 1960 it has been established in all West
European countries (except Greece), Australia, New Zealand, Israel,
Japan, the Philippines, South Africa, Singapore and Hong Kong.

1   The Agent Factor: Parent of the Credit Factor

A   ORIGIN

The mists of time conceal the origin of the agent factor but it seems
certain that its roots go back to the emergence of trade which followed
the dawn of civilisation. Man, to provide himself with more than the
meagre essentials of life, found it necessary to trade, at first in his own
right, and then through representatives or agent factors. To enable
trade to exist, commercial practice evolved, broadly speaking, in three
stages. The earliest stage was that of the travelling merchant who took
his goods to the distant market and bartered or sold them and with the
proceeds purchased other goods for the return journey. In time such
merchants could afford to retain others (travelling agent factors) to
perform these functions for them. In the third and final stage there
emerged the agent factor resident in or near the market to whom goods
were consigned for sale and who might also buy and despatch other
goods to his principal.

B   ENGLISH AGENT FACTORS

Agent factors have always been used extensively in England. They
were originally most prominent in the woollen textile industry which
dates back to within a century of the Norman Conquest. By the

fourteenth century and for many centuries thereafter this was England's most important industry—indeed, to this day, Britain is the world's biggest exporter of woollen textiles. In 1397 Blackwell Hall (adjoining the Guildhall in London), which was built in the first half of the thirteenth century as a private mansion, became public property and was immediately converted into a market house for the sale of woollen cloth. Employed for this purpose for more than four centuries, it became a natural centre for the activities of many agent factors.

Agent factors, who very often sold in their own names without disclosing their principals' names, might appear several times in the line between manufacturer and ultimate consumer. For example, to obtain cloth from a market in the north, a Blackwell Hall factor might negotiate the purchase with a factor located in Yorkshire. The Blackwell Hall factor, if he did not sell to a draper, might arrange a sale of the same merchandise to an exporter who would dispose of it through yet another factor abroad, or to a foreign factor in England representing a foreign importer.

The position of agent factors as middlemen came under a fair amount of criticism, often because of a feeling of resentment against their power to make or mar the fortunes of those who dealt with them. In the cloth industry suppliers were reliant on agent factors to advise on market trends and demands, to supply raw wool, to store merchandise pending sale, to find buyers and to provide finance both for the supplier, by means of advances, and for the buyer through extension of credit.

The custom in the cloth trade was for a supplier to provide a factor with material, usually in advance of orders, and to advise the factor by letter a short time before the material arrived of the alternative prices which he hoped to receive for it—a higher price, usually, for a credit sale than for a cash sale. The factor would store the material and send pieces on approval to prospective buyers. He was a commission agent, charging the supplier a percentage of sales as his fee.

In addition, he filled a financing role because credit was needed at every stage of manufacture and sale. Buyers often wanted long periods of credit; in exports a year or more might be required. Such credit was not readily forthcoming from the supplier, who in fact was often short of money with which to purchase raw material and pay wages. The factors being of good repute and substance, were able to obtain the backing of English banks and financiers and furnish the necessary credit—thus becoming middlemen in finance as well as in goods. The method commonly used was that the factor would accept a bill of exchange drawn on him by the supplier which the latter could then either discount or use for making payments, for such bills were virtually as negotiable as cash. Normally bills would only be drawn when the goods were sold, although factors would often accept them prior to this time against the security of goods in their possession. So significant did such financing become, that by the eighteenth century it had become the most valuable part of the agent factor's business.

English foreign trade used to be dominated by the great trading companies, such as the East India, Muscovy and Levant Companies, which each operated in defined areas of the known world. They were necessarily vested with wide discretion in their choice of buyers, terms of sale and forecast of local demand. Commonly they were represented abroad by sons of or apprentices to members of the company who would spend a period of time training in England before being sent abroad either as resident or travelling factors.

Selling on credit terms was popular throughout the medieval period as instanced in the earliest records of the wool trade. Then as now credit extension was intrinsically risky, a fact which prompted the Levant Company, in 1672, to forbid their factors in Turkey to sell on credit and to direct them to give oaths to this effect. This was met with considerable resistance by their factors who saw the credit sale as the most effective way of disposing of merchandise. The prohibition was finally lifted in 1744 following parliamentary criticism.

Some of the tales of English agent factors abroad make good adventure stories and indicate the peril which many of them faced. For example, in 1583 a factor named Sonnings was hanged in Tripolis for attempting to free an Englishman who had been enslaved there for failing to pay a debt. In sixteenth century Brazil, Baker and Gouglasse were imprisoned by the Spaniards on a false charge of piracy. There are droll stories concerning their morality: in 1589 Brown, author of *The Merchants Avizio*, a kind of handbook for factors, urged them to avoid "wine, wealth and women" and to pray daily; in 1782 Gigone, a Genoese factor, solemnly contracted to abstain from sex and gambling for the whole of the four years he was to be abroad on his principal's business.

Many of the earliest English traders dealing with the new-found colonies, entered into partnerships or contracts with the colonialists to supply goods of one kind in exchange for goods of another. This practice soon lost favour and traders sold through the captain of the outgoing vessel, a travelling agent factor or a resident agent factor. The advantage in using the captain or a travelling agent factor was the minimisation of unfaithfulness, for at least they had to face the trader at the end of the voyage and account for their actions. On the other hand, they could not be expected to have much knowledge of local requirements or the creditworthiness of the colonialists.

The unfaithfulness problem was often tackled by appointing a blood relative, such as a son or a brother, as resident factor. The decision whether to use a resident or travelling factor was also influenced by geography. Where a settlement was above the lowest navigable point of a river the ship had direct access to buyers, but when settlements grew beneath this point, resident factors necessarily came into existence at the nearest accessible port. As the settlements expanded inland, so did the necessity to use resident factors increase.

There appears to have been a general tendency in colonial trade for a proportion of factors resident in the colonies to become merchants on their own account. In this respect they were, no doubt, tempted by the prospect that their profits as merchants would exceed their factoring commissions.

C   AMERICAN AGENT FACTORS

In America, the selling and buying agent factor was to grow and prosper until a combination of industrial, commercial and legal developments resulted in the emergence of the credit factor. The selling and buying factor was an intimate part of American life, literally from the time of the Pilgrim settlement in 1620, for three of the London merchants who financed the voyage of the *Mayflower* were subsequently to enter into a mutual agent factoring agreement with a partnership representing the Pilgrims. The English merchants, described in the agreement as "agents and factors", purchased merchandise in England on behalf of the Pilgrim partnership, which sold it to settlers, Indians, and European fishermen on their annual journey to the fishing grounds of Newfoundland and Nova Scotia. The English merchants also sold on behalf of the partnership all shipments from the colony—mainly furs, fish and timber.

As the American population increased, so did trade between Europe and the colony. At first it was common for merchants to send employees or blood relatives to act as their agent factors in the colony but it became increasingly common to use independent resident factors. By the second quarter of the nineteenth century, the terms "factor" and "commission agent" had become synonymous.

The dramatic increase in the American population during the first half of the nineteenth century (5,308,000 in 1800; 17,069,000 in 1840) created a great demand for European merchandise, particularly textiles, for manufacture into clothing, bedding and home furnishings. This caused a mushrooming of agent factors representing European mills and a concentration of agent factoring in the textile industry, a fact which was to later have great significance for the development of American credit factoring. Agent factors came to be concentrated in New York City because it was an important centre for importing and for textile distribution and selling. and there credit factors are mainly to be found to this day.

The agent factor's activities ran the gamut of selling, buying, storage, extending credit, guaranteeing credit,[1] undertaking collections, financing, litigating and handling drafts and bills of exchange. During the middle part of the nineteenth century his usual commissions were as follows:

For selling foreign products	5%
For selling domestic products	2½%
For guaranteeing customers' credits	2½%
For undertaking collections	2½%
For engaging in litigation	5%
For purchasing, remitting and collecting drafts or bills of exchange	1%
For drawing, endorsing, accepting or selling drafts or bills of exchange	2½%

The 1870s and 1880s witnessed a rapid expansion of American domestic manufacturing concerns and a transformation of the nation from a primarily agricultural to a primarily industrial society. Domestic textile mills began to spring up. Some had occasion to use factors but most preferred to develop their own sales forces and storage facilities. Consequently, agent factors' activities remained concentrated in textile imports.

2   Emergence of the Credit Factor

A   1889–1890: EVOLUTION OR REVOLUTION?

In 1889 there occurred the first step in what might have become a gradual evolutionary process; New York agent factors, Oelbermann, Dommerick and Co., decided to drop their selling and storage functions but to continue to perform their other services for European principals. Revolution rapidly succeeded evolution. The following year, 1890, witnessed the introduction of the McKinley tariff which increased the general level of all import duties to 49·5 per cent. Almost prohibitive duties were imposed on textile imports causing the agent factor's traditional business to drop off with alarming rapidity and European mills and merchants to seek other markets. It was natural that the factors should turn to the industry which they knew best—textiles—and adapt their previous expertise to the requirements of that industry domestically. To a large extent the domestic textile industry preferred to use its own sales forces so the opportunities for the factors' traditional selling activities were restricted. Many factors went out of business. Others adapted by dropping the selling function but otherwise they provided their old services; that is, all the facilities which credit factors provide today plus, often, storage of the clinet's merchandise. Because

[1] See Chorley, Del Credere Agency (1929), 45 L.Q.R. 221; (1930), 46 L.Q.R. 119.

the agent factor and the new credit factor performed most of the same functions, the credit factoring embryo conceived in 1889 was born a year later as an exceedingly well developed baby.

B   1890 TO THE GREAT DEPRESSION

This period marked the rapid growth of credit factoring within the textile industry and the development of a formidable body of credit knowledge due in no small part to the factor's overlapping experience of the same customer in relation to a number of clients. Not every segment of the industry was factored. Clients were textile mills and converters with customers who were clothing manufacturers, department stores and chain stores. Clients selling to retail trades aside from department and chain stores—such as clothing, specialty and haberdashery stores—accounted for only one per cent. of clients and were regarded as fringe accounts.

The 1890s witnessed the commencement of lending against the security of accounts receivable, in effect invoice discounting, by commercial banks. This was purely a cash facility without notification to customers and with bad debt losses borne by the client. In 1904 the first non-bank accounts receivable financing company was established. Its activities were initially somewhat different from the commercial banks. It took an assignment of debts with recourse to the client, but gave routine notice of assignment to customers. However, under mounting pressure from objecting clients an alternative non-notification plan was soon developed accompanied, because of the greater risk element inherent in a non-notification scheme, by strict auditing procedures—the supply of duplicate invoices and receipts to the financier, independent verification of customer accounts and other safeguards.

The commercial banks and discount finance companies did not confine their activities to any particular industry as did the factors. Their clients fell into two general categories; those with minimal working capital whose prospects looked sound, and those who could not obtain any further bank credit. Their advances were always coupled with satisfactory margins to protect against bad debt losses—generally their advances were 70 per cent. to 80 per cent. of receivable assigned as security.

C   THE GREAT DEPRESSION TO 1960

The textile industry was seriously affected by the crash of 1929. As factors' clients and profits shrank they were obliged to look for wider pastures. First, they turned to the former fringe accounts within the textile industry—mills and converters selling to miscellaneous retail stores. Then the search for new business, particularly after World

War II, led them altogether outside the textile industry. By the late 1950s factoring was still very much concentrated in textiles. but it had been used in a wide variety of industries including the following: bedding, chemicals, garments, cosmetics, electrical appliances and supplies, fertilisers, furniture, garden hose, gloves, hardware, hats, hosiery, housefurnishings, housewares, leather goods, metallic yarns, portable organs, nylon, paint, paper, plastics, musical instruments, rubber goods, shoes, fish lines, glassware, radios, thread, sporting goods and toys. The old storage service sometimes accompanied by a packaging and delivery service, and even by the physical location of the client or his selling agent on the factor's premises (the so-called house accounts) rapidly declined in significance and disappeared.

D   1960 TO THE PRESENT

In this period there has been little further expansion of American credit factoring outside the textile industry. There have, however, been three very significant developments which have made the period the most important in the history of credit factoring:

   (i) The entry on a major scale of banks into the factoring field
   (ii) The establishment of factoring in countries outside North America
   (iii) The development of export and import factoring

(i)   Banks enter credit factoring

In America there was a link between banks and factoring as early as 1919 when a corporation was organised under the banking laws of the state of New York to act as factors. However, as late as 1963 only three or four banks had factoring departments. For many years there were two main deterrents to banks entering the factoring field. First, there was considerable uncertainty whether it was a legitimate banking activity. Secondly, there was doubt as to the degree of demand by the business community for factoring by banks.

The first deterrent was removed in 1963 when the Comptroller of the Currency ruled that the national banks had authority to engage in factoring: see: *Comptrollers' Manual for National Banks,* U.S. Comptroller of the Currency, issued 1 June 1963, para 1105. The second deterrent was removed in 1965 as the result of a survey conducted by *Fortune* magazine. The survey was addressed to the top 1,000 U.S. industrial corporations and the 50 largest public utilities, merchandisers, transportation and life insurance companies. One of the questions asked was whether they thought factoring as a bank activity was saleable. The four possible answers were very saleable, saleable, not saleable or no answer. The following results were obtained:

Answer	Percentage
Very saleable	17·8
Saleable	62 0
Not saleable	10·4
No answer	9·0

Relieved of legal worry by the Comptroller's ruling, encouraged by the result of the *Fortune* survey and enticed by the relatively higher return on money employed which factoring offered compared with traditional banking activities, twelve American banks entered the American factoring field between 1965 and 1970, eleven by acquisition of an existing factoring company and one by the formation of is own factoring department.

In England the clearing banks were keeping a sharp eye on the development of the local factoring industry and the large-scale movement of American banks into factoring. Like the American banks, they subscribed to the modern full-service, or supermarket, approach to banking designed to offer a complete range of banking and financial services to their clients, and were attracted by the relatively high rate of return on money employed. Consequently, between 1968 and 1972, all the English clearing banks entered the factoring field and several major American banks have also invested in English factoring since 1960. Throughout America and Europe, today, most factors are either owned by or affiliated with banks. Perhaps the greatest benefits conferred on factoring by bank involvement has been increased confidence in the industry by the business community.

(ii) *Establishment of credit factoring outside America*

Factoring was introduced into Canada during the 1930s. The first factoring company outside North America was founded in England in 1960. The number of established factors in England grew to twelve in 1972, then shrank, through take-overs and mergers, to nine by early 1974. Of these seven are essentially old-line (non-recourse) factors and two recourse factors. All are located in or fairly near London. During the same period invoice discounting has also grown considerably and is carried on by firms specialising in that activity as well as by some of the factors as an alternative facility to factoring.

Very soon after its introduction into England, factoring was established in Germany and soon spread throughout Western Europe. As stated earlier, it is today established in every West European country (except Greece), as well as in Australia, New Zealand, Israel, Japan, South Africa, the Philippines, Hong Kong and Singapore.

Outside North America, there has never been any historical association of factoring with textiles or with any other particular industry. As a result, it has in a little over a decade been applied to more industries and to a relatively greater extent than in America in almost 100 years. Nevertheless, in terms of acquiring comprehensive credit expertise there are obvious advantages in concentrating on a particular industry or industries. Therefore, although no such trend is yet obvious, it is possible that in future years there will be a tendency towards such specialization by individual factors, particularly by those who carry the credit risk.

(*iii*)   *International credit factoring*

The spread of factoring outside North America was the result of the desire by American and non-American enterprises not only to factor domestic foreign trade but also international trade. The types and methods of international factoring and the history of its development have been traced in Chapter One.

CHAPTER THREE

Suitable Clients

"But here, unless I am mistaken, is our client":
Sir Arthur Conan Doyle, *Wisteria Lodge*

Philosophical standards of suitability may and do differ as between factors. A particular philosophy is rarely rigid; it exists within parameters which are not easily defined. At the centre is the ideal client which is, perhaps, a mythical entity, like the ideal woman or the Loch Ness monster. To proceed outwards along the spectrum is to encounter increasing difficulty in perceiving whether the boundaries of suitability have been reached. Thus, whether the facts concerning a particular prospective client fit an abstract, philosophical or conceptual standard is a question on which opinions can differ, in much the same way, for example, as judges who accept that murder is a crime may differ as to what constitutes murder.

Infallibility is not a human quality. Careful analysis of a prospective client does not guarantee that the conclusion to which it leads will not be proven wrong by the passage of time, but it does minimise the potential for error. In the following pages of this chapter, appropriate areas of analysis and analytical techniques for determining suitability are suggested. From the foregoing reference to the subjective nature of the concept and application of a suitability standard, it should be clear that express or implied conclusions hereafter contained are not necessarily universally accepted norms, although, generally, they probably reflect the mainstream of informed opinion.

Suitability should be assessed by the factor before entering into the factoring agreement, and thereafter should be kept under periodic review. Suitability may be analysed under three headings:

1 Risk
2 Profitability
3 Benefits to client

In this chapter each of these aspects will be explored in the following detail:

1   Risk

A   *Debts*: (i) credit terms; (ii) turnover rate; (iii) unfactorable debts; (iv) dilutions.
B   *Customers*:   (i) Quality; (ii) exposures; (iii) location.
C   *Credit Strength*:   (i) Industry; (ii) financial; (iii) history; (iv) owners; (v) management. (vi) methods of operation.
D   *Economic and Political Climate*
E   *Guarantees, Indemnities and other Security*
F   *Power to Conduct Business and to Factor*

2   Profitability

A   *Turnover*
B   *Costs:* (i) Number of customers; (ii) number of invoices; (iii) unusual collection problems; (iv) bad debt provision.
C   *Costing Formula*

3   Benefits to Client

In practice, much time is saved if industry, turnover, average invoice value, number of customers and credit terms are determined by way of preliminary enquiry, in order to dismiss from further consideration, certain businesses, which, in the opinion of most factors, experience has shown to be obviously too risky (e.g. where progress payment terms are involved) or too unprofitable (e.g. where the average invoice value is very low, say less than £40.00) to factor.

1   Risk

A   DEBTS

For the factor, the trade debts owed to the client do not simply form part of the general credit picture: they are his speciality and his chief protection against loss. He invests in them not in the same way as one invests in real property or shares, for debts cannot appreciate in value, but by buying them at a discount (the factoring charge); his expectation is to recoup his investment and make a profit. However, this expectation may be ill-founded unless they are first analysed to determine their quality. This may be done by reference to the credit terms allowed, the turnover rate, unfactorable debts and the nature and extent of dilutions in value.

(i)   Credit terms

Factors are essentially short-term financiers and credit guarantors. The maximum contractual credit period which normally qualifies for factoring is 180 days, although it is uncommon to find domestic clients selling on terms of more than 60 days. This rule has, however, been diluted by the trend in some industries towards contracts of sale being executed as much as a year or so before delivery as customers gamble on today's costs for next year's stock. As the factor is usually asked by the client to approve a transaction at the order stage, the factor may be assuming risks for far in excess of a year, even before taking into account slow payments by customers, although he does have the important contractual right to withdraw approval at any time before shipment or delivery.

It is advisable to inspect conditions of sale. If certification by the customer that goods have been delivered in good condition or that work has been satisfactorily completed, is required, it is prudent for advances to be made against invoices accompanied by such certificates.

(*ii*) *Turnover rate*

The payment period allowed by contract and the time in fact taken for payment are two very different things. It is a fact of commercial life, particularly in times of tight money, that the latter is often significantly in excess of the former. The average turnover period of debts may be calculated according to the following formula:

$$\frac{\text{Average monthly debts outstanding}}{\text{net annual sales}} \times \frac{365}{1}$$

Sometimes, instead of average monthly debts, the debts outstanding on the balance sheet are used, but this involves a greater risk of the average turnover figure being distorted. Distortions to the average turnover figure may be due to:

(*a*) seasonal sales fluctuations—debts will be high at the peak of a season, but low in the off-season;

(*b*) rapidly expanding sales where debts will appear to be high;

(*c*) substantial cash sales which will depress the value of debts. If possible, cash sales should be calculated and eliminated from net annual sales.

If the average turnover figure is high and undistorted, it must be due to slow collections, the reason for which should be determined. It may, for example, be due to weak collection procedures, extended credit terms, or delinquent debts which may in turn indicate poor credit control. An aged analysis of debts will identify disputing, slow-paying and delinquent customers, as well as (see below) customers in which exposures are concentrated.

(*iii*) *Unfactorable debts*

There may be debts which have to be eliminated from factoring because of the degree of uncertainty concerning their collectability. They include:

contra accounts, because the factor's right to claim payment from a customer is illusory if that customer has a right of set-off for sales or services rendered to the client;

group inter-company debts, because trading within a group is for administrative or tax purposes, group members are financially inter-dependent and their debts to each other lack a security element. There is also a risk of collusion;

delinquent debts, because there is no security in investing in debts which are manifestly uncollectible;

debts where payment is conditional upon certain events; for example, resale by the customer (the sale-or-return situation), or a machine operating satisfactorily for an agreed period;

progress payments, because failure by the client to complete the contract can give rise to substantial rights of set-off even in excess of progress debts outstanding and assigned to the factor;

retention payments, because they may legally never be paid and because they may involve unacceptably long credit projections;

debts subject to a prohibition against assignment. Sometimes client/customer contracts prohibit assignment of the receivables arising thereunder. In such a case, consent of the customer to assignment should be obtained for the factor may be legally unable to obtain title to the debt and therefore be unable to enforce payment against the customer. Often, the client does not know whether such prohibitions exist, and the only way to conclusively determine the question is to examine the client/customer contracts. If there are a great number, inspection of all will be impracticable but at least the contracts with the main customers should be studied;

encumbered debts: A search should be made at the Companies Registry to determine whether the debts are subject to a charge. A floating charge over debts does not prevent their assignment unless it contains a prohibition against assignment of which the factor is aware at the time of purchase, but assignment without the knowledge of the chargee, will certainly cause annoyance when it is discovered, and may well prejudice a continuing relationship between client and chargee, which is usually a bank. A release of the debts from the charge, or the chargee's consent to factoring, should therefore be obtained. There is no public registry containing details of assignments of debts, except that general assignments of book debts by a partnership or individual should be registered as a bill of sale in order to obtain priority over the assignor's trustee in bankruptcy: Section 43 of the Bankruptcy Act 1914.

(iv) Dilutions

The "dilution" of a debt means that its gross invoice value has been reduced by virtue of a discount, allowance, credit or dispute. Where the percentage of dilutions significantly exceeds the industry standard, it indicates that the quality of the product or of customers, or perhaps both, may be suspect. Experience has shown that in a liquidation it is usual for dilutions to increase by about 15 per cent. of debts' value. This is due mainly to claims arising out of the client's inability to complete contracts or to honour warranties, for example, as to maintenance of goods sold; and because quality is often sacrificed to economy in the last months before liquidation.

As regards trade discounts and allowances, it is safer to allow for those which *may* be taken under the terms of the client/customer contract, and by virtue of trade custom (if any), rather than to make a projection based on trade discounts and allowances in fact taken in the past. On the other hand, provision for credits and disputes can only be made on the basis of the client's historical records. As a check on actual or potential credits and disputes arising from allegations of non-delivery (and also as a check on fraud), it may be prudent to inspect receipts and consignment notes.

B   CUSTOMERS

(i)   *Quality*

By "quality" is meant credit strength, which is determined basically according to the same principles as the credit strength of a client. Customer quality could be regarded as an aspect of debt quality since a debt is only as good as the customer who owes it.

(ii)   *Exposures*

The old-line factor assumes the risk in respect of approved debts and has to be sure that he will generally be able to approve the exposures which the client requires, otherwise, if the client accepts non-approval, his turnover will suffer and he is likely to become dissatisfied; or if he rejects the non-approval and sells at his own risk the factor is also likely to be dissatisfied because he will consider that the client is running undue risks and prejudicing solvency. Special attention should be paid to concentrations, that is, to sales to the main customers, because curtailment of their credit will have a particularly adverse effect on turnover, and because over-reliance on sales to one or a few customers is likely to cause financial problems if their orders cease or diminish and cannot be quickly replaced.

(iii)   *Location*

The location of customers is not important if they are within the country unless located in a trouble-spot, such as Ulster in 1974. But if they are located abroad, the factor has to consider political, credit and exchange fluctuation risks and whether he has the administrative capacity to factor sales to them.

C   CREDIT STRENGTH

(*i*)   *Industry*

Industry analysis contains two fronts of enquiry; the type of industry and the vertical position of the prospect within it. Strictly, the object of industry analysis is not only to assess risk but also profitability.

Type: Prior to World War II, when factoring was confined to North America, it was, mainly for historical reasons, almost exclusively concentrated in textiles. Since those days, North American factoring has spread to a great many industries, although a concentration in textiles still prevails, but in other parts of the world there has never been a concentration in any particular industry.

The following list is probably not exhaustive, but it is illustrative of the industries which have been successfully factored in various parts of the world:

> architecture, artificial fur, bags, bedding, car accessories and parts, caravan accessories, chemicals, cosmetics, cork goods, cement, construction material, cutlery, consultants, communication equipment, children's wear, dry goods, dental supplies, electrical goods and components, engineering, feathers, fertilizer, furniture, floor covering, garden hose, games, glassware, gloves, hardware, hats, home furnishings, hosiery, houseware, infant's ware, jewellery, leather goods, linen, machinery, men's wear, metal, metallic yarn, musical instruments, nylon fishing lines, optical equipment, paint, paper, photographic equipment, piece goods, plastics, pottery, precision instruments, printed matter, pulp, rubber goods, screening, shoes, sporting equipment, steel, suitcases, textiles, threads, timber, tools, toys, typewriters, valves, veneers, wooden goods, women's wear.

Despite this extensive list, there remain the following industries which are usually considered to be unsuitable for factoring:

> Industries where the debts are generally unfactorable, as explained earlier, e.g. building and construction (progress payments) and capital equipment (conditional sales).

> Industries concerned with the sale of perishables such as fresh food, because of the risk of rapid deterioration through delays, which may of course be caused by unforeseeable events, like strikes, beyond the client's control.

> Industries concerned with gimmicks, because they are at the mercy of the public whim and therefore unstable.

High fashion industries (notably clothing), again because of instability, unless there is a good record of success.

Position: The vertical position of a prospect within an industry—its position on the manufacturing or distribution ladders—does not make the prospect *per se* unsuitable for factoring, but, rather, may make it unsuitable from the viewpoint of profitability or risk to a particular factor. To understand this, let us divide clients into two broad categories:

> Wholesale clients, i.e. manufacturers and distributers who sell to customers other than retailers (and consumers).
>
> Retail clients, i.e. manufacturers and distributers who sell to retailers

From the factor's viewpoint, there are advantages and disadvantages with each category of client. The advantages of the wholesale client are, first, that its product is often more basic than that of the retail client, and, therefore, there are usually alternative markets for its product in the event that one market dries up; and secondly, the factor's administrative costs are fairly low because, generally, invoice values are high and the number of customers small. A factor's charges for this type of client are, therefore, usually lower than for the retail client. The disadvantage of the wholesale client is that the spread of customers tends to be fairly narrow and the factor's credit exposure per customer is therefore high.

The retail client's advantages and disadvantages are the converse of the wholesale client's. There is usually a wide spread of customers and the factor's credit exposure is therefore low, although a fairly recent trend towards mass retail distribution has qualified this low risk theory. On the other hand, invoice value is usually small and customers generally numerous so the factor's administrative costs are high. In some cases, such as builders' merchants where invoices can average less than £20·00, the factoring charge would have to be prohibitively high and factoring would be uneconomic from the client's viewpoint. Where a retail prospect can afford factoring, further considerations are that, first, in the event of a retail market drying up there may be no alternative market available, and, secondly, retailers are sometimes more subject than wholesale clients to changes in demand. These matters can influence customer failures, unauthorised deductions, and a high rate of returns and disputes (often spurious) thereby not only posing credit risks but also causing high and unforeseen administrative costs which erode the factor's profits.

A factor may deliberately try to balance his portfolio of clients between wholesale and retail, particularly when his clients are concentrated in one industry, in order to have a spread between relatively low administrative costs, on the one hand, and relatively low risks, on the other; or he may opt for a concentration in one or the other. If any such policy exists, a wholesale or a retail prospect may be unsuitable for the factor according to his policy, yet nevertheless be suitable in the context of another factor's policy. In such cases, suitability cannot be judged from the viewpoint of factoring *per se* but only from the viewpoint of a particular factor's current policy.

The texile industry will serve as an illustration of some of the respective advantages and disadvantages attached to factoring wholesale and retail clients. There are four rungs on the manufacturing ladder:

> yarn producers and processors
> weavers and knitters
> converters
> garment and home product manufacturers

Yarn producers and processers spin yarn from naturals or synthetic fibres and deliver it uncoloured and in bulk to weavers and knitters of a great many items. Yarn is a simple basic product and unlikely to cause many customer complaints unless something drastic like massive quality control failure occurs. It has many end users and as sales are in bulk, invoice size is large. Weavers and knitters of yarn into piece goods constitute the second rung on the ladder. Their product is still fairly basic, has a number of end users, and invoice size is large.

Converters buy the fabric from the weavers and sell to garment and home product manufacturers or to other converters. By adding colour, pattern, design and finish, they inevitably become involved in considertions of fashion. As fashion is by no means always stable, particularly in the garment industry, there is a greater likelihood that their customers will raise disputes particularly to combat periods of slackened customer interest.

Garment and home product manufacturers are manufacturers of end-use products, as opposed to the three previous classes which are non-end-use producers. They sell to retailers such as department stores, discount stores, specialty shops and mail-order firms. Of the four classes this one essentially represents the highest fashion risk—although it is true that the fashion risk can have repercussions along the whole manufacturing ladder—and largest number of customers and invoices.

(ii) Financial

A client's financial strength is relevant because, first, the factor/client relationship is quasi-permanent in nature and there is a need for assurance that it will not be terminated by a client's insolvency. Secondly, in the case of advance factoring, it (a) indicates the extent of the factor's security in the event that collectable debts are inadequate to cover advances and the difference is at the client's risk; (b) it bears on the collectibility of debts because a client in financial difficulties may sacrifice quality for economy causing a high rate of disputes and credits; and (c) it bears on the fraud risk since the typical factoring fraud is committed by a previously honest client under heavy financial stress.

(a) Reliability of financial statements

An important preliminary to financial analysis is to determine the reliability of financial statements. There are four main questions to consider:

is the accountant who prepared them reputable?

are they certified in the usual form or are there qualifications which should be noted?

are the time periods of statements and the business activities undertaken during these periods identical? If not, it may prove difficult to make valid comparisons between figures and to establish trends.

have the statements been prepared in accordance with generally accepted accounting principles, and have there been any changes in these principles?

(b) Method of analysis

Financial analysis falls into two broad categories:

Unitary analysis: the study of items, groups of items and ratios in one set of accounts ,the most important of which are, or effect, working capital, tangible net worth, profitability and liquidity .In the case of balance sheet items, the valuation is on both a going concern and liquidation basis, since the value of most assets is lower in a forced sale. Neither law nor accounting practice govern or necessarily coincide with methods of financial analysis. Indeed, in valuation and categorsation, the financial analyst tends to be more conservative than the accountant.

Trend analysis: the comparative study of the same items, groups of items and ratios in two or more sets of accounts. This analysis reveals the direction in which a concern is going. For example, unitary analysis of A and B may show identical financial strength at 31 January 1974, but trend analysis may reveal that for several years A has been experiencing a deteriorating position while B's position has been improving. The fact that their paths happened to coincide on a particular date is of little significance compared with the fact that A's path is down while B's is up. The reality of their respective financial conditions cannot be gleaned only from a frozen moment in time, however recent.

Every interpretation of financial strength is based upon a dynamic, moving position.

(c)   Assets

There is no compulsory format for balance sheets, but the traditional method is to list assets in the reverse order of liquidity: fixed assets first, then miscellaneous assets, and, finally, current assets in reverse order of liquidity. American balance sheets, on the other hand, essentially adopt the opposite format, by listing assets in order of liquidity. The American method seems more logical since the first important point to establish, surely, is the adequacy of current assets to meet current liabilities.

The Companies Act 1967 says that "fixed assets, current assets, and assets that are neither fixed nor current shall be separately identified" (see the Second Schedule, paragraph 4(2)) but does not define these terms, although, in practice, classification presents no problem. A recommended definition of current assets is cash and assets held for conversion into cash during the operating cycle of the business or one year, whichever is longer.

Current assets include:

cash and bank balances available for current operations.

Marketable investments if they are temporary investments of excess cash and, therefore, likely to be converted into cash within the normal operating cycle of the business.

amounts due from debtors.

stock.

Prepaid costs are commonly listed as current assets in the balance sheets. These are items, such as rent, rates, insurance, and advertising for which a company has paid before the benefits are received. The accountant's rationale in listing them as current assets is that they would be represented by cash, a current asset, in the balance sheet if they had not been paid for in advance. However, since they neither fit the definition of current assets nor have any value in a liquidation, it is better to treat them, for credit analysis purposes, as assets which are neither current nor fixed.

Cash and Bank Balances: If there are restrictions on cash or bank balances, such as amounts held in escrow pending completion of an agreement, or amounts set aside for the purchase of fixed assets, they should be treated as assets which are neither fixed nor current. These most liquid of assets normally have 100 per cent value in liquidation. However, where cash or bank balances are represented by foreign currency, exchange fluctuations should be borne in mind. If located in a foreign country, there might be legal restrictions in removing the money from that country. There should be adequate cash and bank balances (or an overdraft facility) available to cover at least several weeks expenses.

Marketable Investments: Investment instruments include government securities, bonds and company shares, stock, debentures and commercial paper. Investments may be either short or long term. Short term investments are those which are made temporarily to utilise excess cash, and, if readily marketable, are current assets. Long term investments are not current assets, even if readily marketable, since there is no intention to convert them to cash within the normal operating cycle of the business. They may bear no relation to the firm's operations, in which case they should be regarded critically, particularly if they are of a speculative nature, since creditors may have helped to finance them.

By the Companies Act 1967 the respective aggregate values of quoted and unquoted investments must be stated in the annual balance sheets filed at the Companies Registry (see Second Schedule, paragraph 8 (1)(a)), and income from each must be stated in the profit and loss account (see Second Schedule, paragraph 12 (1)(g)). In the case of quoted investments, if the aggregate market value differs from the balance sheet value, it must be shown, as must the stock exchange value of any investments of which the market value is shown and is taken as being higher than the stock exchange value (see Second Schedule, paragraph 11(8)). The up-to-date market value of quoted investments can be obtained from the stock exchanges pages of the financial press. In the case of unquoted investments consisting of equity share capital of other companies, either the director's estimate of their value or other specified details must be revealed (see Second Schedule, paragraph 5(A)).

Shares in subsidiaries and amounts owing to and by subsidiaries must be shown as separate items in the balance sheet (see Second Schedule, paragraph 15 (2)).

Debtors: Debtors have been analysed above.

Stock: Stock is an important item for analysis because, of all the balance sheets items, it represents the greatest area for discretion as well as for honest and dishonest misrepresentation of value. Its valuation effects not only working capital but also profits and net worth. Gross profit equals net sales—Cost of goods sold (i.e. opening stock + cost of goods purchased—closing stock). Therefore, if closing stock is overvalued profits will be overstated, as will net worth if the profits are retained. If such paper profits are paid out in dividends or taxes, liquidity and solvency may in due course be imperilled. In a forced sale on liquidation, the balance sheet value of stock can easily be halved, but if the stock has also been overvalued the attrition will be proportionately higher. Until 1961 the usual practice was to state in the balance sheet that stock was valued at "the lower of cost or market value". In 1961 the Institute of Chartered Accountants rejected the expression "market value" as ambiguous on the ground that it could mean either net realisable value or replacement price. It therefore recommended that, in the absence of a special valuation method, one of the following formulae should be used in the balance sheet:

"lower of cost or net realisable value". This is the most commonly used formula.

"lowest of cost, net realisable value and replacement price";

"at cost less provision to reduce to net realisable value";

"at cost less provision to reduce to the lower of net realisable value and replacement price".

"Net realisable value" is defined as the amount which is estimated, as at the balance sheet date, will be realised for disposal of the stock in the ordinary course of business, either in its existing condition or as incorporated in the produce normally sold after allowing for all expenditure to be incurred on or before disposal.

"Replacement price" is defined as an estimate of the amount for which in the ordinary course of business the stock could have been acquired or produced, either at the balance sheet date or in the latest period up to and including that date.

Valuation of the cost of stock is an allocation process. Part of the cost of stock available for sale during the period is allocated to the cost of goods sold and the balance to closing stock. There are various methods of stock valuation. The Companies Act 1967 stipulates that if the amount of stock or work in progress "is material for the appreciation by its members of the Company's state of affairs or of its profit or loss for a financial year", the manner of computation shall be stated (Second Schedule, paragraph 11(Bb)). The manner of computation of the cost of stock is always relevant when prices are rising or falling. For example, the commonly used FIFO (First-In-First-Out) method assumes that stock first purchased or produced is first sold so that in a period of rising prices only the older, less expensive purchases are included in cost of goods sold and the rest are allocated to stock thereby producing high profits, stock, working capital, and, if the profits are retained, net worth. The method has the opposite effect in a period of falling prices. In contrast, LIFO (Last-In-First-Out) assumes that stock last purchased is first sold and therefore has the opposite effect to FIFO in a period of rising or falling prices.

An important point to note is whether there is any change in the basis of valuation from one accounting period to the next, since this may affect working capital, profits and net worth. In the absence of special circumstances, such as where one company has been acquired by another and changes its method of valuation to that of a new parent, there is dubious justification for a change in the basis of valuation, and its occurence may indicate an attempt to mislead interested parties by showing a better financial condition in a poor year, or, conversely, by reducing profits and taxes in a good year. This underlines the importance of always carefully scanning the notes to the accounts because any change in the basis of accounting should be stated by way of note, if not otherwise shown (Second Schedule, para. 1(4)).

Sometimes a company will claim that there is a "cushion" in its balance sheet stock (meaning that it is understated) in order to understate profits, and, therefore, taxes; that profitability, working capital and net worth are therefore actually much better than they appear; and that its credit should be assessed according to the "real" position. Such a company is trying to have its cake and eat it. It would not be unreasonable to ignore the cushion on the ground that analysis must be based on financial statements and not on a conflicting "confidential" representation of the true position. On the other hand, if satisfied that the cushion really does exist, it is difficult not to make an allowance for it. The chief clue as to whether a cushion really exists is that the average stock turnover figure is too quick for the industry. In addition, a remarkably low and steady gross profit figure points to manipulation of stock.

In the case of manufacturers, a breakdown of stock between raw material, work in progress and finished goods is helpful in that it enables the analyst to determine whether the right proportion of stock is represented in each category. For example, a knitwear manufacturer's principal selling season is June to October. Therefore, in April and May we would expect to see heavier raw material than in June and July, and in June and July heavier work in progress and finished goods than in October and November. If the right proportions did not exist at the right time, there might be cause for concern.

A visit to the prospect's premises is a useful way of gauging the amount, age and condition of stock. For example, in the case of a present-day men's suit wholesaler, it might reveal that there are a large number of narrow lapel suits in stock, purchased several years earlier when they were fashionable, which have not been written off or down from their original valuation.

Cash surrender value of life insurance (CSVLI): This is really a form of investment. Sometimes, a business insures the lives of its main officers to combat any possible adverse financial consequences of their deaths and, where they are stockholders, to finance the repurchase of their stock. During the lives of the officers the business also has the advantage of being able to use the insurance policy as security for borrowings. For credit analysis purposes, CSVLI should be classified as an asset which is neither fixed nor current because, although it is easily convertible to cash, there is usually no intention that it should be used for this purpose. CSVLI does not vary in liquidation.

Fixed assets: Fixed assets normally include land, buildings, plant, machinery, furniture and fixtures, tools and motor vehicles. The key inquiry concerning fixed assets is whether they have been fairly valued. The Companies Act 1967 prescribes subject to limited exceptions that the value of a fixed asset is its cost, or, if it stands in the company's books at a valuation, the amount of the valuation, less the aggregate amount of depreciation or diminution in value since acquisition or valuation, as the case may be: see Second Schedule, paragraph 5(1). Most fixed assets, other than freehold property, have a limited life because they either wear out or become obsolete. Depreciation is the process of spreading the original cost of the fixed asset over its useful life in a fair manner, so that at the end of its useful life, the amount in the depreciation account will equal the original cost of the asset less its residual realisable value, if any. During the useful life of the asset, depreciation is shown in successive balance sheets as a cumulative deduction from the value of the asset, and in each successive profit and loss account there is a corresponding charge against income.

There is a two-fold rationale underlying the concept of depreciation. First, it satisfies the accounting principal that costs should be matched against the revenue which they help to produce. Thus, if a machine has a useful life of ten years, it helps to generate revenue over a ten-year period. To charge the whole of the original cost against revenue in the year of acquisition is considered to place an unreasonably heavy burden on that year's revenue, while allowing subsequent years' operations to enjoy the benefit of the acquisition without being charged for it. Secondly, depreciation ensures that, on the expiry of the asset's useful life, resources have been conserved in the business equal to the original cost of the asset less its residual realisable value if any. This is because the annual charge against income is merely a bookkeeping entry and not an actual cash outlay—which occurred in the year of acquisition only. Thus, year by year, over the useful life of the asset, funds, reflected in the depreciation account, are retained in the business and, upon the expiration of the useful life of the asset, are available to contribute to the asset's replacement. It must be noted, however, that the funds are not necessarily available in liquid form. Furthermore, they are usually inadequate to replace the asset because the process of depreciation does not take inflation into account, and the replacement cost is usually in excess of the original cost. It is therefore a wise precaution for a firm to create a special replacement reserve to counter the effect of inflation, otherwise a financing problem may arise when the time for replacement arrives. The rate of depreciation to be applied is necessarily an estimate, because the life of the asset and its residual value cannot be known with certainty. Consequently, it is legitimate to adjust the estimate if this is dictated by the circumstances, such as technological advances rendering a machine obsolescent. It is important that the depreciation schedule reflects the economic life of the asset with reasonable accuracy because of its impact on profits, net worth and dividends. If the rate of depreciation is too slow, the net profit will be inflated since an inadequate amount will be charged against revenue; net worth will also be inflated if a fictitious net profit is retained. Conversely, if the rate of depreciation is too fast, net profit and net worth will be understated.

When fixed assets stand in a company's books at a valuation, there is a legal requirement that the names and qualifications of the valuers be shown by a note, or in an annexed statement or report, or otherwise (see Companies Act 1967, Second Schedule paragraph 11 (6A)). This is a sensible rule, since it helps the analyst to judge the reliability of the valuation according to the reputation of the valuer.

In liquidation, freehold property will probably hold its value but a 25 per cent. attrition to leasehold values would not be surprising.

Other assets: The main category of other assets is intangibles. Intangible assets include goodwill, patents, trade-marks, franchises, capitalised expenses and discounts on the cost of issuing shares and debentures. The general rule is that all intangible assets should be deducted in calculating net worth, because they are not normally convertible to cash and therefore are worth nothing. Occasionally, qualifications to this rule do arise; for example, if a patent or a trade-mark relates to a marketable product, or if a franchise is clearly saleable.

(d) Liabilities

Liabilities fall into two categories:

Current liabilities—those which, in the normal course of business, fall due for payment within the operating cycle of the business or one year, whichever is less.

Deferred liabilities—liabilities other than current liabilities.

Trade creditors: This balance sheet item arises as a result of purchase of merchandise for resale on credit. They are normally current liabilities. They usually are open accounts payable, but occasionally are represented by bills of exchange. While not unusual for purchases from overseas countries, bills of exchange are rarely required by domestic suppliers except in certain industries such as timber and furniture. Their presence may indicate that there are past due amounts in respect of which a supplier has insisted upon the additional security of a bill. A high ratio of trade creditors to stock or debtors probably indicates a past due condition, in which case it may be a sensible precaution to ask suppliers for their recent experience and to obtain an aged analysis of creditors.

Loans and overdrafts: Overdrafts, loans repayable on demand, other short-term loans and the current portion of long-term debt are current liabilities, while other loans are deferred liabilities. For analytical purposes, loans fall into three broad categories:

> Bank loans, usually primary borrowings carrying the lowest available interest rates.
>
> Loans due to other financial institutions, usually secondary borrowings carrying higher interest rates.
>
> Loans due to affiliated companies, stockholders and directors. These often carry no interest.

Only if a lender enters into a formal agreement that his loan is subordinated should his loan, which would otherwise be a current liability, be treated as a deferred liability.

Taxes: In the absence of a profit and loss account, a provision in the balance sheet for corporation tax provides a clue to the profitability of a company. The basis on which a corporation tax provision is computed must be shown: Companies Act 1967, Second Schedule, paragraph 11(10). It is common for a current taxation item as well as a deferred taxation item to appear in the balance sheet.

Accrued costs and expenses: This current liability represents normal accrued operating liabilities, e.g. salaries, wages, rent, insurance premiums.

Customer pre-payments: This current liability usually indicates demand for the firm's product as evidenced by willingness of customers to make advance payments. On the other hand, it may indicate that the firm has a financial problem, in that it is obliged to ask for prepayments to improve its cash flow. If the circumstances so warrant, the correct explanation should be established by inquiry.

(e) Equity capital

Equity capital represents the funds which shareholders have paid into the business, plus capital gains and profits earned by and retained in the business. It is an extremely important item, because it represents the owners' financial commitment to the business, which reflects their confidence in it. Issued but uncalled capital should be treated as a debt.

Many companies, at the end of a financial year, transfer the year's profit from the profit and loss account to reserves. Although the transfer of funds to a reserve indicates a commercial intention to retain the funds in the business, all reserves, with two exceptions, may nevertheless be legally distributed as dividends subject to any restriction in the company's articles of association. Indeed, previous years' trading profits may be distributed in a year that a loss is made, and, surprisingly, the commercially unwise course of paying dividends out of a current year's profit even when there is a deficit in the cumulative reserve account, is legally permissible.

Two capital reserves are the creatures of statute. They may not be distributed in any manner, except as specified by statute and must be identified separately in the balance sheet. They are:

The share premium reserve: Where a company sells shares in excess of their par value, the excess is regarded as a profit and must be paid into a share premium reserve account. This differs from share capital (which can never be reduced without the court's consent) in that it may be reduced without the court's consent for a few limited purposes: to issue bonus shares, to write off preliminary expenses, and the expenses of, or commission paid or discount allowed on, the issue of shares or debentures, or in providing the premium payable on redemption of redeemable preference shares or debentures: Companies Act 1948, Section 56.

The capital redemption reserve fund. In the event of redemption of redeemable preference shares out of profit available for dividend, a sum equal to the nominal value of the redeemed shares must be transferred to this reserve, which, like all share capital other than redeemable preference shares, cannot be reduced except with the sanction of the Court, except that it may be used, as with the share premium reserve, for the issue of fully paid bonus shares: see Companies Act 1948, Section 58.

(f)   Financial ratios

A financial ratio is the arithmetical relationship of one financial statement item to another. Viewed in isolation, ratios have limited significance and can sometimes cause wrong conclusions to be drawn. They only assume real significance when compared historically and with industry norms, and when weighed against seasonal and economic influences and the company's method of operation. Practical ratio analysis can normally be limited to a maximum of eleven ratios, which are considered below.

Current Ratio: This ratio is also known as the working capital ratio. The formula is:

$$\frac{\text{current assets}}{\text{current liabilities}}$$

In the past, a minimum current ratio of 2:1 was often considered satisfactory on the basis that it would take a 50 per cent shrinkage of current assets before current liabilities began to be uncovered. Realistically, however, the ratio has to be regarded in the light of the constituent elements of current assets: for instance, the extent to which current assets are represented by cash, debtors and stock is significant because they do not all have the same degree of value in liquidation. In some industries, like haulage and service industries, little or no stock is carried and a low current ratio is therefore acceptable. The ratio can be misleadingly high if obsolete stock, which should be written down or off, is included; or if stock has been over-valued—a possibility where it is unaudited or subject to a limited audit.

Liquid Ratio: This ratio is also known as the quick ratio and the acid test ratio. The formula is:

$$\frac{\text{liquid assets}}{\text{current liabilities}}$$

"Liquid" assets may be defined as cash and assets which can be converted to cash without further sales effort, notably trade debts and marketable investments. This is a very useful ratio for it reveals the extent to which short-term creditors are covered by assets which are subject to little shrinkage in value. A ratio of at least 1:1 is generally satisfactory when the average debtors turnover period does not approximately exceed suppliers' selling terms. If it does, payment of current liabilities depends on the extent to which the ratio is higher than 1:1 or on liquidation of stock

The ratio will be misleadingly high unless care is taken to eliminate from debtors a realistic bad debt provision, as well as debts which either will not be, or are unlikely to be paid within the current business cycle, such as amounts due under instalment contracts not payable within one year, inter-company debts and amounts due from officers and stockholders. The ratio may be misleadingly high due to an unusual occurrence such as the inclusion in cash of the proceeds of sale of fixed assets designed for reinvestment.

Seasonal industries experience wide fluctuations in both their current and liquid ratios because an increase in current liabilities reduces both ratios despite a corresponding increase in current assets. For example:

    (i) *Before increase*

liquid assets	£50,000
current assets	£100,000
current liabilities	£50,000
liquid ratio	1:1
current ratio	2:1

    (ii) *After £20,000 increase in trade debt represented by £20,000 of stock*

liquid assets	£50,000
current assets	£120,000
current liabilities	£70,000
liquid ratio	0·7:1
current ratio	1·7:1

Stock Reliance Ratio: The formula is:

$$\frac{\text{stock}}{\text{current liabilities} - \text{liquid assets}}$$

Where the liquid ratio is less than 1:1, this ratio measures the proportion of stock that must be converted to cash in order to liquidate current liabilities. For example, if the liquid ratio is 0·8:1, stock £80,000, liquid assets £80,000 and current liabilities £100,000, stock reliance is 25 per cent. In other words, current creditors are reliant on the liquidation of 25 per cent in value of stock for payment of current debts. Naturally, current creditors prefer to see no or little stock reliance.

Stock Turnover Ratio: The formula is:

$$\frac{\text{cost of goods sold}}{\text{average stock (i.e. } \dfrac{\textit{opening stock} + \textit{closing stock}}{2})}$$

The resultant figure may be converted to days by dividing it into 365. This number of days is the average age of the stock. Whenever this number of days is higher than is normal in the industry, it may indicate obsolescent stock, which should be written off or down, or poor stock control resulting in an unnecessary amount of working capital being tied up. On the other hand, a high figure may be justified, for example if it is due to taking advantage of an unusual price reduction or to stock piling in anticipation of a shortage or a price rise. A low figure, provided it is not so low that it causes loss of sales due to delay in meeting orders, is generally a good sign, indicating the liquid nature of the stock and reducing the loss potential in the event of a down-turn in selling-prices.

In the case of a manufacturer, the production period has to be taken into account in determining whether stock turnover is reasonable. For example, if 60 days stock is on hand and the production period is 30 days, the stock on hand is about right, assuming that a reasonable amount of finished goods must be on hand to ensure economical production and in order to meet orders for immediate delivery. On the other hand, if 90 days stock was carried, stock might be regarded as too heavy by 30 days.

Purchases/trade liabilities ratio: The formula is:

$$\frac{\text{monthly purchases}}{\text{trade creditors}}$$

When viewed in light of suppliers' terms, this ratio is a useful guide to the age of trade liabilities. For example, if purchases for the month are £100,000 and trade liabilities at the end of the month are £200,000, the ratio is 0·5:1, i.e. monthly purchases are half of the outstanding trade liabilities. If suppliers' terms are net 60 days, trade liabilities would appear to be current. On the other hand, if suppliers' terms are net 30 days, a current position would be reflected by a ratio of 1:1 and a ratio of only 0·5:1 would indicate trade liabilities are paid on average 30 days beyond terms.

Where this ratio indicates that prompt payment discounts are not being taken it is *prima facie* evidence of a liquidity problem. On the other hand, where there is no prompt payment discount, there is no direct monetary inducement to pay within terms, or the shortest terms, and it may merely mean that suppliers are being used as a convenient source of interest free funds. The seriousness of such "leaning" on suppliers largely depends upon the tradition of tolerance in the particular industry, and the financial muscle of the customer. Prompt payments might be the norm in one industry or segment of an industry, whereas payment 30 days beyond terms might be acceptable in another industry or segment. Again, a prime risk concern can largely call the tune over the time it takes to pay suppliers, whereas a marginal risk concern might be obliged to pay promptly in order to continue to obtain credit.

Where trade liabilities appears to be unduly high in relation to monthly purchases, confirmation or elucidation of the past due position may be obtained through an aged analysis and by obtaining the sales ledger experience of other suppliers and factors.

Current Liabilities/Tangible Net Worth Ratio: A high ratio usually points to overtrading which is potentially dangerous because the retirement of current liabilities is heavily dependent on the absence of disruption in the sale of merchandise and collection of debts. A slump in sales or slow collection of debts may well mean that it is impossible to pay current liabilities, at least according to their terms. This then places creditors, particularly major creditors, in a powerful position because they may sue or institute winding-up proceedings or decline to extend further credit.

Liabilities/Tangible Net Worth Ratio: This ratio indicates the degree to which owners and creditors, respectively, are financing the business. A low ratio indicates a reasonably substantial equity commitment by the owners and indicates that they have confidence in the success of the business and would not allow it to fail without a struggle. A high ratio, on the other hand, indicates that their philosophy is to reap equity rewards without running equity risks; i.e. that they are operating a business without adequate capitalisation. The further possibility of a high ratio is that equity has been diluted by losses.

It is not uncommon for owners to have money in the business in the form of liabilities rather than equity capital. Sometimes this represents undrawn remuneration for services, which is commendable provided the remuneration is reasonable and there is a need for the money to be left in the business. However, although this represents a welcome addition to any unreasonably small capital contribution, the owners' game plan is only marginally altered: equity rewards are their prize, but the risk they are running is only that of a creditor. Consequently, a factor may be justified in trying to improve the ratio by seeking capitalisation of all or part of the liabilities to the owners or the subordination of such liabilities to the claims of other creditors or the factor.

Stock/Working Capital Ratio: This ratio provides a clue as to whether the company is being properly financed. A ratio of 1:1 or less indicates a satisfactory situation, i.e. that stock is being financed out of working capital. Where the ratio is higher, the company is probably either under capitalised or carrying obsolescent or slow-moving stock.

Profitability Ratios: These ratios are usually expressed as percentages.

$$\frac{\text{gross profit}}{\text{net sales}} \times 100$$

This ratio reveals whether and the extent to which profits and losses are attributable to cost of goods sold or to expenses. Fluctuations in the gross profit percentage between accounting periods warrants investigation to determine what particular item or items have grown or shrunk and the reasons.

$$\frac{\text{net profit}}{\text{net sales}} \times 100$$

$$\frac{\text{net profit}}{\text{tangible net worth}} \times 100$$

When comparing a company's historical profitability or its profitability compared with other companies in the same industry, it is sufficient to look at the net profit/net sales ratio. However, when comparing companies in different industries, it may be necessary to look further to the net profit/tangible net worth ratio because high turnover industries have a lower net profit/net sales ratio than industries involving substantial fabrication.

(iii)   History

There are three main aspects of historical enquiry:

> number of years in business
> principal developments
> insolvency, litigation and fire record

Other things being equal, it is easier to conclude that there is a proven demand for the product of a prospect which has been selling its product for many years, and that it will continue trading indefinitely, than it is to reach the same conclusion of a prospect which has been operating for only a short time. Furthermore, a long-established prospect is more likely than a newcomer to have established relationships with suppliers which will prove beneficial in times of financial stress.

Factors like to see a prospect's financial statements covering a minimum of two years trading, although exceptions are often made to this principle. There is, however, a sound rule that companies starting from scratch should not be factored, unless they are well capitalised and managed, because factoring money is not in the nature of venture capital.

Here is an example of a start-up situation where factoring was feasible:

A promoter in the electronics industry had obtained the exclusive UK distributership rights for two foreign suppliers, famous names and world leaders in their fields. The promoter formed a distribution company and capitalised it at £25,000.00. He had previously had marked success in a similar venture in the same field, and he gathered together for the new undertaking experienced management who had worked for him in the previous venture and who had very good track records. Based upon previous experience in the venture and a certain demand for the supplier's product, sales of approximately £2 million were projected for year one, and £4 million for year two. Within the first month of trading, orders were already pouring in. The likely customer portfolio showed that the customers were of sufficiently good quality for the projected exposures to them to be considered reasonable. In these circumstances there was actually competition for the business among leading factors, and the company entered into factoring agreement within two months of commencement of trading.

If the litigation, insolvency or fire record is poor, a prospect will probably be rejected unless economic or other circumstances are mitigating. For example, an insolvency which occurred during the Depression would probably not be significant.

(iv) Owners

The identity of the owners of a corporate prospect is relevant for three reasons. First to determine who controls the company; secondly, to assess the integrity of the owners, since the reputation of a private company is only as good as that of its owners; and thirdly, because substantial shareholders, and sometimes even small shareholders, are commonly required to provide indemnities or guarantees.

(v) Management

Management strength and depth is one of the most important elements considered. Nearly all factoring clients are corporations. A corporation is an inanimate and intangible entity, a mere concept. It is the flesh-and-blood people controlling and running its day-to-day affairs who determine its success or failure. It is therefore essential to pierce the corporate veil and assess their qualifications, experience and achievements.

A history of frequent job changes may indicate instability. Health and age are considered: the principal managers may be dynamic but on the point of retirement, or previously dynamic but now in poor health. How will their departure or death affect the company? Is there anyone of sufficient calibre to take their place? Young management should never be thought less of because of their youth *per se,* although the task of assessing their competence may be more difficult than with older men because of the more limited record to which to refer.

Above all else, are management honest? Do any of them have a bankruptcy, litigation or criminal record? Their shareholdings, ability to work well together as a team, working conditions and material compensation (including pensions) are valuable indications of whether they are likely to continue to stay with the company.

(vi) *Method of operation*

Clearly, a key element in a client's viability is its method of operation. A factor will, therefore, want to look into the sources of supply, capacity to meet orders promptly, product quality, costing, price levels, and marketing and sales methods.

He should ask whether sources of supply are adequate to meet sales requirements, whether they are the best sources of supply, and whether alternative sources are available to replace them, if necessary. In order to promote and maintain customer goodwill, the prospective client's capacity to meet orders promptly is important. If goods are sold from stock, are adequate stock levels maintained? If goods are made or purchased against orders, are the orders met within a reasonable time? Do factory, outworker, storage and delivery facilities have the capacity to meet present and foreseeable sales levels?

Product quality is particularly significant because shoddy products undermine the factor's security in purchased receivables, cast doubts on the future of the prospect's business, and make sales ledger administration and collections difficult because of the high rate of disputes, claims and returns. Product quality is determined by physical inspection (which, in the case of technical items, may reveal little to a non-technical person like a factor), by assessment of quality control methods, by obtaining customers' references, and by analysing the sales ledger to determine the historical incidence of disputes, returns and credits.

The factor should be interested in the client's marketing methods;

the extent to which agents and representatives are used; their basis of remuneration and allocation of sales territories; whether they participate in the collection process; how quickly orders are processed; whether the historical sales record indicates that the marketing methods are successful or could be improved; orders in hand; and the effect of any seasonal selling on financing requirements.

D   ECONOMIC AND POLITICAL CLIMATE

Economic and political conditions have to be taken into account because they are matters essentially beyond the prospect's control which can have an impact, perhaps devastating, on production, sales and delivery. The matters to be considered at every stage of the buying, producing and selling cycle are industrial harmony, availability of raw materials, climatic conditions, sales tax, tariffs and quotas, war, revolution, civil disturbance and change of government. In the case of importers and exporters, these considerations necessarily extend abroad.

E   GUARANTEES, INDEMNITIES AND OTHER SECURITY

A guarantee is a collateral promise or agreement to pay any debt or perform any duty owed by client to factor if the client fails to do so. An indemnity differs from a guarantee in that it is not a collateral promise but an independent promise to answer for any debt or duty owed by client to factor regardless of default by the client. Thus a guarantor's liability is dependent upon default by the client whereas an indemnifier's liability is independent of the client's liability. To put it another way, a guarantor is secondarily liable to the factor, an indemnifier primarily liable. A further distinction and advantage of an indemnity is that a guarantee which is collateral to a void agreement will normally itself be void whereas an indemnity will not be invalidated.[1]

There are four reasons why a factor seeks indemnities or guarantees. First, the financial strength of indemnifiers or guarantors may enable a prospect to be factored where the financial strength of the client alone would militate against it. Secondly, they are a safeguard against channeling of funds to associated companies, shareholders or their wives. Thirdly, they are of psychological value in preventing fraud and promoting responsibility. Fourthly, they are of practical advantage in ensuring the co-operation of parties most closely associated with the client in the event of the client's insolvency or bankruptcy, for they will be aware that co-operation will help to reduce or eliminate their own potential liability toward the factor.

There are seven main categories of indemnifiers or guarantors:

---

[1] *Yeoman Credit, Ltd. v. Latter*, [1961] 1 W.L.R. 828, at p. 831.

1 Parent company
2 Subsidiary companies
3 Co-subsidiary companies, i.e. companies with the same parent as the client.
4 Related companies, i.e. companies in which substantial shareholders of client or parent company also have a substantial interest.
5 Substantial shareholders.
6 Minor shareholders.
7 Wives of shareholders.

Indemnities or guarantees are not normally required in maturity factoring or where the advance percentage is low, because the client's equity in debts, against which the factor may offset, is adequate to absorb merchandise disputes and other charge backs. In the case of normal advance factoring the suitability of a prospect tends to increase if the factor can obtain indemnities or guarantees. Sometimes they are not available because, for example, potential indemnifiers or guarantors do not consider that the circumstances warrant impairment of their prospects for raising other finance by weakening their own financial strength through entering into contingent liabilities towards the factor; or shareholders feel that they have enough of their own money at risk in the form of equity. Here the factor must make a commercial judgement whether to waive guarantees and indemnities or some of them.

There is no alternative to waiving guarantees or indemnities of individual shareholders where the prospect is a public company because of the multitude of shareholders. With private companies, it is common enough not to insist on the guarantees or indemnities of minor shareholders, or to allow them to enter into a more limited form of guarantee or indemnity than substantial shareholders. For example, liability may be limited to a specified amount or to losses arising only from the client's fraud or other limited circumstances. The theory behind obtaining wives' guarantees or indemnities is that they are a safeguard against the legal syphoning of shareholders' wealth to their wives so that their own indemnities or guarantees become virtually valueless. But shareholders understandably resent the involvement of their families in their company's liabilities, so that in practice it is rare for a wife to give such security or indeed, for a factor to request it. Collateralised indemnities or guarantees (for example, secured by real property, shares or bank deposits) are unusual but sometimes necessary.

Other security arrangements include agreements by shareholders to

(*a*) subordinate their loans to the client to any liability of client to factor;

(*b*) not to call for repayment of their loans to the client while factoring continues; and

(*c*) to increase equity capital.

2 Profitability

A   TURNOVER

At present, most UK factoring clients have an annual sales volume of between about £100,000 and £5,000,000 (at current money val.es). Most factors look for a minimum annual turnover of about £100,000 on the basis that an insufficient profit is generated on smaller turnovers unless the factoring charge is so high as not to be in the prospect's best interests. Nevertheless, exceptions are made in respect of smaller turnovers, notably where the client shows good growth potential, where a factor is likely to be prepared to give support for a relatively low immediate return in anticipation of improved profitability through the client's future growth. Also, there are a few factors which do factor clients with small turnovers for various reasons such as the fact that the market is less competitive or their own resources are more limited than larger factors.

Subject to the factor's policy concerning exposure to capital and his ability to handle large volumes of work, there is no turnover ceiling. However, a client with a turnover of more than £5 million is unusual because it can generally obtain money more cheaply from other sources; has sufficient specialisation and economies of scale to enable it to discharge the credit control and sales ledger at a reasonably low price and at a reasonably high standard; and probably has credit insurance facilities or regards itself as large enough to be self-insuring. Sometimes a client which has grown large while factoring, although usually able to obtain money more cheaply elsewhere, may be so satisfied with the factor's non-financial services that it will continue to factor on a maturity basis rather than incur the trouble and expense of establishing its own credit collection and sales ledger departments, and of negotiating and administering a credit insurance policy which will, in any event, not protect its gross profit margin.

B   COSTS

For the purpose of determining the profitability of a factoring account, all the factor's budgeted costs may be represented by four cost items: cost per customer, cost per invoice, a provision for unusual collection problems, and a bad debt provision.

(*i*) *Number of customers*

A credit file has to be opened on every customer. Much of the information therein and the time involved in collating and analysing it cost money. Of course, where more than one client sells to the same customer, the cost can be spread among them. There are also costs attached to establishing an account for each customer and following for collections. An average of one customer per £1,000 of turnover (at current money values) is generally about the maximum which can be handled at a reasonable cost to the client. The actual cost per customer is calculated on the basis of experience.

(*ii*) Number of invoices

Every debt is evidenced by an invoice. Every invoice has to be physically processed by the factor. The factor's administrative costs are therefore heavily influenced by the number of invoices which it has to handle, or, to put it another way which is more adaptable to changes in turnover, by the average invoice value. The general experience of the factoring industry is that it is unprofitable to factor where the average invoice value is less, than, say, £40 (at current money values) without a factoring charge which is too expensive for the client. Indeed, many factors look for a higher minimum average invoice value. Highly advanced computerised book-keeping systems tend to lower the unit processing cost and enable factors with such systems to accept low average invoice values. Again, the cost per invoice is calculated on the basis of experience.

(*iii*) Unusual collection problems

If the level of adjustments, allowances, returns, credits and disputes is unusually high, the factor will be involved in more expense than is normal. The degree and nature of such collection problems should therefore be ascertained, and, if unusual, a provision made.

(*iv*) Bad debt provision

Many old-line factors use a bad debt provision of 0·1 per cent. of factored turnover as the norm, but each case should be looked at individually since it may warrant a much higher provision.

C COSTING FORMULA

The following is a hypothetical example of the application of a suggested costing formula:

Income	£	
Factoring charge at 1·5% of £300,000 of turnover	4,500	
Factor's discount 1% after cost of money on average advances of £30,000	300	
		£4,800

Expenses

250 customers at £6 each	1,500	
2000 invoices at £0·75 each	1,500	
Unusual collection problems	100	
Bad debt provision	300	
	———	3,400
Net income		£1,400
Net income as a percentage of average advances		4·7%

3 Benefits to client

To this point, the suitability assessment has been almost completely from the factor's viewpoint. However, even if the prospective client represents a reasonable risk and a profitable account, it cannot be said to be suitable unless factoring will benefit it, otherwise the client will in due course realise it made an error and terminate the factoring relationship, perhaps with ill-feeling towards the factor. It is therefore advisable to assess whether such benefit exists, and to make the cost/benefit comparison suggested in Chapter One.[2]

To ensure the adequacy of factoring finance, a cash flow projection may be advisable, especially where the prospect has liquidity problems or seasonal needs. This may reveal the need for supplementary, temporary, or periodic financing which the factor might provide by increasing the percentage of the advance purchase payments and/or through secured or unsecured loans. Liquidation of such supplementary financing would probably be by offset against the purchase price of debts which it helps to generate.

[2] See p. 23, *ante.*

CHAPTER FOUR

The Mechanics of Credit Factoring

"The worm's-eye point of view": Ernie Pyle, *Here is Your War*

In entering into a factoring relationship, a client trusts the factor to carry out the credit, collection and the sales accounting functions in a manner which will constitute a clear improvement over the pre-factoring situation, and to pay promptly for receivables in accordance with the factoring agreement. For the factor's part, it is essential that his internal organisation is both sophisticated and efficient in order to justify the trust and to ensure a mutually satisfactory continuance of the relationship. The procedures, systems and techniques which the factor uses to discharge its functions may be called the mechanics of factoring. Our analysis of the mechanics of factoring is detailed, but does not imply industry-wide uniformity as to all details. On the contrary, differing viewpoints and degrees of computerisation make variations inevitable. Hence, some of the more important alternative practices are examined.

Before beginning the day-to-day relationship, special steps have to be taken to equip the client to co-ordinate its activities with the factor on a continuing basis. When the legal documents governing the factoring relationship have been executed, the client is given certain standard forms: schedules of receivables and of credits, dispute notices, applications for credit approval, change of terms requests. He will also be given a rubber notice of assignment stamp or printed notice of assignment stickers if alternative arrangements for printing or typing of notice of assignment have not been made. It will assist the client if he is provided with written guidelines to the day-to-day operating relationship, and introduced to the account executive and credit man or credit men responsible for its account. Where the factor is computerised, the client will be informed of his computer number for coding schedules or invoices and credit notes; and if the client is to be responsible for coding customers, he will also be given a list of their numbers. One sophisticated development is that the client's computer (used for example, for stock control) is programmed to output directly into the factor's computer; i.e., the client's computer "speaks" to the factor's computer.

It is helpful, also, if the factor assists with the assignment of receivables on the client's ledger at the commencement of factoring, and a member of the factor's staff may attend the client's premises for this purpose. Since this intital assignment will usually cover a large number of receivables, the sales ledger itself or a photocopy or micro-film thereof may be used as evidence of receivables instead of copy invoices. Sometimes the old-line factor will not assume the credit risk with respect to receivables in existence at the commencement of factoring because he had no prior control over them.

When the takeover of the client's ledger has been completed, day-to-day operations begin. These involve five functions, which may each be handled by a different department:

1   Credit control
2   Document processing
3   Customer accounting
4   Client accounting
5   Client relations

1   Credit Control

A   CREDIT

(*i*)   *Decision-making*

There are four steps in the credit decision-making process:
(*a*)   Collation of all the information which is available and necessary in the circumstances.
(*b*)   Analysis of this information.
(*c*)   A conclusion as to whether the customer is entitled to credit.
(*d*)   A conclusion as to the amount of credit to which the customer is entitled.

(*a*)   Credit Information

The credit information with which the factor is concerned covers a customer's financial condition and prospects, history, owners, and economic and political influences. The sources of this credit infor-mation are credit agencies, the Companies Registry, banks, suppliers, the financial press, the factor's own sales ledger records and those of other factors, and the customer itself.

It is usual for the majority of credits to be approved on the basis of information obtained indirectly rather than from the customer itself. In the first place, this is because it is manifestly undesirable to take up any of the customer's time if the required information is available from other sources. But, secondly, it is because there is widesprerad reticence among customers to disclose information, particularly financial information, to the trade. This appears to be based on a philosophy that such information is private and the trade have little or no right to know about it. The paradox is that credit information is readily disclosed to a bank where even a small loan is being sought, yet the trade is expected to extend much larger amounts of credit without the same information. The philosophy is unfortunate, not merely from the viewpoint of the risk which the trade creditor has to take but also from the customer's viewpoint, because credit is based on confidence and confidence on information, and non-disclosure of the information may therefore result in more limited credit than would be the case if it was revealed.

It is inevitable that cases will arise where information available from indirect sources is inadequate for any or the required amount of credit. Subject to the client's consent, there is then no choice but to contact the customer, which may be done by phone, letter, or personal visit, depending on the circumstances. Since, as stated, many customers have a bias against disclosure, direct contact can be a delicate task, and in order to win the customer's confidence, it may be necessary for the factor to pledge that any information received will be treated in strict confidence.

Disclosure of information by a customer is, in the last analysis, a matter of supply and demand: if the customer wants the client's merchandise sufficiently, it will disclose the required information. Disclosure is also a question of degree: a customer is more likely to consider a disclosure request reasonable if the amount of credit is substantial relative to its financial strength.

As far as financial information is concerned, Parliament has mitigated the trade's problem in obtaining such information by requiring all limited companies to annex to their annual return filed at the Companies Registry, a duly certified copy of the following:

1   Balance sheet and abridged profit and loss accounts
2   The auditor's report on accounts
3   The director's report[1]

Most of the detailed information required to be in the accounts are contained in the Second Schedule to the Companies Act 1967. There are some unfortunate statutory limitations in the information which is required to be contained in the profit and loss account. First, there is no requirement to disclose cost of goods sold, gross profit or operating expenses. It is, therefore, impossible to measure the ratio of these items to sales, or changes in such ratios, and analyses of the causes of profits and losses and trends is thereby severely limited. Secondly, a company whose sales do not exceed £250,000 per annum need not disclose its sales figure, provided it is neither a holding company, nor a subsidiary

---

[1] Companies Act 1948, ss. 127 (1) and 157 (1).

company.[2] Legally, a company has to deliver its annual return and accounts to the Registrar of Companies within 42 days after the annual general meeting.[3] Not more than 15 months must elapse between one annual general meeting and the next.[4]

Unfortunately, the financial information available through a search of the Companies Registry is often out of date, due to the tendency of many companies to file out of time and lax enforcement of the penal provisions concerning late filing. The Companies Act 1948 contains two sanctions for failure to comply with the statutory filing provisions. First, if the directors do not lay the balance sheet, profit and loss account and, where applicable, group accounts before the annual general meeting of the company within 18 months of incorporation, and at least once in each calendar year thereafter, they are liable to a fine not exceeding £200 or imprisonment not exceeding six months, except that a sentence of imprisonment cannot be imposed unless the court is satisfied that the offence was committed willfully.[5]

Secondly, the Registrar of Companies, or any member or creditor, may serve notice on a company which has defaulted in complying with any provision of the Act requiring filing of a return, account or document with the Registrar of Companies, and if the default is not made good within 14 days of service, the court may, on application of any member, creditor, or the Registrar, order the company to remedy the default within a specified time.[6] The company or any officer bears the costs of an incidental to this application.[7] If the officers of the company fail to comply with the order, they are guilty of contempt of court and may be fined or imprisoned.[8] Section 428 would be a potent weapon if it was properly enforced. Clearly, the primary responsiblity for enforcement should rest on the Registrar of Companies, but, unfortunately, tardy filing is common enough, and the Registrar has done little to systematically correct the situation.

(b)   *Analysis*

Analytical techniques for determining credit strength are basically the same for a customer as for a prospective client, and have been canvassed in Chapter Three.

An additional point to bear in mind is the risk of fraud. A customer may provide false financial information or delay providing financial information in order to conceal a deteriorated position which would prejudice its credit. Occasionally, the professional business criminal

---

[2] The Companies (Accounts) Regulations 1971, S.I. 1971 No. 2044.
[3] Companies Act 1948, s. 126 (1).
[4] *Ibid.,* s. 131 (1).   [5] *Ibid.,* ss. 149(6), 150(3).
[6] *Ibid.,* 428 (1).   [7] *Ibid.,* s. 428 (2).
[8] *Re George Dowman, Ltd.,* (1960), *Times,* 26 July.

may be encountered whose basic technique is to establish a favourable credit standing, obtain credit and disappear with the profits leaving creditors stranded. His methods of obtaining a favourable credit standing include the following:

> buy an established business, drain it of funds, and desert it;
> put available funds in a bank account so as to obtain a banker's reference;
> establish worthwhile references through a business not associated with the fraudulent activities;
> establish a good payment record with suppliers until ready to make a criminal move.

(c) Credit worthiness and (d) Amount of Credit

These are related questions. Trade credit is founded on the answers to two questions:

> 1 Is the customer entitled to credit? This is a question of confidence.
> 2 If so, how much? This is a question of quantifying the confidence.

A customer is entitled to credit if the factor has confidence that the customer is and will be able to retire its current liabilities in an acceptably prompt manner during the period of credit under consideration. This confidence is implicit in the Latin root of the word "credit": *credere,* to believe or to trust. In so far as the basis of such confidence is an opinion as to a future course of events, the confidence can never be absolute for no one can read the future. Credit worthiness—entitlement to credit—therefore covers a wide spectrum, ranging from customers commanding the greatest confidence, called prime risks, to customers commanding little confidence, called marginal risks. The answer to the second question—how much credit should be given—reflects this fact for it involves the monetary quantification of confidence, i.e. the pound amount of credit extended should reflect the degree of confidence. Hence, a prime risk customer is entitled to virtually as much credit as it reasonably requires, whereas a marginal risk customer should receive carefully controlled credit of a relatively modest amount. Since marginal risks represent the greatest loss potential, they constitute the most important area for credit control, involving accurate, initial assessment of the risk, constant alertness to any change and close attention to collections.

In cases where confidence is not high, either because of paucity of information or because the information leads to that conclusion, prudence says that the amount of credit should be limited. In these situations, rough rules of thumb regarding credit exposure are often used. Perhaps the commonest is that there should be a maximum exposure of one-tenth of tangible net worth or one-fifth of working capital, whichever is less. Hutson and Butterworth say of customers with whom there has been some experience of payments that "a crude but useful rule of thumb here is to assess credit at twice the highest payment made on time and free of any duress. This applies particularly to accounts with monthly credit terms.[9] Although paucity of credit information may compel the use of such arbitrary rules, they can be unfair both to the customer and to the client and generally should be shunned wherever sufficient information is available for an individual judgement to be passed, because every situation is different and warrants a personalised opinion of a host of variables, including such subjective impressions as managerial ability, which cannot be reduced to mathematical formulae. If this was not the case, the whole area of credit assessment could be relegated to a computer.

To the rule that the amount of credit reflects the degree of risk there are three qualifications or compromises. The first two are based on economic considerations, and the third on a point of principle.

First, where the amount of credit required is not warranted by the risk alone, it may nevertheless be extended if the likely profit generated by taking the risk outweighs the potential loss. Thus, if a supplier sells £500,000 of merchandise per annum to a customer, on which it generates a net pre-tax profit of £50,000, and this level of sales requires a credit line of £40,000 which does not seem to be justified in view of the risk, the potential loss could be weighed against the profit to determine whether the risk is worth while. If this supplier was being factored, the factor might adopt similar reasoning in weighing the income which the client generated for the factor, overall, against the risk. This policy favours the larger, more economically important client. In order to minimise the risk of impairing good-will with such a client, the factor is likely to take greater risks than he would for a less economically significant client. For example, two clients, A and B, each pay a factoring charge of one per cent. and A has a £5,000,000 annual sales volume and B £500,000. The annual factoring charge income generated by A is £50,000 and by B £5,000. Clearly, A is economically more important to the factor than B, and the income generated by B is more easily wiped out by a loss than that generated by A. The factor is, therefore, more likely to take greater risks on A's account than that of B. It is not that B is being penalized but that A is being favoured.

The second economic qualification relates to small credit exposures. Credit investigations cost money and the more detailed an investigation the greater the cost. If a client who pays a factoring charge of one per cent. sells to customers X and Y responsible for annual sales by the

[9] Hutson and Butterworth, *Management of Trade Credit* (1968, Gower, London), p. 74.

client of £100,000 and £100, respectively, the cost of a detailed investigation of each may be the same, but X is responsible for £1,000 of income for the factor and Y for only £1. A thorough investigation of X is economically justified, but not of Y. Consequently, the form of compromise made in respect of small orders is that they are approved on the basis of little or no investigation. For example, the policy may be:

(*a*) to approve exposures (i) under £100 automatically without any investigation; (ii) between £100 and £500 on the basis of a satisfactory credit agency rating; (iii) between £500 and £1000 on the basis of a satisfactory credit agency report; and, (iv) between £1000 and £2000 on the basis of a satisfactory credit agency report and bankers reference;

(*b*) to launch more detailed investigations only in respect of larger exposures, to the degree that circumstances warrant.

There may, of course, be small customers like Y, responsible, in aggregate, for a fairly substantial sales volume. To apply such a liberal credit policy across the board to all of them constitutes taking a calculated risk, based on experience, that the cost of investigating them in depth or at all will substantially outweigh the likely losses flowing from the policy, and that the cost of investigation is therefore not justified. Another way of dealing with small orders is to agree that the first £100 of debts outstanding on a customer's insolvency is at the client's risk.

The third compromise is that if a factor has two or more clients who are selling to the same customer, they each are entitled to be treated as though the other did not exist for the purposes of determining the amount of credit which should be extended to that customer. For example, suppose that client C asks the factor to approve a line of credit for a customer and the factor concludes that the risk warrants a line of £50,000, and C accordingly sells to the customer up to the limit of the line. Client D then receives a £40,000 order from the same customer. This is the classical dilemma of every old-line factor, which has to be particularly borne in mind when the factor is concentrating on one industry. To be fair, there is only one route the factor can take and that is to approve the orders D has received and to continue to do so, if necessary, up to the limit of £50,000.

(*ii*) *Approval methods*

Factors use two methods of credit approval, either in conjunction or independently: the order approval method and the credit limit method. There are two types of credit limit: the outstanding receivables limit and the shipping limit. As stated above, as an adjunct to whatever method is used, a system of automatic approval of small orders, perhaps those less than £100, is often also used.

The order approval method means simply that a client is required to submit individual orders for approval. By this method, the factor is able to exercise tighter credit control than with limits. The order approval method may, therefore, be appropriate where customers have to be closely watched, for example, because they are marginal accounts or because they are part of a volatile industry. On the other hand, the order approval method involves a significantly greater workload than the credit limit method, which, therefore, for economic reasons, is used wherever possible.

The outstanding receivables limit means that any receivable which, when aggregated with all the other outstanding receivables owing by the same customer, falls in whole or in part within the credit limit established by the factor, carries the factor's credit approval to the extent that it does not exceed the credit limit. For example, if the factor establishes a £10,000 limit for customer X, and the client sells goods worth £2,000 to X, and assigns the resultant receivable to the factor when X owes £9,000, the factor assumes the credit risk as to £1,000, and the client bears the credit risk as to the other £1,000 which exceeds the credit limit. Under the usual terms of a factoring agreement, any unspecified payment by X is appropriated, first, to receivables at the factor's risk, and, secondly, to receivables at the client's risk. However, in the event of the customer's liquidation, factor's and client's claims would rank pari passu by statute. Since the client is no longer maintaining its own sales ledger, it cannot be sure at any given moment how much a customer owes the factor. Consequently, it is necessary, in case of doubt as to whether the limit is full for the client to contact the factor to determine the question. However, a recent American innovation by-passes this necessity: there, a factor has provided some of its larger clients with a video screen linked to the factor's computer, which enables them, at the push of a button, to determine by themselves how much is outstanding on any account.

The shipping limit places the amount of credit extended in the context of the credit historically taken by the customer. For example, if the advisable exposure is £8,000, the trade terms net 30 days, and the customer has historically paid, on average, 30 days after due date, the client could be authorised to ship, at the factor's risk, £8,000 of merchandise to the customer in any 60 day period, or £1,000 per week, or £200 per day. More simply, if the frequency of orders is, say, weekly or daily, the customer could be informed that orders of up to £1,000 or £200 respectively, are automatically approved. The system is administratively simpler than the outstanding receivables limit, but is a looser method of control: there is no automatic adjustment, as with an outstanding receivables limit, if a customer's payment habits change. In other words, the factor has to be alert to the customer who begins to take longer to pay because this will result in the exposure on which the shipping line was based being exceeded.

Where a client decides to ship without the factor's approval, the factoring agreement may require it to advise the factor immediately the decision is made rather than when the account receivable is offered for assignment. This is in order that the factor may receive the earliest possible notice as to whether the client is imperilling its own solvency by selling to a poor risk.

Regardless of the method of credit approval used, it should be remembered that the factoring agreement usually allows the factor to withdraw approval at any time before goods are shipped or delivered. The normal procedure is to advise the client to stop shipment. The rationale is that if a change in a customer's credit circumstances occurs, the factor should not be expected to enter blithely the yawning jaws of disaster, paralized by a credit decision made on the basis of circumstances which have changed, when the common-sense remedy is to stop ship-ment and resell the merchandise, like any supplier bearing the credit risk itself would do in the same situation. Although factoring agreements do not usually say so (a matter which a client might justifiably resent and try to remedy), it is traditional for responsbile old-line factors to absorb losses resulting from withdrawal of approval.

In recourse factoring, there is sometimes a tendency for the client to be more relaxed about obtaining credit approval before shipment, and the first that a factor may know about a new customer or order is upon receipt of the assignment or offer to assign the receivable. Although this means that the client is inadequately protecting his own interests by not seeking the factor's credit advice, the reason for this relaxation is, in a sense, understandable: the recourse client cannot shed the credit risk by obtaining approval of an order or by staying within approved credit lines, and therefore does not have the same incentive as the old-line client to ensure that the factor's credit advice is obtained and accepted.

(*iii*) *Approval procedures*

Where credit limits are used, they are established at the outset of factoring, excepting any customers to be considered on an order approval basis. The limits take the form of specific amounts for all the client's active customers.

When individual orders are submitted for approval, a recommended procedure, which can also be used where a new credit limit is being requested, is as follows: the client applies for approval in duplicate on a standard form provided by the factor (see Appendix IV), or, where delivery is required at once or very soon, by telephone. Clients located at great distances form the factor may use a telex. The factor notes telephone applications in duplicate on a standard form. Whichever method of communication is used, the factor is notified of the customer's name and address, the amount, the terms, and the delivery date. By the end of the same day, the credit man involved should take one of four courses of action:

> approve the order;
>
> decline the order—this means that it is considered that the customer is not entitled to any credit;
>
> decide that the order cannot be approved at that time because of a (probably) temporary problem: for example, the credit limit may be full or the customer may owe the factor amounts which are unacceptably past due. The client should be advised to resubmit the order for approval at such time in the future as it is considered that the problem will probably be resolved;
>
> hold the order in order to obtain more information.

Details of the order and the decision are noted in the credit file which may consist of computerised information. The procedure of many, but not all, factors is for the credit man to assign an approval number to an approved order, which is noted on the credit approval request standard form and in the credit file, and subsequently endorsed by the client on the resultant invoice to facilitate the factor's subsequent internal verification of approval. The original form is mailed to the client and the duplicate is retained for the factor's record. Meanwhile, because it is urgent, the decision on a telephoned approval request is telephoned to the client.

In practice, the time required to decide whether an order should be approved or declined varies from a few moments, where all the relevant information is on file and the credit man if familiar with the account, to as much as a couple of weeks where the customer is unknown and there is difficulty in obtaining information. In the great majority of cases a decision is made on the same day or within a few days after it is requested. A practical control is for the factor's clerk to confer with one of the client's staff at the end of each week to check whether their respective records agree as to orders which are being held or have not been processed.

(iv)   Review

The skill and experience of credit men naturally vary. Each should be given authority to approve exposures up to an amount which it is considered fairly reflects his skill and experience. Above this amount, the decision should be referred to a more senior credit man or to the credit manager for confirmation.

Large exposures, for example above £10,000, should be formally reviewed by a committee of senior management on a regular basis, say every six months although individual committee members may keep a constant informal eye on exposures. The credit man should also have a discretion to, at any time, refer credits of any amount extended to marginal customers to this committee for their consideration. The committee should meet, say, monthly under normal circumstances, but should be convened at any time to meet an urgent situation.

(*v*) *Personnel organisation*

There are clearly advantages of specialisation if a credit man is assigned to handle a specific industry or a segment of an industry. Within industry divisions, opinions and practice differ as to whether (*a*) one credit man should handle one client, or (*b*) the customer list within an industry, or segment, should be carved into alphabetical blocks and a credit man assigned to each block. Where there is a concentration of clients in one industry, opinion (*b*) has merit because typically, several or even many clients will be selling to the same customers and there is some point in one credit analyst having control over all credit extended to one customer. On the other hand, some factors prefer that one credit man should handle the whole of a client's customers because they feel that this promotes a closer relationship between client and factor than would be the case if the client dealt with several creditmen.

In the interest of economy, the various tasks involved in the approval procedure should be allocated to personnel according to their degree of skill. Skilled, highly paid credit men should be relieved of time-consuming, routine tasks in order to have maximum time for analysis and decision-making. The reception of approval applications, their distribution and the distribution of credit files to the right credit man, the transmission of decisions to the client, the obtaining of routine information, and the like, should be delegated to clerical staff. At the intermediate level there may be investigators to obtain and analyse routine information and generally assist the credit men.

B   COLLECTIONS

Collections have a dual importance. They are an element in credit control and they effect cash flow. Basically, collection procedures are designed to effect collections as quickly as possible without losing goodwill. For the sake of efficiency, standard procedures are employed but they should not be rigid because allowance has to be made for the different tolerances, that is the normal collection habits, of industries and segments of industries, and the varying financial strength and importance of customers.

The payment habits of industries and segments of industries can vary considerably. For example, payment one month after maturity of an invoice may be normal in one industry or segment, unacceptably slow in another, and unusually fast in a third. Similarly, prompt payment discounts may only be allowable in one industry or segment if payment is made strictly according to terms yet in another some latitude may be permissible.

Three categories of customers require the greatest degree of personalised attention:

(*a*) The main customers of a client. These are important to the client because of the large sales volume, and particular care has to be taken not to impair goodwill.

(*b*) Slow paying but financially solid customers. Typically, these are prime risks who take a long time to pay suppliers, particularly in high interest money conditions when they regard suppliers as a convenient source of free credit. They assume, correctly, that this will not impair their credit because their suppliers generally need them more than they need the suppliers, and because in the last analysis there is minimal doubt that they will pay.

(*c*) Marginal risks. This category obviously presents the greatest problems and need for attention.

In each of these three categories the recommended collection formula is polite persistence and, wherever possible, a rapport with the customer's bought ledger personnel and the executive who signs the cheques. Polite persistence cannot offend a reasonable man, but it is a nuisance and tempts him to pay up for the sake of peace and quiet. A personal visit to the customer's premises may be warranted to establish and maintain rapport, and also, as a last resort, to demand payment when all other methods have failed.

Subject to the foregoing, the standard collection procedures and time-table might be as follows:

1 April	Month end statement: for a specimen, see Appendices VI and VII
20 April	REMINDER: for a specimen, see Appendix VIII
30 April	SECOND REMINDER: for a specimen, see Appendix IX
10 May	Standard letter
20 May	Telephone call, confirmed by letter
30 May	Further telephone call, confirmed by letter
10 June	Decide further action according to amount involved, financial strength of customer and any other relevant circumstances. Further action could include another

telephone call, another letter, a final letter threatening legal proceedings, a telex, or a personal visit. Substantial amounts, say over £2,000, should be referred to the credit man handling the account for a decision.

Disputes generally arise over quality, quantity, specifications or discounts. Where a dispute arises, a notice of dispute (for a specimen, see Appendix X) is sent to the client inviting him to either issue a credit, if he admits the customer's claim, or to advise the factor of the answer to the claim. The factor will attempt to resolve the dispute but if it cannot be resolved within a reasonable time—normally about 30 days—the amount involved will be charged back to the client since disputed items are always at the client's risk. If the client so wishes, the factor will, at the client's expense, handle legal proceedings for the collection of debts at the client's risk. Such debts, of course, include not only disputed items but also debts which have not been approved by the factor.

Occasionally, a factoring agreement may provide for the automatic charge back of small deductions, say £10 or less, from customer payments. These small amounts commonly relate to prompt payment discounts wrongly taken by the customer after the periods in which they are allowable have expired. The rationale behind their automatic charge back is, first, that it can cause loss of goodwill to pursue such relatively small amounts; and, secondly, the time involved in collecting them may be significant although the aggregate amount is insignificant and the factoring charge can be kept down if the factor does not have to collect them. Where there is no such automatic charge back provision, or to provide for the situation where the unallowable discount exceeds the amount of the provision, the client's attitude towards unallowable discounts should be ascertained at the commencement of factoring. Some clients prefer to be charged with such amounts, at least in the case of important customers, rather than risk losing goodwill by chasing them.

In recourse factoring, any past due debt may, by the terms of the factoring agreement, be charged back to the client. In practice, however, the recourse factor exhausts his collection procedures before charging back a past due debt.

Except in the case of credits, where a charge back arises, a recourse notice (for a specimen, see Appendix XI) is sent to the client with a copy to the factor's client accounting and customer accounting departments so that the client's current account may be debited and the customer's account credited. It is advisable for charge backs arising out of disputes and for the institution of legal proceedings to be approved beforehand by the credit man handling the account, and for substantial charge backs to be approved beforehand by the credit manager or the client executive whose function is analysed below under "client relations".

2 Document Processing

On a regular basis, the client forwards to the factor schedules of receivables (for a specimen see Appendix XII) and schedules of credits issued. A credits schedule is normally called a notification, but the receivables schedule may be designated as an assignment, an offer to assign or a notification, depending on the practice of the particular factor concerned. This may happen as often as invoices and credit notes arise, but more commonly it is agreed that, for mutual administrative convenience, schedules will be forwarded once or twice a week. Upon receipt, schedules are usually numbered by the factor for reference. Schedules may be in duplicate, triplicate or even in quadruplicate. Where duplicate schedules are used, the client retains the copy for his records, and the original goes to the factor. In the case of triplicate schedules, the extra copy may be returned to the client as the factor's receipt. In the case of quadruplicate schedules, the factor may send the original to his client accounting department and the exra copy to his customer accounting department.

As a minimum contractual requirement, copy invoices are attached to receivables schedules and copy credit notes to credit schedules in order that the factor should have documentary evidence of receivables should customers (or indeed, the client or its liquidator) subsequently require such proof. Occasionally, in order to guard against the fraudulent assignment of fictitious receivables and to ensure that original invoices contain the required notice of assignment, factors require the original invoices to be forwarded with the receivables schedules, and undertake responsibility for mailing the invoices to customers. Despatch/delivery notes may also be required. They may not be available until after schedules are received because of the client's despatch procedures; for example, the client's head office may prepare invoices and schedules, but area offices deliver the merchandise.

Original credit notes are also sometimes forwarded to the factor for inspection and mailing on the reasoning that credits are contractually subject to the factors' approval and this procedure therefore gives the factor the opportunity to veto the credit. In practice, however, a credit veto rarely occurs. Schedules may contain all the salient details of invoices or credits, i.e. customer name, address, amount, terms, invoice number and date and, possibly, computer input number. Alternatively, they may merely refer to the attached invoice or credit note numbers and the total amount.

Where the factor is computerised, and most are, items input into the computer have to be coded with the client's and customer's' computer numbers. Often, the client is required to code items on the schedule or on invoices and credit notes. However, some factors do this job themselves either (1) to minimise the client's workload for competitive reasons, and/or (2) because it is considered that the client will make too many errors and foul up the factor's computer system. Where the factor does the coding, it is easy for a backlog to build up at the point of coding, unless careful control is excercised.

All these documents have to be checked for accuracy, completeness and validity. Routine checking should embrace the following:

(*a*) Invoices contain the required notice of assignment
(*b*) Schedules are signed by the client's authorised signatory
(*c*) Schedules contain all the required details
(*d*) Totals of schedules correspond with totals of attached invoices or credit notes
(*e*) Invoices are not post-dated
(*f*) There does not appear to be any double invoicing
(*g*) Invoices do not contain unacceptable terms e.g. sale or return, or progress payments.
(*h*) Credit notes do not significantly pre-date attached credit schedules
(*i*) Dispatch/delivery notes do not post-date the schedules assigning the debts to which they relate
(*j*) There are no missing dispatch/delivery notes

3 Customer Accounting

Customer accounting is handled in most respects in the same fashion as it would be by any trading concern. Receivables purchased are debited, and collections, credits and charge backs to the client are credited to the respective customers' accounts. Posting of receivables and credits may be from the schedules or the invoices and credit notes. Charge backs are generated either by the customer accounting department, or by the collection department, in either case with the approval of the credit man handling the account, at least where amounts are significant.

Some factors commingle all receivables purchased so that a particular customer's account may show receivables purchased for more than one client, although the various assignors will be identified because of possible client risk items, credits and charge backs. One statement may therefore relate to more than one client. Other factors segregate customers by client.

The customer accounting of most factors is computerised. Customer accounts are usually maintained on an open item system, that is, a balance is struck after each transaction is recorded by keying off or matching cash received against specific invoices. The system is usually maintained on an aged basis (for a specimen, see Appendix XIII). This aged analysis is for the use of the credit and collection department, as well as the customer accounting department. Clients are often provided with an aged analysis relating to their particular debts. Aged analyses are produced as often as required, either in the form of hard-copy, or on a video screen by a direct computer link or micro-fiche. Under the most sophisticated systems, input is fed directly into the computer and almost simultaneously shows on the video screen at the touch of a button. On a less sophisticated plane, micro-fiches may be produced periodically and viewed by insertion into the video screen. Micro-fiches and hard-copy analyses could be produced daily, but where, in order to cut costs, they are produced less frequently, say weekly or monthly, they are supplemented by hard-copy daily activity reports. The video screen system constitutes a simpler reference method than leafing through computer-produced hard-copy or manually produced ledger cards.

The application of collections to receivables can be a time consuming task, unless a computerised, automatic cash application system is operative. Under one such system, each collection is coded and input and the computer then automatically matches the collection to the receivable of the same amount. In the event of two receivables of the same amount, the collection is applied to the older. This system is, however, unsuitable for accounts such as department stores, where there is a likelihood of many items of the same, or similar amount. This system rejects all amounts which it cannot match by this automatic process and these are then applied manually and input accordingly. In practice, such an automatic cash application has proved extremely effective and reduced the workload by approximately 70 per cent. A further time-saving device is to use the customer's checking account number, endorsed on his check, as a computer input number.

In order to verify the existence and collectibility of debts it is not uncommon for factors to conduct a continuous audit programme to confirm balances outstanding. This is done by circularising a certain percentage of customers monthly. The percentage circularised depends on the factor's policy: once a year for each customer, or 10 per cent. of receivables outstanding per month are typical policies.

4   Client Accounting

It is usual for the factor to keep the client informed of the state of the account between client and factor by providing the client periodically, and usually monthly, with (*a*) A summary of debts purchased. The specimen contained in Appendix XIV is credited with the value of all debts offered as they are purchased and debited with their value as the purchase price is paid on their agreed maturity date. A factor who pays for debts on collection rather than on maturity might instead maintain this as a memorandum account merely showing the value of purchased debts although in his own books he would debit it with collections.

(*b*) A client current account. The specimen contained in Appendix XV is credited with the value of debts on their maturity date. This is appropriate where the debts, apart from the advance payments arrangement would be paid for on maturity, but where they would be paid for on collection, which is the practice of some factors, the account would instead be credited with collections as they are received. The account is also credited with any other amount to which the client is entitled, for example, customer discounts recovered for which he had previously been debited, or interest on credit balances left with the factor. The account is debited with the factoring charge (sometimes called the service charge), factor's discount, value added tax payable on the factoring charge, credits issued to customers, disputes and any other items which may be debited under the terms of the factoring agreement.

The format of client accounting documentation varies among factors. For example, the specimens contained in Appendixes XIV and XV follow the normal banking practice of not setting out detailed calculations of the factoring charge and factors discount, but some factors' client account documents do contain these details.

It is also common for clients to be provided with a daily activity report, and an aged analysis of debts (for a specimen see Appendix XIII) or at least of debts at the client's risk.

5 Client Relations

The soundest system of maintaining client relations is the client executive system. At the commencement of factoring, a member of the factor's management is designated to assume primary responsibility for relationships with the client. The responsbiilities of this client executive, as he is usually called, embrace the following:

(*a*) ensure that the factoring facility is being properly administered and that the client is satisfied;

(*b*) decide or make recommendations on applications by the client for changes in the factoring facility or for additional facilities such as seasonal financing;

(*c*) advise the client, as required, with respect to its business problems generally;

(*d*) periodically review the profitability of the account in the light of changing conditions, such as increases or decreases in turnover, number of customers and the average invoice value;

(*e*) keep under review the client's credit. Whereas the credit department is responsible for customer's credits, client executives are responsible for client's credits. This means keeping information up to date, analysing and reporting on it periodically and as necessary.

Fraud

The client executive's credit responsibilities include fraud prevention. Factoring is entered into on the basis of mutual trust. However, frauds on factors are usually committed by previously honest clients who drift into fraud because of a desperate credit situation or greed. Once fraud has been committed losses usually follow so prevention through continuous vigilance is necessary. Vigilance has to be tempered by practicality: fraud p evention systems should not be prohibitively expensive nor prejudice the goodwill of a reasonable client. It may be reasonable to conclude that factoring fraud prevention systems are effective from the fact that losses through fraud have historically been very small compared with credit losses. Because of his close relationship with the client, the account executive has direct responsibility for the most important anti-fraud technique: continuing assessment of the client's honesty. The rest of the factor's fraud prevention system consists of the document validity checks of the document processing department; debt verification by the customer accounting department; and information obtained during the course of collection. All detected frauds or attempts, or suspicions thereof, should be reported to the client executive.

The main frauds committed by clients are as follows:

(*a*) Providing false financial statements or deliberately delaying providing financial statements in order to conceal a deteriorated credit position.

(*b*) Selling fictitious debts. This is difficult to get away with where original invoices are channelled through the factor, but there have been instances of the following methods which, until detected, were successful. First, the client double invoices, which confuses the customer; then, when challenged, claims that it was an administrative error and issues a credit for which it is debited by the factor; but by the time the matter is sorted out the client has had the use of the factor's funds for some time. Secondly, the client connives with a member of the customer's staff to pass the invoices for payment. Thirdly, the client connives with a member of the factor's staff to pass the invoices.

(*c*) Debts are assigned prior to shipment of the goods to which they relate, in order to accelerate cash flow.

(*d*) Concealment of or delay in notifying the factor of credits in order not to impair cash flow.

(*e*) Collection of payments directly from a customer or customers, or concealing or delaying the forwarding of such payments to the factor.

Part Two : Law

CHAPTER FIVE

The Assignment of Book Debts

1 Legal Objectives

The legal method of conducting factoring in England has been for the factor to take assignments, by way of purchase, of client's book debts which

(*a*) are enforceable against the client;[1]

(*b*) are enforceable against the customers;[2]

(*c*) have priority, as far as possible, over competing interests of third parties;[3]

(*d*) avoid payment of *ad valorem* stamp duty;[4]

(*e*) avoid the restrictive provisions of the Moneylenders Acts 1900–1927, which, however, are about to be repealed;[5]

(*f*) avoid public registration of assignments on the reasoning (which not everyone shares) that such registration would deter some businesses from factoring. The point is related to the priorities question above, because the two statutory provisions requiring public filing of assignments of book debts affect priorities as between the factor and, (i) in the case of general assignments, the trustee in bankruptcy of a client who is a sole trader or partnership (section 43 of the Bankruptcy Act 1914); and, (ii) in the case of charges or assignments by way of mortgage, the general creditors of a corporate client in liquidation (Companies Act 1948, s. 95).

Mortgages and charges are similar to purchases in commercial effect but they are not normally used in factoring because they do not achieve all the desired legal results. Purchase, mortgage and charge are distinct legal concepts with different legal consequences in some respects. Purchases and mortgages are both forms of assignment whereas a charge is not. However, a purchase is an absolute transfer of property for consideration, whereas mortgages and charges are secured loans. The chief characteristic of a loan, distinguishing it from a purchase, is a promise to repay.[6] A mortgage is an absolute transfer of property subject to a proviso for redemption upon repayment of the

---

[1] Pp. 98 *et seq., post.*   [2] Chap. 6, *post.*   [3] Chap. 7, *post.*
[4] P. 104, *post.*   [5] Chap. 8, *post.*
[6] *De Vigier* v. *Inland Revenue Commissioners*, [1974] 2 All E.R. 907; [1964] 1 W.L.R. 1073.

loan.[7] An assignment of debts "by way of continuing security" has been held to be a mortgage and not a sale,[8] for in such a case equity implies a right of redemption.[9] Although section 136(1) of the law of Property Act 1925 excludes from its operation an "assignment purporting to be by way of charge" and although a charge has been judicially described as an "equitable assignment",[10] such equations of charges with assignments are, strictly, inaccurate because a charge only gives a right to payment out of a particular fund or particular property without transferring that fund or property.[11] Even the assignment of part of a debt is not a charge.[12]

A further point of distinction has to be made between a fixed and a floating charge. A fixed charge attaches to a particular fund or property immediately, whereas a floating charge "attaches to the subject charged in the varying condition in which it happens to be from time to time. It is of the essence of such a charge that it remains dormant until the undertaking charged ceases to be a going concern, or until the person in whose favour the charge is created intervenes. His right to intervene may of course be suspended by agreement. But if there is no agreement for suspension, he may exercise his right whenever he pleases after default.[13]

The conceptual differences between purchase, mortgage and charge have the following differing legal consequences which are difficult, if not impossible, to justify in principle. First, a purchaser of debts, but not a mortgagee or chargee avoids the highly inconvenient and much criticised[14] provisions of the Moneylenders Acts 1900–1927, which, fortunately, are about to be repealed, since they apply only to the business of moneylending and not to the business of purchasing debts. As the Judicial Committee of the Privy Council said in *Chow Yoong Hong* v. *Choong Fah Rubber Manufactory*:[15] "There are many ways of raising cash besides borrowing. One is by selling book debts . . .". Secondly, charges and mortgages but not purchases have to be registered with the Registrar of Companies to be valid against any liquidator of the company.[16] However, a factor, as a purchaser of debts, is not a creditor and an unregistered charge is therefore valid as against him.

[7] *Halliday* v. *Holgate* (1868), L.R. 3 Exch. 299; *Durham Brothers* v. *Robertson*, [1898] 1 Q.B. 765, at p. 722.
[8] *Hughes* v. *Pump House Hotel*, [1902] 2 K.B. 190.
[9] *Durham Brothers* v. *Robertson*, supra.
[10] *Webb* v. *Smith* (1885), 30 Ch.D. 192, at p. 201, *per* Lindley, L.J.
[11] *Tancred* v. *Delagoa Bay and East Africa Rail. Co.* (1889), 23 Q.B.D. 239, at p. 242, *per* Denham, J.
[12] *Re Steel Wing Co., Ltd.*, [1921] 1 Ch. 349; *Walter and Sullivan, Ltd.* v. *J. Murray & Sons, Ltd.*, [1952] 2 Q.B. 584; [1955] 1 All E.R. 843.
[13] *Governments Stock and Other Securities Investment Co.* v. *Manila Rail. Co.*, [1897] A.C. 81, at p. 86, *per* Lord MacNaghten.
[14] Chap. 8, *post.*
[15] [1962] A.C. 209; [1961] 3 All E.R. 1163.   [16] Companies Act 1948, s. 95.

But in commercial reality, the sale of debts to a factor, except in the case of maturity factoring, is similar in effect to giving security whatever the law may say. For this reason it is treated, generally, in the same way as a loan secured by book debts by the American Uniform Commercial Code,[17] and the Crowther Committee recommended the same treatment in its proposal for a Lending and Security Act modelled on the Code.[18]

A considerable amount of legal weaving and threading is necessary to make an umbrella of the desirable applicable law under which to shelter from the torrent of inconvenient or harsh law.

2 The Factoring Agreement

It has been found that the best solution to the various problems is to use a master agreement (the "factoring agreement") providing for the sale and purchase of book debts. Usually, the factoring agreement is only an "agreement to agree". For specimens, see Appendices II and III. By its terms, specific existing debts are to be offered for sale to the factor as they arise on the terms set out in the factoring agreement and thus no purchase occurs until the factor accepts the offer. This is the best method of avoiding payment of *ad valorem* stamp duty.[19] However, some factoring agreements are not agreements to agree but agreements for the purchase of present and future debts and (*a*) for the legal assignment of those debts as they arise in the terms set out in the master agreement; or (*b*) for notification to the factor of those debts as they arise. For a specimen of the latter see Appendix I. The last two types of factoring agreement rely on less certain methods of avoiding *ad valorem* stamp duty[20] and if entered into with a sole trader or partnership, they have to be registered as bills of sale in order to be valid against clients' trustees in bankruptcy: Bankruptcy Act 1914, section 43.

A factoring agreement is likely to contain the following principal provisions (refer to Appendices I–III for full details):

(*a*) the client agrees to sell or to offer to sell all its debts to the factor;
(*b*) The client warrants and covenants that the debts are valid, enforceable, undisputed, bona fide, arise in the normal course of business; that information, etc. furnished to the factor by the client in respect of them is correct; and that contract terms giving rise to the debt will not be changed without the factor's consent (credits may be excepted);
(*c*) the old-line factor assumes the credit risk (i.e. the risk of financial

---

[17] UCC, Article 9–102 (1) (*b*). However, the assignments of debts as part of the sale of a business or for the purpose of collection are not.
[18] Report of the Committee on Consumer Credit (The "Crowther Report"). Cmnd. 4596, para. 5.5.2.
[19] P. 104, *post.*   [20] P. 104, *post.*

inability of the customer to pay) in respect of debts which it approves.[21]

As regards unapproved debts, a right of recourse to the client arises if they are unpaid by their due date or if matters in the nature of acts of bankruptcy occur to the customers who owe them;

(*d*) notice of assignment in a form required by the factor is to be endorsed on invoices sent to customers;

(*e*) specified documents (invoices, credit notes, receipts) are to be sent to the factor with schedules;

(*f*) the minimum period of notice of termination (usually three months) is specified (although the factor often has a right to terminate upon any breach by the client), as is the minimum period for which the agreement is to run (usually about a year), and, perhaps, a minimum annual factoring charge which tends to have the effect of making the agreement run from year to year;

(*g*) the factor has a power of attorney to execute assignments and to endorse negotiable instruments received from customers in respect of payments;

(*h*) matters of accounting and administrative detail are sometimes set out, although it might be argued that it is not essential to do so, and they might be more conveniently excluded since such details tend to change from time to time causing the inconvenience of amendment to the agreement.

3 Corporate Client's Capacity to Factor

Important changes to the previous law were effected by section 9(1) of the European Communities Act 1972 which states that:

> "In favour of a person dealing with a company in good faith, any transaction decided on by the directors shall be deemed to be one which it is within the capacity of the company to enter into, and the power of the directors to bind the company shall be deemed to be free of any limitations under the Memorandum or Articles of Association; and a party to a transaction so decided on shall not be bound to enquire as to the capacity of the company to enter into it or as to any such limitation on the powers of the directors, and shall be presumed to have acted in good faith unless the contrary is proved."[1]

The section protects a dealing with a company in good faith in that, subject to a proviso, it abolishes the *ultra vires* rule. By this rule, a transaction which was outside the ambit of a company's powers contained in the objects clause of its Memorandum of Association was void and could not be ratified even with the unanimous consent of all the members.[2] Thus, due to the judge-made doctrine of constructive

[21] P. 6, *ante.*
[1] For a critical analysis, see Prentice, D.D., "Section 9 of the European Communities Act" (1973), 89 L.Q.R. 518.
[2] *Ashbury Railway Carriage and Iron Co.* v. *Riche* (1875), L.R. 7 H.L. 653.

notice of the contents of the Memorandum and Articles of Association,[3] it used to be essential for a factor to inspect the objects clause of the Memorandum to ensure that a company had the power to factor and to carry on its business. This is no longer necessary since the *ultra vires* doctrine can no longer be relied on *provided* the transaction was decided on by the board of directors. It is prudent for a factor to obtain a copy of the enabling board resolution certified as correct by the secretary or a director.

A further protection for a factor dealing with a corporate client is afforded by the rule in *Turquand's Case* (1855),[4] otherwise known as "the indoor management rule", which states that third parties are entitled to assume that the internal procedures of a company, both at directors' and at shareholders' meetings, have been regularly conducted in the absence of actual notice to the contrary .

4 Power of Client's Agents

Clients use agents to act on their behalf. Indeed, corporations, which constitute the vast majority of clients, are abstract concepts and can only act through agents. The question of the power of agents to bind clients is therefore important to factors, particularly in relation to the execution of the factoring agreement and the signing of assignments and other documents thereunder.

Agents include directors in relation to whom section 9(1) of the European Communities Act 1972, cited above, has the effect of modifying the doctrine of constructive notice. Previously, a third party was deemed to have constructive notice of any limitation of directors' powers contained in the Memorandum or Articles of Association. Therefore, any such limitation in the Memorandum or Articles would invalidate a transaction to which it applied although the transaction could be ratified subsequently by ordinary resolution at a general meeting.[5] Now, by section 9(1), a third party is protected if he acted in good faith and did not have actual knowledge of a limitation of the directors' power, contained in the Memorandum or Articles.

The section does not cover the important question whether an individual director or other person who purports to act for the company is duly authorised to do so by the board of directors. This question continues to be governed by the general principles of agency law. A client is bound by the acts of its agent who has actual authority (whether express or implied).[6] This is partly reflected in section 32(1)(b)

[3] *Ernest* v. *Nichols* (1857), 6 H.L. Cas. 401.
[4] *Royal British Bank* v. *Turquand* (1856) 6 E. & B. 327.
[5] *Grant* v. *United Kingdom Switchback Rail. Co.* (1888), 40 Ch.D. 135; *Re Bank of Hindustan, China and Japan, Campbell's Case* (1873), 9 Ch. App. 1.
[6] Powell, *The Law of Agency* (2nd Edn.), 1961, p. 36.

of the Companies Act, 1948 which says that a contract which is by law required to be in writing may be made on behalf of the company in writing signed by any person acting under its authority, express or implied. By section 74(1) of the Law of Property Act 1925, in favour of a bona fide purchaser for value without notice, a deed is deemed to be validly executed by a company if its seal, or a seal purporting to be the company seal, has been affixed in the presence of a director and the secretary, or persons purporting to be the director and the secretary, and attested by them

A client is also bound by the act of its "agent" who has no actual authority but who has either apparent authority or usual authority. Apparent authority means that the agent appears to have authority as a result of a representation by the client to the factor on which the factor acts to his detriment. Here the client is estopped from denying the agent's authority. Usual authority means that the agent has the authority which a person in his position usually possesses to act on behalf of the client. A managing director has a very wide usual authority extending to the ordinary business of the company.[7] Other individual directors have very little usual authority,[8] but they do have the authority to sign cheques on behalf of the company, and to clothe a transaction with formal validity which has already been authorised by the board or the managing director.[9] Thus, it seems likely that a director who signs an assignment or other document pursuant to a factoring agreement which has been authorised by the board, has usual authority to do so.

If a factor has paid part or all of the purchase consideration for a debt to the client; the assignment is then discovered to be not binding on the client because of want of authority of the agent who assigned it; and the client will not ratify the assignment, the factor may be entitled to recover the money paid to the client in quasi contract. This is the species of obligation imposed by law in the absence of contract or tort to redress unjust enrichment of the recipient.[10]

5   Meaning and Nature of Book Debts

In *Independent Automatic Sales, Ltd.* v. *Knowles and Foster*,[11] Buckley, J., approved the following definition of book debts established a century earlier in *Shipley* v. *Marshall*:[12]

[7] *Freeman and Lockyer* v. *Buckhurst Park Properties (Mangal), Ltd.*, [1964] 2 Q.B. 480; [1964] 1 All E.R. 630, C.A.
[8] *Rama Corporation, Ltd.* v. *Proved Tin and General Investments, Ltd.*, [1952] 2 Q.B. 147; [1952] 1 All E.R. 554.
[9] *Re Land Credit Co. of Ireland Ex parte Overend, Gurney & Co.* (1869), 4 Ch.App. 460.
[10] *Kelly* v. *Solari* (1841), 9 M. & W. 54, at p. 59; 152 E.R. 24, at p. 26; Birks, "The Recovery of Carelessly Mistaken Payments", 1972 Current Legal Problems, 178; Goff and Jones, *The Law of Restitution*; Stolar, *The Law of Quasi-Contract*.
[11] [1962] 3 All E.R. 27.   [12] (1863), 14 C.B.N.S. 566.

"So far as I am aware, no more precise definition of the term 'book debts' has ever been attempted judicially and I shall not attempt one. *Shipley* v. *Marshall,* I think, establishes that if it can be said of a debt arising in the course of a business and due or growing due to the proprietor of that business that such a debt would or could in the ordinary course of such a business be entered in well-kept books relating to that business that debt can properly be called a book debt whether it is in fact entered in the books of the business or not."[13]

A book debt belongs to the species of property called choses, or things, in action. A chose in action has been defined as a personal right to property which can only be enforced by action and not by taking physical possession.[14] Legal choses in action, which include debts arising under contracts, are those over which the common law courts had exclusive jurisdiction prior to the Judicature Act 1873. Equitable choses in action, such as legacies or interests in trust funds, are those over which the Chancery Courts had exclusive jurisdiction prior to the Judicature Act 1873. By the Judicature Act 1873, the jurisdictions of the Common Law and Chancery Courts were fused.

English legislation virtually invariably uses the expression "book debts" but the equivalent expressions "accounts receivable" or "receivables", which are American in origin, are now commonly used in England by commercial men including factors.

6 The History of Assignment of Debts[15]

The earliest English legal records of assignments of debts date back to the twelfth century and indicate that they were by and to Jews who at that time had a virtual monopoly on moneylending because they were the only class whose property was substantially in the form of money, and the Church threatened excommunication to Christians who (presuming they had the money) charged interest on loans. When the king needed money he found it convenient to tax the Jews who might pay him by assignment of debts due to them. This period of royal patronage ended with the expulsion of the Jews from England at the end of the thirteenth century. Thereafter the royal judges adopted a hostile policy towards the assignment of choses in action and to this day the common law refuses to recognise them, excepting crown debts and by the law merchant, bills of exchange and promissory notes.

[13] At p. 34; See also *Re Haigh's Estate, Haigh* v. *Haigh* (1907), 51 Sol. Jo. 343, at p. 343, *per* Parker, J. In *Paul and Frank, Ltd.* v. *Discount Bank (Overseas), Ltd. and The Board of Trade,* [1967] Ch. 348; [1966] 2 All E.R. 922; it was held that an assignment of a credit insurance policy did not of itself create a book debt in favour of the assignee.

[14] *Torkington* v. *Magee,* [1902] 2 K.B. 427, at 430.

[15] See the learned and valuable article by S. J. Bailey "Assignment of Debts in England from the Twelfth to the Twentieth Century", 47 L.Q.R. 516 (1931); 48 L.Q.R. 248, 547 (1932).

The common law had four main objections to the assignment of legal choses in action. First, there was a deeply entrenched notion that property, whatever its nature, could not be transferred without delivery of possession. Since a chose in action is an intangible with a merely notional existence, it is impossible physically to deliver possession of it and the common law therefore regarded it as unassignable.

The second objection was that it constituted maintenance. In 1620 Coke claimed that such an assignment would be "the occasion of multiplying of contentions and suits of great oppression to the people, and the subversion of the due and equal execution of justice".[16] On the other hand, it had been established as early as 1305 that the maintenance objection was overcome if, at the time of the assignment the assignor was answerable to the assignee for a pre-existing debt.[17] Thus, in case after case there appears the allegation of the existence of a pre-existing debt. But with the development of assumpit and the doctrine of consideration, by the sixteenth and seventeenth centuries this allegation began to disappear from the record. By 1749 the phrase "valuable consideration" was used in connection with the assignment of choses in action and thereafter the allegation of a debt precedent was unnecessary.[18] Indeed, by the end of the seventeenth century the presumption of maintenance had disappeared to the extent that if the assignment were by deed it bound the assignor on the covenant and he could be sued for damages.[19] But this development did not overcome the common law hurdle because the assignee still could not bring an action in his own name against the debtor.

The third objection was that a debt was too personal to be assigned.[20] Bailey has convincingly argued that the "too personal" objection was rooted, although perhaps subconsciously, in the fear of imprisonment of the debtor, for a debtor who defaulted in payment could face the horrors of the debtors' prison.[1] A debtor therefore sought a creditor whom he could trust and from whom he could obtain extension of time, if necessary, for payment of a debt since the consequences of imposing a stranger as creditor against the debtor's will could be severe. The theory that the fear of imprisonment was the basis of the "too personal" objection is borne out by the fact that within five years of the virtual abolition of imprisonment of debtors by the Debtors Act

---

[16] *Lampet's Case* (1612), 10 Co. Rep. 46b, 77 E.R. 994.

[17] Y.B., 33 Edw, 1 Mich. R.S. 86–89.

[18] *Row* v. *Dawson* (1749), 1 Ves. Sen. 331, 27 E.R. 1064, *per* Lord Hardwicke.

[19] *Deering* v. *Farrington* (1674), 1 Mod. 113, 86 E.R. 772; followed and applied in R. v. *Aickles Inhabitants* (1702), 12 Mod. 553 at p. 556, 88 E.R. 1513; *Ward* v. *Audland* (1847), 8 Beav 201, 50 E.R. 79; *Aulton* v. *Atkins* (1856), 18 C.B. 249, 139 E.R. 1364; *Gerard* v. *Lewis* (1867), L.R. 2 C.P. 305.

[20] See *Fitzroy* v. *Cave*, [1905] 2 K.B. 364, at p. 372, *per* Cozens-Hardy, J.

[1] See 48 L.Q.R. at p. 550.

1869, direct assignments of debts at law became possible by the Judicature Act 1873, section 25(6).

The fourth objection was that a debt or other legal chose in action was too uncertain to be assigned. The subject-matter of a grant must be certain, so that, according to Bracton, "There is no donation of an uncertain thing."[2] He claimed that a chose in action could not be bequeathed unless it had been liquidated by judgement or recognizance. However, by the fifteenth century it was established that a liquidated debt was sufficiently certain[3] although unliquidated claims or money payable in an uncertain event were considered to be too uncertain until the nineteenth century.[4]

In 1648 the common law courts, perhaps uneasy about the rationale of their doctrine, evolved the theory of novation by which it could be avoided.[5] Strictly, novation is not an assignment at all, although its effect is the same. It is a tripartite agreement between assignor, assignee and debtor whereby the original debt between assignor and debtor is extinguished and the latter becomes bound anew to the assignee. The distinguishing feature of novation as compared to assignment is the consent of the debtor to the arrangement.

The common law also sanctioned another device which effectively skirted its own doctrine. This device was the use of a power of attorney to the assignee to collect and recover the proceeds of the debt. Theoretically, this meant that the assignee held the proceeds as agent of the assignor, but if the instrument appointed him as attorney "sans accompt render" (meaning, without having to account for the proceeds) he was entitled to keep the proceeds. By the end of the seventeenth century this device had become an established method of avoiding the common law doctrine against assignment of debts.[6] Theoretically, this device could be used by factors today, but, because assignments are now possible by statute and are procedurally easier to enforce in equity against customers, there is no reason to resort to such artifice.

If there was no such power of attorney or novation, the assignee could only sue the debtor at common law by bringing an action in the name of the assignor. This required the assignor's consent, which might be refused. Moreover, even if the assignor gave his consent he might do or threaten to do something to prevent the assignee from recovering in the action. The assignee received no help from the common law courts to compel the assignor to lend his name to the action

[2] See Bracton, *De Leg.* ff. 15b–16b at f. 15b.
[3] Y.B. 5 Edw. 4, 8.
[4] Sweet, "Choses in Action", 10 L.Q.R. at p. 304 citing *Brice* v. *Bannister* (1878), 3 Q.B.D. 569, C.A.; *Walker* v. *Bradford Old Bank, Ltd.* (1884), 12 Q.B.D. 511.
[5] *Baker* v. *Edmonds* (1647), Sty. 62, 82 E.R. 531; see also *Tatlock* v. *Harris* (1789), 3 Term. Rep. 174, at 180, 100 E.R. 517, per Buller, J.
[6] Malynes: "*Lex Mercatoria*" I, c. xv, p. 78.

or to restrain the assignor's action or threat because the common law did not recognise the assignment.

The attitude of the Chancery judges to the common law prohibition against assignment was blunt: "Courts of equity", said Buller, C. J. in 1791, "from the earliest time thought the doctrine too absurd for them to adopt."[7] Prior to the Judicature Act 1873, equity courts had exclusive jurisdiction over equitable, but not legal, choses in action, so they could not directly adjudicate in an action against a debtor of a legal chose in action. But where the assignee was faced with a recalcitrant assignor, equity regarded the latter as bound in conscience and implied an agreement to lend his name to a common law action. The procedure for an assignee to follow was to bring a Chancery suit against a recalcitrant assignor in order to compel him to lend his name as plaintiff in an action against the debtor. By this circuitous route, the assignee brought its claim before a common law court, but by subterfuge, for the assignor was the nominal plaintiff.

It is in the light of this history that one should read the claim of Willes, J. in 1857 that the common law doctrine "has, as everyone must know, long since been exploded".[8] True, there had been an explosion, in fact several, but they had not demolished the doctrine. His honour probably meant that the doctrine could be avoided by suing in the assignor's name with the assistance of equity if the assignor would not consent, by the doctrine of novation and by the power of attorney "sans accompt render".

Thus, immediately prior to enactment of the Judicature Acts 1873, the course which the assignee of a debt had to take in order to sue the debtor was either:

(*a*) to obtain the assignor's consent and co-operation to a common law action against the debtor in the assignor's name as plaintiff; or

(*b*) if this was not possible, to bring a chancery suit against the assignor to compel him to lend his name to a subsequent common law action against the debtor.

The need for law reform was glaring. It came with section 25(6) of the Judicature Act 1873 which was subsequently transplanted into the Law of Property Act 1925 as section 136(1). This enables a factor whose assignment complies with the requirements of the section to sue the customer without joining the client as a party.

7 Requirements of Statutory Assignments

Section 136(1) of the Law of Property Act 1925 says:

---

[7] See *Master* v. *Miller* (1791), 4 Term. Rep. 320, at p. 360, 100 E.R. 1042, at p. 1053.
[8] *Balfour* v. *Sea Fire Life Assurance Co.* (1857), 3 C.B. N.S. 300, 140 E.R. 756.

"Any absolute assignment in writing under the hand of the assignor (not purporting to be by way of charge only) of any debt or other legal thing in action, of which express notice has been given to the debtor, trustee or other person from whom the assignor would have been entitled to claim such debt or thing in action, is effectual in law (subject to equities having priority over the right of the assignee) to pass and transfer from the date of such notice:

    (*a*) the legal right to such debt or thing in action
    (*b*) all legal and other remedies for the same, and
    (*c*) the power to give a good discharge for the same without the concurrence of the assignor."

There are three formal requirements of an effective statutory assignment: the assignment must be absolute and not purporting to be by way of charge only; it must be in writing under the hand of the client; and express notice of the assignment must be given to the customer.

A   ASSIGNMENT MUST BE ABSOLUTE AND NOT PURPORTING TO BE BY WAY OF CHARGE ONLY

The assignment must clearly indicate the intention of the parties to transfer all the assignor's rights to the debt. In *Hughes* v. *Pump House Hotel*.[9] Matthew, L.J. said as follows:

"the defendants . . .contend that the instrument in question constituted an absolute assignment. . . . In every case of this kind, all the terms of the instrument must be considered; and, whatever may be the phraseology adopted in some particular part of it if . . . it is clear from the instrument as a whole that the intention was to pass all the rights of an assignor in the debt or chose in action to the assignee, then the case will come within section 25 [of the Judicature Act 1873, since repealed and replaced by Section 136 of the Law of Property Act]."

The fact that an instrument uses the word "absolutely" shows that it is intended, in point of form, to be an absolute assignment and this is evidence that the parties also intended it to be absolute in substance.[10]

In *Durham Brothers* v. *Robertson*,[11]. Chitty, L.J. said,

"Where the Act applies it does not leave the original debtor in uncertainty as to the person to whom the legal right is transferred; it does not involved him in any question as to the state of the accounts . . . the legal right is transferred and is vested in the assignee."

In the same case it was held that an assignment is not absolute if it is

---

[9] [1902] 2 K.B. 190, at pp. 193–194.
[10] *Comfort* v. *Betts* (1891), 1 Q.B. 737 at p. 740, C.A. *per* Fry, L.J.
[11] [1898] 1 Q.B. 765, at p. 773.

conditional. Future debts[12] and parts of debts[13] are not assignable under the section although assignable in equity. A "future" debt is "not merely not payable but not earned at the date of the assignment".[14] A mortgage is within the section[15] but a charge is expressly excluded.

B   THE ASSIGNMENT MUST BE IN WRITING UNDER THE HAND OF THE CLIENT

Any written assignment suffices. It need not be by deed nor need it be for valuable consideration: *Re Westerton, Public Trustee* v. *Gray*.[16]

The phrase "under the hand of the assignor" raises the question precisely who can execute the assignment. Most clients are corporations, and a corporation, of course, is only an abstraction with neither a mind nor a body, let alone a hand, of its own. It possesses no "hand" which it can put to an assignment and has to act through its directors and agents whose power to bind their principal is analysed above.[17] The representative capacity of the signatory must be made clear otherwise it will not be "under the hand of the assignor". In the Canadian case of *Mahoney* v. *Traders Finance Corporation, Ltd.*[18] the court considered a section equivalent to section 136(1). An automobile company purported to assign a debt, secured by a chattel mortgage, to a finance company. The assignment was executed by a duly authorised officer of the auto-mobile company in his own name and without any statement of his representative capacity. However, the assignment said, "the undersigned hereby absolutely assigns . . ." so that the document read as an assign-ment by the officer of a debt owing to him personally. The court held that the assignment was not under the hand of the assignor because the officer "did not purport to sign in a representative capacity on behalf of the vendor. He executed the assignment as an individual when no title to the chattel mortgage was vested in him". It is clear that the court would have held the assignment was "under the hand of the assignor" if the representative capacity of the officer had been stated.[19]

C   EXPRESS WRITTEN NOTICE TO THE CUSTOMER

The principal method used in factoring to give notice of assignment is by printing, typing, stamping or sticking it on the invoice. Usually the client attends to the placing of notices on invoices and their mailing

[12] *Tailby* v. *Official Receiver* (1888), 13 App. Cas. 523, H.L.; *Holt* v. *Heatherfield Trust, Ltd.,* [1942] 1 All E.R. 404, at p. 408.
[13] Re *Steel Wing Co., Ltd.,* [1921] 1 Ch. 349; *Williams* v. *Atlantic Assurance Co.,* [1933] 1 K.B. 81; *Walter and Sullivan, Ltd.* v. *Murphy & Sons, Ltd.,* [1955] 2 Q.B. 584; [1955] 1 All E.R. 843.
[14] *G. & T. Earle, Ltd.* v. *Hemsworth Rural District Council* (1928), 44 T.L.R. 605, at p. 609, *per* Wright, J.
[15] *Tancred* v. *Delagoa Bay and East Africa Rail Co.* (1889), 23 Q.B.D. 239; *Hughes* v. Pump House Hotel Co., *supra.*
[16] [1919] 2 Ch. 104.   [17] P. 93.   [18] (1958), 17 D.L.R. (2d) 432.
[19] Cf. *Wilson* v. *Wallani* (1880), 5 Ex. D. 155.

to customers. As an additional precaution, notice of assignment may also be contained on statements of account sent to the customer by the factor. A typical notice of assignment on an invoice would say that "the debt due under this invoice has been assigned to and is payable only to our factors, X Factors Ltd.; of (address) whose receipt alone will be recognised." As regards debts already invoiced and on the sales ledger and assigned to the factor at the commencement of factoring, notice is typically given in a letter from client or factor to the customer.

The notice is considered to have been given when it is received by the customer.[20] The statute prescribes no time limit within which notice must be given,[21] but it will be ineffectual if given after an action has commenced.[22] The statute does not say who has to give notice so either assignor or assignee may give it.

If the customer is a company, notice sent to the address of a branch or plant of the company is sufficient. It is not necessary to address it to a particular individual within the company for the company's internal arrangement as to the officer responsible for payment are of no concern to the client or to the factor.[1]

The section does not speak of "a notice" but of "notice". A separate document, therefore, is not essential, and a copy of the actual assignment instrument sent to the customer could constitute notice,[2] although, in the context of factoring, this would be an impractical course.

In *Denney, Gasquet and Metcalfe* v. *Conklin*[3] Atkin, J. said that in order to comply with the section, the notice must bring to the customer's attention with "reasonable certainty" the fact that the debt had been assigned. Nevertheless, he was rather liberal in upholding the sufficiency of the notice which he was considering. One Derham had assigned a debt to trustees under a deed of arrangement. The solicitors of the trustees wrote to the debtor in the following words: "The trustees of the deed of arrangement dated the 5th of December, 1907, and executed by Mr Walter Derham have instructed us to apply for an account showing all of the dealings between yourself and Mr Walter Derham. The reason of this application is that there appears from Mr Derham's books to be a considerable debt due from you to him for money advanced." It will be noted that there was no mention of the amount assigned, the trustees were not actually identified by name nor as assignees, and the last sentence of the letter seemed to negate the idea of an assignment in that it indicated the debt was still due to Derham.

[20] *Holt* v. *Heatherfield Trust, Ltd.,* [1942] 2 K.B. 1; [1942] 1 All E.R. 404.
[21] *Bateman* v. *Hunt,* [1904] 2 K.B. 530, C.A.
[22] *Compania Colombiana de Seguros* v. *Pacific Steam Navigation Co.* [1965] 1 Q.B. 101, at p. 129.
[1] *William Brandt's Sons & Co.* v. *Dunlop Rubber Co.,* [1905] A.C. 454, at pp. 459, 465.
[2] *Van Lynn Developments, Ltd.* v. *Pelias Construction Co., Ltd.,* [1969] 1 Q.B. 607, at p. 615, *per* Widgery, J.
[3] [1913] 3 K.B. 177; cf. the Canadian case of *Imperial Bank* v. *Georges* (1909), 2 Alta L.R. 386.

In *James Talcott, Ltd.* v. *John Lewis & Co. Ltd.*[4] Du Parcq, L.J. held that "it is not enough that the notice should be capable of being understood to mean that the debt is assigned. It must be plain and unambiguous, and not reasonably capable when read by an intelligent business man, of a contrary construction."[5] In the same case, Mac-Kinnon, L. J. said "the language is immaterial if the meaning is plain". The court there held that the following notice, which was stamped on the invoice, was ineffective because it did not satisfy the plain and unambiguous criterion:

> "To facilitate our accountancy and banking arrangements, it has been agreed that this invoice be transferred to and payment in London funds should be made to James Talcott Ltd., 6–8 Sackville Street, London, W.I. Errors in this invoice must be notified to James Talcott Ltd. immediately."

It has been held that if the date of assignment is wrongly stated on the notice it is ineffectual as notice under the section.[6] The short ground of the decisions holding to this effect is that notice with a wrong date is notice of a non-existent document.[7] They therefore left open the question whether it is necessary to give the date of the assignment on the notice. That question was resolved in the negative in *Van Lynn Developments, Ltd.* v. *Pelias Construction Co., Ltd.*,[8] Denning, M. R. said:

> "It seems to me to be unnecessary that it should give the date of the assignment so long as it makes it plain that there has in fact been an assignment so that the debtor knows to whom he has to pay the debt in the future . . . the notice itself is good, even though it gives no date."[9]

The court also held that erroneous but superfluous statements on the notice do not affect its sufficiency. Denning M. R. said, "This notice, does, however, go on to make an inaccurate statement. It says that 'notice of this assignment has already been given to you'. But, as Davies, L. J. said in the course of argument, that it is merely an inaccurate surplusage. It can be ignored." Possibly, a misstatement of the amount of the debt will invalidate the notice.[10]

In the light of *Hockley and Papworth* v. *Goldstein*[11] it seems that the written notice requirement is always mandatory and no circumstances

---

[4] [1940] 3 All E.R. 592.   [5] At p. 599.

[6] *Stanley* v. *English Fibres Industries, Ltd.* (1899), 68 L.J.Q.B. 839; approved in *W. F. Harrison & Co., Ltd.* v. *Burke*, [1956] 2 All E.R. 169, C.A. But such a mistake does not affect an equitable assignment: see *Whittingstall* v. *King* (1882), 46 L.T. 520.

[7] See *Van Lynn Developments, Ltd.* v. *Pelias Construction Co., Ltd.*, [1969] 1 Q.B. 607, at 612 *per* Denning, L.J., C.A.

[8] Note 2, *supra*.   [9] *Ibid.*, at p. 613.

[10] *W. F. Harrison & Co., Ltd.* v. *Burke, supra* at 421.

[11] (1921), 90 L.J.K.B. 111.

will excuse it. In that case the debtor was not given written notice of assignment because he could neither read nor write and it was not thought worth while to give him written notice. Instead, the assignment was read over to him twice and he understood its contents. Bailhache, J. held that written notice was mandatory and verbal notice consequently insufficient.

8 Requirements of Equitable Assignments

The statute does not affect the efficacy of equitable assignments of debts in any way.[12] Hence an assignment which does not qualify as a statutory assignment may still be effective as an equitable assignment with slightly different procedural consequences. For example, as stated, a mistake in the notice as to the date of assignment will render it ineffective as a statutory assignment, but it will still be effective as an equitable assignment. The formal requirements of an equitable assignment of a debt are very relaxed. No particular form of words is required provided the meaning is plain that the assignor intends the assignee to have the benefit of the debt. In *William Brandt's Sons & Co.* v. *Dunlop Rubber Co.*[13] Lord MacNaghton delivered a classic statement on the formalities of equitable assignments in the following words:

> "But, says the Lord Chief Justice, 'the document does not, on the face of it, purport to be an assignment nor use the language of assignment. . . .' An equitable assignment does not always take that form. It may be addressed to the debtor. It may be couched in the language of command. It may be a courteous request. It may assume the form of mere permission. The language is immaterial if the meaning is plain. All that is necessary is that the debtor should be given to understand that the debt has been made over by the creditor to some third person. If the debtor ignores such a notice, he does so at his peril. If the assignment be for valuable consideration and communicated to the third person, it cannot be revoked by the creditor or safely disregarded by the debtor."[14]

His Lordship was referring to the equitable assignment of a chose in action not yet in existence which, as he indicated, has to be for valuable consideration, even if by deed. However, it is unnecessary for the equitable assignment of an existing debt to be for value provided the assignor has done everything required of him to transfer the debt.[15] In

[12] See *William Brandt's Sons & Co.* v. *Dunlop Rubber Co.,* [1905] A.C. 454, at p. 461, *per* Lord MacNaghten.
[13] [1905] A.C. 454, at p. 462, H.L.
[14] At p. 462; followed in *German* v. *Yates* (1915), 32 T.L.R. 52, at p. 53, *per* Lush, J.; *Letts* v. *Inland Revenue Commissioners,* [1956] 3 All E.R. 588, at p. 592, *per* Upjohn, J.; see also *Tailby* v. *Official Receiver* (1888) 13 App. Cas. 523, at p. 563, *per* Lord MacNaghten.
[15] *Holt* v. *Heatherfield Trust, Ltd.,* [1942] 2 K.B. 1; [1942] 1 All E.R. 404; *Re McArdle,* [1951] Ch. 669; [1951] 1 All E.R. 905.

this context, "for valuable consideration" includes in satisfaction of an antecedent debt or part of a debt.[16]

Although the formal requirements of an equitable assignment are very relaxed, there are nevertheless certain minimum requirements which must be observed. An equitable assignment of an existing debt must be in writing signed by the client, or by his agent duly authorised in writing, because "a disposition of an equitable interest or trust subsisting at the time of the disposition, must be in writing signed by the person disposing of the same, or by his agent thereunto lawfully authorised in writing or by will": Law of Property Act 1925, section 53(1)(c).

There must be an actual assignment; a mere mandate or authority is insufficient.[17] The assignment must sufficiently identify the debt concerned[18] and be communicated to the assignee.[19]

Notice of an equitable assignment is conceptually different from notice in a statutory assignment. Notice is part of the definition of a statutory assignment: the legal title does not pass until notice is given. In contrast, an equitable assignment transfers the equitable title without notice being given. Thus, absence of notice of an equitable assignment does not impair the efficacy of the transaction as between factor and client in the slightest degree. Nevertheless, notice of assignment is highly desirable for three reasons:

(a) To prevent the customer paying the amount of the assigned debt to to the client and obtaining a good discharge,[20]

(b) to prevent the customer setting up further equities against the factor,[21]

(c) to obtain priority, so far as possible, over other competing interests.[1]

9 Stamp Duty

Stamp duties are taxes imposed by Parliament on certain legal instruments. They are taxes on documents and not on transactions.[2] The Stamp Act 1891 imposes the duties and the Stamp Duties Management Act 1891 contains administrative provisions. Both Acts have been amended and supplemented by annual Finance Acts and by the Revenue Acts.

---

[16] See *Norman* v. *Federal Commissioner of Taxation* (1963), 109 C.L.R. 9, particularly the judgement of Windeyer, J. where the authorities are reviewed.

[17] *Re Williams, Williams* v. *Ball*, [1917] 1 Ch. 1, at pp. 6–8.

[18] *Percival* v. *Dunn* (1885), 29 Ch.D. 128; *Palmer* v. *Carey*, [1926] A.C. 703; *Brice* v. *Bannister* (1878), 3 Q.B.D. 569.

[19] *Re Hamilton, Fitzgeorge* v. *Fitzgeorge* (1921), 124 L.T. 737, at 739.

[20] Pp. 111–112, *post*.   [21] Pp. 112 *et seq.*, *post*.   [1] Chap. 7, *post*.

[2] *Inland Revenue Commissioners* v. *Angus* (1889), 23 Q.B.D. 579, *per* Esher, M.R.

An instrument of assignment of book debts is classified as a conveyance on sale for the purpose of assessing the stamp duty payable thereon.[3] Any contract of agreement for the sale of any equitable interest in debts is charged with the same *ad valorem* duty as a conveyance on sale.[4]

An instrument of conveyance on sale is subject to *ad valorem* duty at the rate of one per cent. of the consideration paid[5] except that:

(a) it is exempt from duty if the amount or value of the consideration is £10,000 or under and the instrument is certified within the meaning of section 36 of the Finance Act 1958, at £10,000.

(b) it is subject to duty at a reduced rate if the value of the consideration is £15,000 or under and the instrument is so certified at £15,000.[6]

The said section 34 certificate says that the transaction effected by the instrument does not form part of a larger transaction or series of transactions in respect of which the amount or value of the consideration exceeds £10,000 or £15,000, as the case may be.

If an assignment instrument is not stamped within thirty days of execution, the following additional amounts must be paid:

(i) where the unpaid duty exceeds £10, a penalty equal to the amount thereof;

(ii) interest at 5 per cent. per annum on the unpaid duty from the date of execution of the instrument;

(iii) a fine of £10.[7]

The penalty does not have to be paid if:

(i) a reasonable excuse for the delay is afforded to the satisfaction of the Commissioners or of the court, judge, arbitrator or referee to whom it is produced;

(ii) the Commissioners omit the penalty; or

(iii) within the 30 day period, the opinion of the Commissioners has been sought.[8]

The fine may be recoverable by proceedings in the High Court but the only method of enforcing payment of the penalty, and presumably also the interest, is by refusing to stamp unless it is paid.[9]

The real incentive for stamping is that the assignment instrument is inadmissable in evidence unless it is stamped in accordance with the

[3] Stamp Act 1891, s. 54.   [4] Stamp Act 1891, s. 59.
[5] Stamp Act 1891, First Schedule.
[6] Finance Act 1963, as amended by Finance Act 1970, Sched. 1, para. 10 and Finance Act 1972, s. 125 (1)
[7] Stamp Act 1891, s. 15.   [8] Stamp Act 1891, s. 15.
[9] *Sergeant on Stamp Duties* (6th Edn., 1972), pp. 10, 61.

law in force at the time it was executed,[10] except that it may be received in evidence on payment to the court of the unpaid duty, the penalty and a further sum of £1 (curiously, the fine is not mentioned in this context).[11] Also, unstamped instruments may be admitted to refresh a witness' memory,[12] to prove fraud.[13] or an act of bankruptcy[14] and in an action to set aside the instrument and to prevent it being carried into effect where, if the action succeeded, the instrument would be void.[15]

The Lord Chief Justice has reminded judges that they should always ask to see the originals of documents required to be stamped.[16] This duty of judges exists whether or not objection is taken to the admissibility of the document and even if the parties consent to the admission of an unstamped document.[17] However, it is the settled practice of the courts to allow an unstamped document to be admitted in evidence upon the undertaking of the solicitors, representing the party who wishes to adduce it in evidence, to stamp it and produce it so stamped.[18] Anomalously, counsel will not take any initiative in aiding the judges in their duty because the General Council of the Bar has ruled that it is unprofessional for counsel to take stamp objections other than in revenue cases.[19]

Payment of one per cent ad valorem duty on all assignments would cripple the factoring industry. The factoring charge is usually between 0·5 per cent. and 2·5 per cent. of turnover. It would make factoring unprofitable for the factor if he paid one per cent duty out of the factoring charge which may even be inadequate for the purpose, and it would make factoring far too expensive for the client if he had to pay it on top of the factoring charge. It is therefore essential to the survival of the industry that the duty is legally avoided. Four legal devices have been used to avoid payment of the duty:

(*a*) *The first device* relies on the principle that stamp duty is a tax on documents and not on transactions Therefore if no stampable document comes into existence no tax is payable. A written offer to assign and an unwritten acceptance does not bring a stampable document into existence.[20] An offer and an acceptance, supported by consideration,

---

[10] Stamp Act 1891, s. 14 (4).   [11] Stamp Act 1891, s. 14 (1).
[12] *Birchall* v. *Bullough*, [1896] 1 Q.B. 325.
[13] *Re Shaw, Ex parte Official Receiver* (1920), 90 L.J.K.B. 204.
[14] *Re Gunsbourgh, Ex parte Trustee (No. 2)* (1919), 88 L.J.K.B. 562.
[15] *Mason* v. *Motor Traction Co., Ltd.,* [1905] 1 Ch. 419.
[16] *Law Journal* 1959, Vol. CIX, 395.
[17] *Bowker* v. *Williamson* (1889), 5 T.L.R. 382; *Nixon* v. *Albion Marine Insurnace Co.* (1867), L.R. 2 Exch. 338.
[18] *Re Coolgardie Goldfields, Ltd.,* [1900] 1 Ch. 475, at p. 477; *Parkfield Trust* v. *Dent,* [1931] 2 K.B. 579.
[19] The annual statement of the General Council for the Bar 1956, p. 28; Boulton, *Conduct & Etiquette at the Bar,* 5th Edn., p. 70.
[20] *Carlill* v. *Carbolic Smokeball Co.,* [1892] 2 Q.B. 484; on appeal [1893] 1 Q.B. 256.

constitute an agreement and an agreement to assign is an equitable assignment.[21] Although equitable assignments are usually subject to ad valorem duty, if they are in the form of a written offer and unwritten acceptance duty is avoided. Factors utilise this device by requiring a client to make a written offer which, by the terms of the factoring agreement, is accepted by conduct, such as payment of the purchase consideration, or by lapse of time, such as expiration of 48 hours after receipt of the offer unless non-acceptance or a counter-offer is communicated to the client. The agreement will also normally contain a covenant for further assurance requiring the client to execute a statutory assignment if required by the factor.

(*b*) *The second device*, applicable to statutory assignments, is to ensure that each assignment instrument is in respect of debts whose value does not exceed £10,000 and contains a certificate of value. However, it is arguable that this is ineffective because in reality the assignment, contrary to the assertion in the certificate, forms part of a series of transactions (i.e. assignments) in respect of which the aggregate value exceeds £10,000. In *A.-G.* v. *Cohen*[22] Greene, L.J. hypothesised an agreement under which a builder developing land had under one contract an option to purchase different parts at different times so that the options, when exercised, would produce a series of contracts, in which case, he concluded, there would be such an integral relationship as to constitute each part of a series of transactions. Monroe has applied this dictum to "block discount agreements whereby dealer's trade debts are financed", which do not commit either party, to reach the conclusion that such agreements, even if they gave both parties an option as to assignments thereunder, would be part of a series of transactions.[1] If he is correct, by analogy, the same can be said of factoring assignment instruments pursuant to a factoring agreement.

(*c*) *The third device* is where the factoring agreement envisages that the assignment shall be effected by a "notification" of debts by client to factor. Apparently, the idea is that a notification is not an assignment instrument. However, this seems doubtful and it may be that the notification would be construed as an assignment instrument and be subject to ad valorem duty.

(*d*) *The fourth device* can be used in the case of foreign clients. Assignments executed outside the UK are not subject to duty unless they are brought into the country. If the original is required as evidence in legal proceedings it will not attract a penalty if it is stamped within 30 days of being brought into the country.[2]

---

[21] *Tailby* v. *Official Receiver, supra.*
[22] [1937] 1 K.B. 478, at pp. 490, 491, C.A.
[1] Monroe, *The Law of Stamp Duties* (4th Edn., 1964, Sweet & Maxwell), p. 78.
[2] Stamp Act 1891, s. 15.

10 Enforcement Procedures against Customers

Originally, a statutory assignment had important procedural advantages over an equitable assignment,[3] but today the procedural advantages are only of a minor nature. The reason is that there have been three important developments since 1873 relating to the enforcement of rights under an equitable assignment. First, in 1904, it was held that an assignee could, without obtaining a Chancery Court order as was previously necessary, join a recalcitrant assignor as co-defendant with the debtor rather than be obliged to institute chancery proceedings to have him joined as plaintiff: see *Bowdens Patents Syndicate, Ltd.* v. *Herbert Smith & Co.*[4] Secondly, in the following year, it was held that the debtor may waive the requirement that the assignor be joined as a party to the action: see *William Brandt's Sons & Co.* v. *Dunlop Rubber Co.*[5] Thirdly, the rules of the Court now provide that no cause of action is to be defeated for non-joinder of a party, and the Court may direct that an assignor be joined as a party to the case at any stage of the proceedings (see R.S.C. Ord. 15, r. 6; C.C.R. Ord. 15, r.1.) although this requires the agreement of the assignee.[6] Thus, the modern procedural law is as follows:

(*a*) If the factor has a statutory assignment he may take proceedings against the customer without joining the client as a party;

(*b*) If the factor has an equitable assignment:

    (i) he may still take proceedings against the customer without joining the client as a party if the customer waives that requirement;

    (ii) otherwise, he should take proceedings and join the client as co-plaintiff if he consents or as co-defendant if he does not.

(*c*) If the factor fails to join the client as a party initially the court may at any stage of the proceedings order the client to be joined, but if the factor does not consent to the joinder, the action will be dismissed.

11 Summary of Modern Significance of Statutory and Equitable Assignments

As far as factors are concerned, the modern significance of statutory and equitable assignments is their different consequences in three repects: *ad valorem* stamp duty, enforcement procedures against customers, and priorities as between competing legal and equitable interests in the debts. The first two consequences have been discussed above; the third is analysed in Chapter Seven.

[3] See p. 95 *et seq., supra.*
[4] [1904] 2 Ch. 86, at p. 91, *per* Warrington, L.J.
[5] [1905] A.C. 454.
[6] *Performing Rights Society, Ltd.* v. *London Theatre of Varieties, Ltd.,* [1924] A.C. 1, H.L.

12   Conflict of Laws in International Credit Factoring

In international factoring,[7] customers, and sometimes clients, are located abroad. As regards the legal relationships between factor, client and customer, two questions arise: do the English courts have jurisdiction? If so, what law should they apply?

The jurisdiction of the English courts is primarily dependent on the presence of the defendant in England when the writ is served.[8] A corporation is "present" in England if it is registered in England;[9] if it is incorporated outside England but has established a place of business in England;[10] or if it is incorporated outside England but carries on business in England.[11] Alternatively, the courts will assume jurisdiction where they would not otherwise have it if the parties submit to their jurisdiction, for the courts of England are open to the whole world. A plaintiff submits to jurisdiction by beginning an action,[12] a defendant by appearing voluntarily as a defendant provided it is not simply to contest the jurisdiction of the court. [13] Alternatively, parties submit to jurisdiction by contract between them.[14] It is usual for English international factoring agreements to provide for the submission of the parties to the jurisdiction of the English courts.

The assignability of a debt is governed by the proper law of the debt. The expression "proper law" is explained at the end of this section. "Assignability" covers two matters: whether the debt is capable of assignment;[15] and the conditions under which it can be assigned insofar as they effect the customer—for example, whether the factor takes subject to customers' equities and whether notice of assignment has to be given to the customer.[16] Morris considers that the question whether the client has to be joined as a party to an action against the customer, as is the case with English equitable assignments, falls under this latter heading of conditions.[17]

The intrinsic validity of an assignment is governed, subject to the qualifications below, by the proper law of the assignment,[18] which is not necessarily the same as the proper law of the debt. "Intrinsic validity" covers three matters:

[7] P. 23, *ante.*

[8] Dicey and Morris, *The Conflict of Laws* (8th Edn., 1967, Stevens), Rule 22.

[9] Companies Act 1948, s. 437 (1).

[10] Companies Act 1948, ss. 407 (1) (*c*), 412.

[11] *Newby* v. *Van Oppen and Colts Patent Firearms Manufacturing Co.* (1872), L.R. 7 Q.B. 293.

[12] R.S.C. Ord. 15.   [13] R.S.C. Ord. 10.

[14] *Montgomery Jones & Co.* v. *Liebenthal & Co.,* [1898] 1 Q.B. 487; R.S.C. Ord. 10.

[15] *Re Fry, Chase National Executors and Trustee Corporation,* [1946] Ch. 312; [1946] 2 All E.R. 106; *Campbell Connelly & Co., Ltd.* v. *Noble,* [1963] 1 W.L.R. 252, at p. 255; *Compania Colombiana de Seguros* v. *Pacific Steam Navigation Co.,* [1965] 1 Q.B. 101, at pp. 128–9; Dicey and Morris (*supra*), Rule 83; Morris, *The Conflict of Laws* (1971, Stevens), p. 316.

[16] *Kelly* v. *Selwyn,* [1905] 2 Ch. 117.

[17] Morris (*supra*), p. 316.   [18] Dicey and Morris (*supra*), Rule 84.

(*a*) Formal validity. The assignment is valid if it complies either with the formal requirements of its proper law or of the place where it was made (called the *lex loci actus*).[19]

(*b*) Capacity of factor and client to make the assignment. Although leading extra-judicial writers consider that the proper law governs,[20] there is also authority that it is governed by the law of the domicile of the party or by the *lex loci actus*.[1]

(*c*) Essential validity. This includes matters such as the necessity for consideration. Again, leading extra-judicial writers consider that the proper law governs;[2] there is also authority that the *lex loci actus* governs.[3]

"Proper law" means the law which the parties agree should govern provided that law has a "real and substantial connection"[4] or, if their agreement is not expressed and cannot be inferred from the circumstances, by the law which has the closest and most real connection.[5] In the latter case, the courts try to decide what reasonable and sensible businessmen would have decided should be the proper law if they had thought about it. All the relevant circumstances are considered, the principal ones being the place of the transaction, the place of performance, the places of residence or business of the parties, and the nature and subject matter of the transaction.[6] It is usual for an English international factoring agreement to stipulate that it is governed by English law.

[19] *Republica de Guatemala* v. *Nunez*, [1927] 1 K.B. 669.
[20] Dicey and Morris (*supra*), Rule 84; Morris (*supra*), p. 319.
[1] *Republica de Guatemala* v. *Nunez, supra, per* Scrutton and Lawrence, L.JJ.; *Lee* v. *Abdy* (1886), 17 Q.B.D. 309, *per* Day and Wills, JJ.
[2] Dicey and Morris (*supra*), Rule 84; Morris (*supra*), p. 319.
[3] *Re Anziani, Herbert* v. *Christopherson*, [1930], 1 Ch. 407.
[4] *Re Helbert Wagg & Co., Ltd.'s Claim*, [1956] Ch. 323, at p. 341, *per* Upjohn, J.; cf. *Boissevain* v. *Weil*, [1949] 1 K.B. 482, at p. 491 where Denning, L.J. said the intention of the parties was only one of the matters to be taken into account.
[5] Dicey and Morris (*supra*), Rules 85, 127.
[6] *The Assunzione*, [1954] P. 150; [1954] 1 All E.R. 278; Morris (*supra*), p. 225.

CHAPTER SIX

Customers' Rights and Liabilities

A New Way to Pay Old Debts: title of play by Philip Massinger.

1 Duty to Pay Factor

A customer's duty to pay the factor arises when he receives notice of assignment. As from that moment, the general rule is that he ignores such notice at his peril,[1] and must treat the factor as his creditor so far as the assigned debt is concerned. Payment to the factor after receipt of notice of assignment insulates the customer from further liability to the client, for, as Cranworth, L.C. said in *Jones* v. *Farrell*,[2] "if my creditor tells me to pay AB, and I accordingly pay AB, and the creditor afterwards sues me I have a good plea of payment". Conversely, payment to the client after receipt of notice of assignment does not discharge the customer's liability in respect of the assigned debt, and the customer can be compelled to pay again by the factor.[3] If, before he receives notice of assignment, the customer has given the client a cheque for the debt and the client is still holding the cheque and has not yet presented it, the customer is not obliged to stop payment on the cheque and may disregard the notice.[4]

There appears to be a conflict of authority as to whether a customer can question the validity or enforceability of the assignment. In *Walker* v. *Bradford Old Bank*,[5] Smith J. said:

> "It is not competent for a mere stranger to the assignment to successfully raise any point as to whether a Court of Equity would or would not enforce it, and I am of opinion, even if the point now taken by the defendants as to what the Court of Equity under the circumstances of this case would or would not do, be correct, that it is not open to the defendants, being mere debtors to the estate of the deceased assignor or to his assignee, now to impeach the settlement."[6]

On the other hand, in *Van Lynn Developments, Ltd.* v. *Pelias Construc-*

---

[1] *William Brandt's Sons & Co.* v. *Dunlop Rubber Co.,* [1905] A.C. 454, H.L.
[2] (1857), 1 De G. & J. 208, at p. 218; 44 E.R. 703 at p. 707.
[3] *Brice* v. *Bannister* (1878), 3 Q.B.D. 569, C.A.
[4] *Bence* v. *Shearman*, [1898] 2 Ch. 582, at p. 585, C.A.
[5] (1884), 12 Q.B.D. 511.   [6] *Ibid.*, at p. 515.

tion Co. Denning, L.J. said with reference to a statutory assignment that:

> "after receiving the notice, the debtor will be entitled of course, to require a sight of the assignment so as to be satisfied that it is valid and that the assignee can give him a good discharge."[7]

Lord Denning's dictum is commercially inconvenient in the context of factoring because of the large number of customers who could require such sights of assignment. It is also difficult to see any point in his rule as an anti-fraud device where it is the client who gives notice of assignment, because there is no risk of fraud as there is where a stranger to the client/customer contract purports to be an assignee and to give notice of assignment. Where it is the client who gives notice of assignment, Lord Denning's rule could have the mischievous result of providing customers with a technical excuse to delay payment. If his Lordships' dictum is correct, it is submitted that is should be confined to cases where the assignee gives notice of assignment.[8] This would mean that a customer who receives notice of assignment on an invoice could not require a sight of the assignment because notice of assignment on an invoice, which is a document prepared by the client, is notice from the client and not from the factor.[9]

2   Customers' Equities

By section 136(1) of the Law of Property Act 1925, a factor with a statutory assignment takes "subject to equities having priority over the rights of the assignee". This means subject to all equities which would be enforced in a Court of Equity.[10] Thus, the same principle applies whether the assignment is statutory or equitable.[11] By "equities" is meant any defence or claim which a customer could raise against the client as at the time of receipt of notice of assignment. In *Roxburghe* v. *Cox*[12] James, L.J. said:

> "Now an assigneee of a cho e in action, according to my view of the law, takes subject to all rights of set-off and other defences which were available against the assignor, subject only to this exception, that after notice of an assignment of a chose in action the debtor cannot by payment or otherwise do anything to take away or diminish the rights of the assignee as they stood at the time of the notice."[13]

---

[7] [1969] 1 Q.B. 607, at p. 613; [1968] 3 All E.R. 824, at p. 826.

[8] "Even if the assignment is defective, the debtor must pay the assignee if the latter can give him a good receipt (i.e. if he has authority from the assignor)": Bailey, 48 L.Q.R. 547, at p. 570, n. 1.

[9] *James Talcott, Ltd.* v. *John Lewis & Co., Ltd.,* [1940] 3 All E.R. 592, at p. 595, *per* MacKinnon, L.J.

[10] *Young* v. *Kitchin* (1878), 3 Ex D. 127, at p. 130, *per* Cleasby, B.

[11] *Phipps* v. *Lovegrove* (1873), L.R. 16 Eq. 80; In Re Pain, *Gustavson* v. *Haviland,* [1919] 1 Ch. 38, at p. 46.

[12] (1881), 17 Ch.D. 520, C.A.   [13] *Ibid.,* at p. 526.

Thus, the crucial point of time is receipt of notice of assignment. It is insufficient that the equity is accruing at the time of notice: to be set-off against an assigned debt it has to have actually accrued. This is illustrated by *Re Pinto Leite and Nephews, Ex parte Des Olivaes*, [14] where a debt of £100,000 was assigned by A to B and notice of assignment given to the debtor, C. Subsequently, A became indebted to C in the sum of £15,000 arising out of a contractual obligation entered into before notice of assignment. C became bankrupt. It was held that the £15,000 could not be set-off against the assigned debt. Clauson, J. said:

> "the assignee of a chose in action . . . takes subject to all rights of set-off which were available against the assignor, subject only to the exception that, after notice of an equitable assignment of a chose in action, a debtor cannot set-off against the assignee a debt which accrues due subsequently to the date of notice even though that debt may arise out of a liability which existed at or before the date of the notice; but the debtor may set-off as against the assignee a debt which accrues due before notice of the assignment, although it is not payable until after that date: see *Watson* v. *Mid-Wales Rail. Co.* (1867), L.R. 2 C.P. 593; *Re Taunton, Delmard, Lane & Co.,* [1893] 2 Ch. 175."[15]

He added that even if the debt due from assignor to debtor has accrued at the time of notice of assignment, it could only be set-off if it was payable before the assigned debt was payable. He said it had been established by the obscurely reported case of *Jeffryes* v. *Agra and Masterman's Bank*[16] that:

> "when the debt assigned is at the date of notice of the assignment payable in futuro, the debtor can set-off against the assignee a debt which becomes payable by the assignor to the debtor after notice of assignment, but before the assigned debt becomes payable, if, but only if, the debt so to be set-off was *debitum in praesenti* at the date of notice of assignment."[17]

Thus, for example, if, at the time of notice of assignment of a debt of £1,000 payable on 30 January, the client owes the customer £400 for a debt payable on 15 January and £300 for a debt payable on 15 February, the customer may set-off the £400 against the assigned debt and pay the factor £600, but he cannot set-off the other £300 which he has to recover, if he can, from the client.

There is one exception to the rule that an equity must have accrued by the time of notice of assignment in order to be offset against the assigned debt. It may be offset, even if it an is unliquidated claim for damages, if it accrues subsequent to notice of assignment provided it arises out of the same contract as the assigned debt and is inseparably

---

[14] [1929] 1 Ch. 221.   [15] *Ibid.*, at p. 233.
[16] (1866), L.R. 2 Eq. 674.   [17] [1929] 1 Ch. 221, at p. 236.

connected with it. This principle was spawned in rudimentary form in two cases decided in 1878, *Brice* v. *Bannister* and *Young* v. *Kitchin,* and was developed a decade later in *Newfoundland Government* v. *Newfoundland Rail. Co.*

In *Brice* v. *Bannister*[18] X agreed to build a vessel for the defendant, the price to be paid in instalments. Before the vessel was finished, X in writing directed the defendant to pay the plaintiff £100 out of monies due to or to become due from the defendant to X. After he had received the direction from X, the defendant loaned money to X to enable him to complete the vessel and recouped the loan out of the balance of the purchase money. The balance of the purchase money, amounting to more than £100, was paid to X. The majority of the Court of Appeal held that the plaintiff assignee was entitled to recover the £100 from the defendant. Cotton L. J., one of the majority said:

> "It was urged that the assignee of a chose in action takes subject to all equities. But these must be equities existing *or arising out of circumstances existing* before notice is given of the assignment; and advances made by the defendant were in no way sanctioned by the contract, and in no sense an equity between (X) and the defendant existing *or arising from circumstances existing* at the date of the notice to the defendant of the assignment to the plaintiff."[19]

In *Young* v. *Kitchin*[20] the plaintiff sued as statutory assignee of a debt due from the defendant to the assignor on a building contract. The defendant pleaded, by way of set-off and counterclaim, that he was entitled to damages for breach of contract by the assignor to complete and deliver the buildings at a specified time. Cleasby, B. held that the damages, which arose out of the same contract, could be set-off to the extent of the value of the assigned debt.

In *Newfoundland Government* v. *Newfoundland Rail. Co.*[1] the Government of Newfoundland contracted with the Newfoundland Railway Company for the latter to construct a railway line over five years. Part of the consideration was a subsidy for each five miles of line completed, payable over 35 years. The Railway Company assigned the subsidies to X, and subsequently failed to complete the line. The Judicial Committee of the Privy Council held that it was in accordance with the principle followed in *Young* v. *Kitchin* that the Government could set-off a claim for unliquidated damages for breach of contract against the assignee's claim for the subsidies in respect of the completed portion of the line.

> "The two claims under consideration have their origin in the same portion of the same contract, where the obligations which gave rise

18 (1878), 3 Q.B.D. 569, C.A.   19 *Ibid.,* at p. 578.
20 (1878), 3 Ex D. 127.   1 (1888), 13 App. Cas. 199, P.C.

to them are intertwined in the closest manner . . . there is no universal rule that claims arising out of the same contract may be set against one another in all circumstances. But their Lordships have no hesitation in saying that in this contract the claims for subsidy and for non-construction ought to be set against one another . . . unliquidated damages may now be set-off as between the original parties, and also against the assignee if flowing out of and inseparably connected with the dealings and transactions which also give rise to the subject of the assignment."[2]

Thus, for example, if, after a customer receives notice of assignment of a debt arising from a contract for the sale of shoes, the shoes are found to be defective, the customer may off-set its damages against the assigned debt.

It was established in *Stoddart* v. *Union Trust, Ltd.*[3] that the equities which a customer can raise against the factor do not include purely personal claims against the client. An assignor fraudulently induced a debtor to buy a newspaper for £800 and then assigned the debt to an assignee who was ignorant of the fraud. The assignee sued the debtor for the debt. The debtor pleaded the fraud and asked for a declaration that no further money was due under the contract. The debtor also counter-claimed against the assignee and the assignor (who was joined as a defendant to the counter-claim) and claimed, if it was liable under the contract, damages equal to the amount payable. The counter-claim against the assignee was struck out, but judgement was recovered against the assignor in the consolidated hearing in which the assignee's claim against debtor was allowed. The debtor appealed and the Court of Appeal affirmed that the debtor could not set-off the damages against the assignee's claim. The reason, as stated by Kenedy, J., one of the members of the Court of Appeal, was that the debtor's claim was a purely personal claim dehors the contract which gave rise to the assigned debt and consequently could not lie against the assignee who was innocent of fraud, although it could lie against the assignor.[4] The whole court indicated that if the debtor had been able to seek rescission of the contract on the ground of fraud rather than counter-claim for damages for fraud, this would have been an effective answer to the assignee's claim.[5] But, in fact, the debtor was helpless to seek rescission because he had resold the newspaper and had thereby affirmed the contract and put it out of his power to rescind.

It may be concluded that a customer who has been fraudulently induced to buy goods from a client may be cancellation and rescission of the contract treat it as void and this will be an effective answer to the factor's claim on the assigned debt. But if the customer does not do this, or cannot do it because it has affirmed the contract, for example

---

[2] *Ibid.,* at pp. 212–213.
[4] *Ibid.,* at p. 194.

[3] [1912] 1 K.B. 181.
[5] *Ibid.,* at pp. 189, 191, 195.

by selling the goods, a claim for damages for fraud is no answer to the factor's claim, although it will lie against the client personally.

The equities which a customer may raise against the factor are limited in value to the amount of the assigned debt. Equities may only be used by way of set-off against the factor's claim and nothing can be recovered from the factor.[6] In other words, equities operate as a shield against the factor, but cannot be used as a sword against the factor. Any excess in value of equities over the amount of the assigned debt may be recovered from the client but not from the factor.

A provision in the client/customer contract that the latter will not raise claims or defences against an assignee is enforceable by the factor.[7] In *Re Blakely Ordinance Co.* Rollit, L.J. said:

> "The right to this money was assignable in equity and though in the absence of anything more than a mere assignment, the assignee would take subject to the equities between the original parties to the contract, I am of the opinion that there is nothing inequitable in allowing the debtor in an obligation to contract with his creditor, that he will not avail himself of any such equities, that he will pay the amount due on the obligation to the assignee of the creditor . . . without regard to any such equities . . . and it would, I think, be inequitable to deny the assignee of the creditor the full benefit of the contract entered into between the original contracting parties."[8]

A release of equities, which may be by words, writing or course of conduct, by the customer is also enforceable by the factor.[9]

Logically, it would seem to follow that if a customer is bound, as against a factor, by a provision, in its contract with the client, not to raise equities against the factor, that it is entitled as against the factor to the benefit of a provision, in its contract with the client, that the benefit of the contract is not assignable. However, there have been differences of opinion on the effectiveness of such a prohibition against assignment and the present state of the law is not clear.[10]

In *Brice* v. *Bannister*[11] Bramwell, B. said it may be, and he hoped it was, the law that a debtor is entitled, as against an assignee, to the benefit of such a prohibition.

In *Re Turcan*[12] the Court of Appeal appeared to nominally uphold the

---

[6] *Young* v. *Kitchin* (1878), 3 Ex D. 127, at p. 131, *per* Cleasby, B.

[7] *Re Blakely Ordinance Co., Ex parte New Zealand Banking Corporation* (1867), 3 Ch. App. 154, at pp. 159–60; *Higgs* v. *Assam Tea Co.* (1869), L.R. 4 Exch. 387, at p. 396; *Phoenix Assurance Co., (Ltd.)* v. *Earl's Court (Ltd.)* (1913), 30 T.L.R. 50, C.A.

[8] (1867), 3 Ch. App. 154, at pp. 159–160.

[9] *Higgs* v. *Assam Tea Co.* (1869), L.R. 4 Exch. 387; *In Re Northern Assam Tea Co., Ex parte Universal Life Assurance Co.* (1870), L.R. 10 Eq. 458, at p. 463, *per* Romilly, M.R.

[10] In America the majority view is that such a prohibition is unenforceable: see Glenn, Garrard, "The Assignment of Choses in Action; Rights of Bona Fide Purchaser", 20 Virginia Law Review 621, at 622–3 (1933–34).

[11] (1878), 3 Q.B.D. 569, at p. 581, C.A.   [12] (1889), 40 Ch.D. 5, C.A.

effectiveness of such a prohibition as against an assignee, while at the same time circumventing it. A marriage settlement contained a covenant by the settlor to "convey or assign" his interest in any property to which he should become entitled during the marriage to trustees of the settlement. He afterwards took out a life insurance policy which contained a condition that it should not be assignable in any case whatever. On his death, it was held that the insurance policy belonged to the trustees of the marriage settlement and not to his estate. Cotton, L.J., with whom the rest of the court concurred, said:

> "Would a Court of Equity in the lifetime of the covenantor have enforced the covenant to settle this policy notwithstanding the condition against assignment? I think it would . . . I think the condition was inserted in order to prevent the insured from availing himself of his power to assign the policy and to give the assignee a right to receive the money from the office. *But though he could not assign the policy*, I think it would have been sufficient compliance with the covenant if he had executed a declaration of trust for the trustees of the settlement."[13]

The *ratio decidendi* of this curious decision is not easy to state. It appears to be based on a liberal interpretation of the marriage settlement covenant and a strict interpretation of the life insurance policy prohibition. That is, the court appeared to hold that a convenant in a marriage settlement (or at least in the marriage settlement before the court) to "assign or convey" included an undertaking, in the alternative, to declare a trust, but that a prohibition against assignment in a life insurance policy (or at least in the policy before the court) should be interpreted literally so as to exclude a declaration of trust. On this basis, the question in the context of factoring would be whether the covenant to assign debts in the factoring agreement would be given the same liberal interpretation, and whether a prohibition against assignment in the client/customer contract would be literally construed. If so, then such a prohibition against assignment could be defeated by the client executing a declaration of trust of debts in the factor's favour.

However, further confusion is generated by the Court of Appeal decision in *Spellman* v. *Spellman*.[14] A husband entered into a hire purchase agreement which contained a prohibition against assignment of the agreement or the benefit thereof. The court considered the question whether the husband could assign the benefit of the agreement to his wife, although the opinions expressed were strictly obiter dicta since the whole court held that, on the facts, there had not been any such assignment. The majority view, expressed by Danckwerts, J., with whom Ormerod, J. concurred, was as follows:

> "It is plain, also, that the fact that there is a prohibition in the docu-

---

[13] *Ibid.,* at p. 11.   [14] [1961] 2 All E.R. 498, [1961] 1 W.L.R. 921, C.A.

ment creating the chose in action against assignment is not necessarily fatal to such a claim: see *Re Turcan*. It is possible, as it seems to me, that if such an equitable assignment had been made there could have been (as between husband and wife) an assignment of the benefit of the hire purchase agreement. . . ."[15]

The majority opinion was that a prohibition was ineffective (at least in the circumstances before the court) which is inconsistent with *Re Turcan* which held that a prohibition against assignment was effective to defeat an assignment but not to defeat a declaration of trust. The minority view of Wilmer, L. J., is contrary to that of the majority and consistent with *Re Turcan*:

"For myself, I am not persuaded that it is possible to overlook the specific provision of the agreement whereby the hirer, that is the husband, has covenanted that he will not assign or charge the goods or the benefit of the agreement."[16]

Perhaps some assistance can be derived from the law of landlord and tenant. If the lessee of real property assigns in breach of a covenant against assignment, the lessor has an option either to forfeit the tenancy and eject the lessee or to sue the lessee for damages for breach of covenant.[17] By analogy, it might be argued that, in factoring, a customer has an option to disregard the assignment or sue for breach of covenant. On the other hand, the analogy is rather superficial because the financial standing and character of a tenant strongly determine whether the rent will be paid and the premises properly looked after, whereas it would not appear to be significant if the customer pays the client or the factor. Thus, it is difficult to imagine the customer recovering more than nominal damages if he sued the client for breach of covenant as he does not appear to have suffered any injury. If no injury is suffered by the assignment of debt, then a covenant against its assignment would seem to be unreasonable and, for this reason, perhaps it would be held to be ineffective at least as between factor and customer.

3 Set-off in Bankruptcy or Winding-up of Customer and Client

By section 31 of the Bankruptcy Act 1914, which also applies to the winding-up of companies by virtue of section 317 of the Companies Act 1948,[18] where there have been "mutual credits, mutual debts or other mutual dealings" between factor and customer, the respective sums due from each to the other may be set-off and the balance claimed provided that the factor cannot claim the benefit of such a set-off if at

---

[15] *Ibid.*, at p. 925.   [16] *Ibid.*, at p. 928.
[17] *Silcock* v. *Farmer* (1882), 46 L.T. 404; *Works Commissioners* v. *Hull*, [1922] 1 K.B. 205; Hill and Redmans *Law of Landlord and Tenant* (15th Edn. 1970), p. 460.
[18] *Mersey Steel and Iron Co.* v. *Naylor, Benzon & Co.* (1882), 9 Q.B.D. 648.

the time of purchasing the debt he had notice of an available act of bankruptcy committed by and available against the customer. A likely situation where such mutual dealings can exist is where the customer is also a client of the factor. For example, suppose that when the customer goes into bankruptcy or liquidation, he owes the factor £12,000 and is owed, as a client, £10,000 (being his equity in debts sold to the factor). Does the factor have to pay £10,000 to the trustee or liquidator and prove for the £12,000? If the distribution to general creditors is only, say, 25p in the £, he will only receive £3,000 on this claim and will have paid out or lost £19,000. Or can the factor set off the £12,000 against the £10,000 and prove for the balance of £2,000, in which case his loss will be only £1,500? The answer depends first, on whether their dealings are "mutual" within the meaning of section 31, and, secondly, when the assignment of the debt owed by the customer occurred. In *Rolls Razor, Ltd.* v. *Cox*[19] Winn, L.J. said:

> "I regard as the type of mutual dealings contemplated by the section although many others less comprehensive and of shorter continuity would also be included, is that by the intention of the parties express or implied, they each extend to the other credit in respect of individual sums of money until such time as such sums are brought into account and in the account set off against other sums in totality, in respect of which the other party has given credit; to be contrasted are dealings of a kind which may occur either in isolation or within the complex of a continuous run of dealings, which are themselves mutual of such a kind that it is clear from their character that the parties intend that the monetary outcome of them shall be separately settled between the parties and not treated as a mere item on the one side or the other of a running account."[20]

This seems to indicate that if the parties intended that they would have no right of set-off, the dealings are not mutual. However, his Lordship only seems to have referred to the keeping of a consolidated current account as an example or as evidence of a mutual dealing rather than stating it as an essential criterion. This is borne out by the judgment of Roskill, J. in *Halesowen Presswork and Assemblies, Ltd* v. *National Westminster Bank, Ltd.,*[21] ultimately affirmed by the House of Lords on appeal,[1] who said that mutuality was not excluded merely because the system of book-keeping used did not provide for consolidated accounts. In fact, factors normally segregate client accounts and customer accounts and do not set-off one against the other unless insolvency occurs. However, it is normal for the factoring agreement to

---

[19] [1967] 1 Q.B. 552.   [20] *Ibid.*, at p. 575.
[21] [1971] 1 Q.B. 1, [1970] 3 All E.R. 473.
[1] *National Westminster Bank, Ltd.* v. *Halesowen Presswork and Assemblies, Ltd.,* [1972] A.C. 785; [1972] 1 All E.R. 641, H.L.

provide that the factor may set-off an amount due from the client to the factor against any amount due from the factor to the client, and this certainly seems wide enough to include the set-off of a debt due from the client as the customer or another client. On the other hand, it seems strongly arguable that the above dictum of Winn, L.J. was rejected by the House of Lords decision in *National Westminster Bank, Ltd.* v. *Halesowen Presswork and Assemblies, Ltd.*[2] and that it is not possible to contract out of section 31. This indicates that intention is irrelevant. If so, mutuality is an objective concept and the reservation of a right of set-off in a factoring agreement is immaterial in bankruptcy or liquidation. Thus, debts between factor and client may be set against each other irrespective of whether this was their intention.

Where mutuality exists, the time of assignment determines whether the set-off is allowable. A factor who at the time of the bankruptcy or winding-up owes a debt to a client cannot acquire a right of set-off by taking an assignment of a debt due from that client to another client.[3] This, is subject to an important exception: if the assignment is taken after the bankruptcy or winding-up, in consequence of any arrangement for that purpose made before the bankruptcy or winding-up—for example, where the assignment is pursuant to a factoring agreement entered into with another client before the bankruptcy or winding-up—then a set-off of the assigned debt will be allowed.[4]

If a debt has been absolutely assigned before the client's bankruptcy or insolvency, the customer has no right to set-off a debt due from the bankrupt or insolvent. The fact that notice of assignment has not been given by the commencement of bankruptcy or winding-up is immaterial.[5] A factor cannot set-off a debt owed by a customer if he knew at the date of assignment that notice convening a meeting of creditors as part of the machinery of voluntary liquidation had been given.[6]

4   Duty to Give Information to the Factor?

In *Etty* v. *Bridges*[7] it was said that a trustee is under a duty to inform a prospective assignee who enquires, of the existence of any other assignment of which the trustee has received notice. *Mangles* v. *Dixon*[8]

---

[2] *Supra.*

[3] *Re Milan Tramways Co., Ex parte Theys* (1884), 25 Ch.D. 587, C.A.; *Dickson* v. *Evans* (1794), 6 Term Rep. 57; 101 E.R. 433.

[4] *Re Moseley Green Coal and Coke Co., Barretts Case* (1865), 12 L.T. 193; *McKinnon* v. *Armstrong* (1877), 2 App. Cas. 531; McDonald Henry & Meeks, *Australian Bankruptcy Law and Practice* (4th Edn., 1968, Law Book Company), 395.

[5] *Re Ashphaltic Wood Pavement Co., Lee and Chapman's Case* (1885), 30 Ch.D. 216, C.A.; *Re City Life Assurance Co., Ltd., Stephenson's Case*, [1926] 1 Ch. 191.

[6] *Re Eros Films, Ltd.*, [1963] Ch. 565, [1963] 1 All E.R. 383.

[7] (1843), 2 Y. & C.Ch. Cas. 486, at p. 493.

[8] (1852), 3 H.L. Cas. 702; 10 E.R. 278.

appears to say that a debtor or trustee has to inform an assignee, who has given him notice, of any fraud affecting the assignee of which he is aware:

> "where there is no fraud, nothing which could lead to a conclusion in the mind of the party who receives the notice, that the party who gives it has been deceived and is likely to sustain a loss, the party receiving the notice is not bound to volunteer information."

Halsbury says, citing *Mangles* v. *Dixon,* that if the notice shows that the assignee has been deceived "if the debtor does not undeceive the assignee, he may be prevented from taking advantage of equities between himself and the assignor".[9] However, *Mangles* v. *Dixon* does not seem to go so far as to say that loss of equities is the sanction against the customer in such circumstances. Furthermore, the case may well have been impliedly overruled by Lord McNaghten in *Ward* v. *Duncombe*.[10] Certainly, he overruled *Etty* v. *Bridges* in holding that a trustee is under no duty to inform a prospective assignee, who enquires, of the existence of any assignment of which he has notice.[11] Although trustees have now been given this duty by section 137(8) of the Law of Property Act 1925, there is no equivalent statutory duty on debtors and it is probable that *Ward* v. *Duncombe* is authority for the view that there is no liability whatsoever on debtors to furnish an assignee who gives notice, or a prospective assignee who enquires, with any information.

[9] 6 Halsbury's Laws of England (4th Edn.) p. 37, para. 62.
[10] [1893] A.C. 369.   [11] *Ibid.*, at p. 369.

CHAPTER SEVEN

Priorities

"In the development of our law, two principles have striven for mastery. The first is for the protection of property: no one can give a better title than he himself possesses. The second is for the protection of commercial transactions: the person who takes in good faith and for value without notice should get a good title. The first principle has held sway for a long time, but it has been modified by the common law itself and by statute so as to meet the needs of our own time.": Bishopsgate Motor Finance Corporation, Ltd. *v.* Transport Brakes, Ltd.,[1] *per* Lord Denning.

This Chapter is devoted to the analysis of priorities as between factors and third parties with competing interests in debts purchased by the factor. By "third parties" we mean parties other than clients and customers. These third parties are:

1. Assignees and chargees
2. Cestuis que trust
3. Clients' solicitors and mercantile agents with liens
4. Client's execution creditors
5. Client's general creditors in bankruptcy or winding-up

"Priority" has two shades of meaning. The priority of an absolute purchaser of a whole debt, or of the client's general creditors in bankruptcy or winding-up, is to the whole debt. Their claims are claims to ownership. In all other cases, the competing party is a creditor, and the claim is not to ownership but to security for indebtedness. Security claims can arise from a variety of legal devices, but they share the common characteristic that they are limited to the amount of the client's indebtedness, secured by the debt, to that party. Any surplus of the debt's value over indebtedness goes to the next party with priority, and so on until the debts are exhausted. Thus, the factor who purchases a debt will be entitled to the whole debt if he has priority; to nothing if another purchaser or the client's general creditors in insolvency or bankruptcy have priority; and to the excess, if any, remaining after the prior rights of other claimants.

The main protection against priority conflicts lies in the honesty and solvency of clients. This is proven by the fact that the competing claims

[1] [1949] 1 K.B. 322, at p. 336.

of all the third parties listed above result either from fraud or insolvency; although, as mentioned in Chapters Three and Four, the latter or its imminence can breed the former. The first two categories—assignees and chargees, and cestuis que trust—are the victims of fraud. The client has fraudulently transferred a security interest in the same debts to two or more parties. The claims of the last three categories—lienholders, execution creditors, and general creditors in bankruptcy or insolvency —arise by operation of law because the client is insolvent. In fact, even a defrauded party joins issue on priorities only as a result of the client's financial inability, actual or estimated, to repay the money obtained by fraud, so in that sense every party to a priority case is there because the client is unable to pay his debts.

1   Assignees and Chargees

There are two types of assignees: purchasers and mortgagees. There are also two types of chargees: fixed and floating. The conceptual and consequential differences between purchase, mortgage, fixed charge and floating charge have been analysed in Chapter Five. Sensibly, for the purposes of priorities, they are regarded identically, subject to inevitable qualifications with respect to a floating charge.

A   EQUITABLE ASSIGNEE V. EQUITABLE ASSIGNEE

The best-known priority rule is known as the rule in *Dearle* v. *Hall*.[2] This rule governs competition between equitable assignees (and chargees) of choses in action. For the sake of brevity the expressions "assignment", "assignor" and "assignee" hereafter used in this section, include, respectively, "charge", "chargor" and "chargee" except where otherwise indicated. The rule is that priority goes to the assignee of whose assignment notice is first given to the customer except that an assignee who is first to give notice cannot obtain priority if he knew of an earlier equitable assignment at the time of his assignment. Where notices are simultaneous or no notice of either assignment has been given to the customer, priority is determined by the chronological order of the assignments provided the equities are equal.[3]

The rule was originally applied to equitable choses in action but has since been applied to trade debts which are legal choses in action. In *Gorringe* v. *Irwell India Rubber and Gutta Percha Works*[4] it was assumed that the rule applied to debts and the matter was put beyond doubt by the decision in *Marchant* v. *Morton Down & Co*.[5] In the latter case, a partnership supplied boxes to a City wholesale house on credit. On

---

[2] (1823) 3 Russ. 1; 38 E.R. 475 (Plumer, M.R.); affd. on appeal (1827), 3 Russ. 48; 38 E.R. 492 (Lord Lyndhurst, L.C.).
[3] See p. 130, *post*.   [4] (1886), 34 Ch.D. 128, C.A.   [5] [1901] 2 K.B. 829.

21 December, money due to the partnership from the wholesale house
on 11 January was assigned by one partner to the defendant. On 4
January the same debt was assigned by the other partner, who was
ignorant of the first assignment, to the plaintiff by deed in consideration
of delaying the execution of a judgement debt. The plaintiff gave notice
of assignment to the debtor before the defendant. Channell, J. held that
the plaintiff had priority over the defendant on the basis of the rule in
Dearle v. *Hall*. In *B. S. Lyle, Ltd.* v. *Rosher*,[6] Viscount Kilmuir said that
for the rule in *Dearle* v. *Hall* to apply there were "at least four requirements, namely: a fundholder, someone who has, or has had, a beneficial interest, assignee no. 1 and assignee no. 2."[7] This puts it rather too
tersely in that the rule applies regardless of the number of assignees.

Original authority for the rule

Plumer, M. R. who formulated the rule at first instance in *Dearle* v.
Hall said that the authority for it was *Ryall* v. *Rowles*[8]. But Lord Mac-
Naghten in *Ward* v. *Duncombe*[9], observed that *Ryall* v. *Rowles* was a
bankruptcy decision concerned with acts necessary to take a chose in
action out of the order and disposition of the bankrupt. He went on to
point out that:

> "The doctrine of reputed ownership is entirely the creature of statute
> and applicable by statute in cases of bankruptcy only. I cannot help
> thinking that in extending the doctrine to cases of equitable assignment
> of personal property where there is no bankruptcy . . . the Court has
> gone perilously near legislating."[10]

On the other hand, this is not so surprising, for as Sir George Jessel
said in his famous judgement in *Re Hallett's Estate Knatchbull* v. *Hallett:*[11]

> ". . . it must not be forgotten that the rules of Courts of Equity are
> not, like the rules of the Common Law, supposed to have been estab-
> lished from time immemorial. It is perfectly well known that they have
> been established from time to time—altered, refined and improved from
> time to time. In many cases we know the names of the Chancellors
> who invented them."[12]

He illustrated his remarks by "such things as the separate use of a mar-
ried woman, the restraint on anticipation, the modern rule against
perpetuities and the rules of equitable waste". Firth commented that he
might have added the rule in *Dearle* v. *Hall* to his list.[13]

In any event, despite his criticisms of the rule, Lord MacNaghten in
Ward v. *Duncombe* concluded that the rule in *Dearle* v. *Hall* is settled

---

[6] [1958] 3 All E.R. 579   [7] *Ibid.,* at p. 602.
[8] (1750), 1 Ves. Sen. 348; 27 E.R. 1074.   [9] [1893] A.C. 369.
[10] *Ibid.,* at p. 394.   [11] (1879), 13 Ch.D. 696.   [12] *Ibid.,* at p. 710.
[13] Firth, "The Rule in *Dearle* v. *Hall*" (1895), 11 L.Q.R. 337.

law. In *Montefiore* v. *Guedalla*[14], Cozens-Hardy, L.J. said "the rule laid down in *Dearle* v. *Hall* is now part of the Law of the Land. . . . it was affirmed and possible extended by the House of Lords in *Foster* v. *Cockerell*"[15]

Rationales of the rule

Originally, there were two rationales for the rule, one substantive and the other conceptual. The substantive rationale was that an assignee who omitted to give notice was at fault in that a subsequent assignee could not discover the existence of the prior assignment by enquiry of the debtor or trustee and therefore would be misled. Plumer, M. R. said that failure to give notice enabled the assignor to "carry the same security repeatedly into the market" and to thereby induce "third persons to advance money upon it in the erroneous belief that it continues to belong to him absolutely, free from encumbrance".[16] The theory therefore originally rested on the fault of the first assignee resulting in a mischief. Indeed, Plumer, M.R. repeatedly characterised the omission as negligence.

This rationale was eroded by the decision of the House of Lords in *Foster* v. *Cockerell*[17] (ironically in a judgement delivered by Lord Lyndhurst who had affirmed Plumer, M. R.'s decision in *Dearle* v. *Hall*) that a subsequent assignee gained priority because he was first to give notice although he had not enquired as to the existence of a prior assignee and, indeed, had not given notice until five years after his subsequent assignment. That decision has been interpreted to mean that the conduct of either assignee—for example, an imputation of laches—is irrelevant.[18] The rule today is as stated by Wright, J. in *Re Lake, Ex parte Cavendish*:[19] "the Court seems to me to have in modern times asked only which assignee was the first to protect his security by notice."

The rationale was battered further by Lord MacNaghten whose opinion in *Ward* v. *Duncombe*,[20] was that the principle underlying the rule in *Dearle* v. *Hall* was so unclear and uncertain that it ought not to be extended to a new case. He held, contrary to earlier decisions, that a trustee is under no duty to inform an assignee of any prior assignment of which he had received notice. This took much of the punch out of the premise that notice was also notice to a subsequent assignee who enquired. Although trustees have since, by statute, been given the duty to provide this information, it was submitted in Chapter Six that it is

---

[14] [1903] 2 Ch. 26, C.A.   [15] *Ibid.*, at pp. 37–8.
[16] (1823) 3 Russ. 1; 38 E.R. 475.
[17] (1835), 9 Bli. N.S. 332; 5 E.R. 1315.
[18] *Timson* v. *Ramsbottom* (1837), 2 Keen 35; 48 E.R. 541; *Meux* v. *Bell* (1841), 1 Hare 73; 66 E.R. 955.
[19] [1903] 1 K.B. 151, at p. 154.   [20] [1893] A.C. 369, H.L.

doubtful whether a debtor is under any such duty.[21] Nevertheless, the rationale has continued to be expressed. In *Re Dallas*[1] Vaughan Williams, L.J. said:

> ". . . whatever view one takes of the principle upon which notice is allowed to affect priorities, it is common to all the theories of the principle that the trustee or other person who legally dominates the fund will inform the person giving the notice whether there is any prior incumbrance in existence."[2]

Apart from the question of legal duty to inform a subsequent assignee or prospective assignee of a prior assignment of which notice has been given, as a matter of commercial reality most debtors, at least if pressed, are likely to give such information, so notice does have some practical effect as an anti-fraud device. The system, in the absence of compulsory public registration, is probably the best anti-fraud measure which could be devised, although, as was perceived long ago in *Etty* v. *Bridges*[3] it is far from perfect:

> "although the notice does not necessarily prevent such a fraud, it renders its commission much less likely; inasmuch as the trustees, if asked, (will) be likely to give information of the notice. . . . It is obvious, however, that unfairness or forgetfulness or negligence on a trustee's part, or his death or infirmity may render the notice, as a prevention of fraud, useless."[4]

The conceptual rationale is that perfection of title to personalty as against third parties is attained by delivery of possession of the personalty. Plumer, M.R. said in *Dearle* v. *Hall* that

> "notice, then, is necessary to perfect the title—to give a complete right in rem, and not merely a right as against him who conveys his interest . . . these are the principles on which I think it to be very old law, that possession, or what is tantamount to possession, is the criterion of perfect title to personal chattels, and that he, who does not obtain such possession, must take his chance."[5]

Of course, a chose in action is intangible and therefore cannot literally be possessed in the same way as a chattel. However, in the words of Lord Lyndhurst on appeal in *Dearle* v. *Hall*, "notice, is, in a certain degree, taking possession of the fund. It is going as far towards equitable possession as it is possible to go".[6] In other words, notice, in the case of choses in action, is regarded as equivalent to possession.

Some picturesque language has been used by the Courts to describe the

[21] Pp. 120–121, *supra*.
[1] [1904] 2 Ch. 385, C.A.   [2] *Ibid.*, at p. 411.
[3] (1843), 2 Y. & C.Ch. Cas. 486; 63 E.R. 218.   [4] *Ibid.*, at p. 493.
[5] (1823), 3 Russ. 1, at p. 24; 38 E.R. 475.   [6] (1827), 3 Russ. 48, at pp. 58, 59.

conceptual rationale. In *Lee* v. *Howlett*,[7] it was said that it meant that the party who first makes himself "master of the chose" had priority. In *Etty* v. *Bridges*,[8] it was said that the assignee must "set his mark" upon the chose.

It is of historical interest to note that the assumption of the court in *Dearle* v. *Hall* that possession of personalty perfected title as against third parties was incorrect in so far as goods were concerned. In *Johnson* v. *Credit Lyonnais*,[9] Cockburn, C.J. said:

> "These authorities fail to satisfy me that at common law the leaving by a vendee goods bought, or the documents of title, in the hands of the vendor, until it suited the convenience of the former to take possession of them, would, on a fradulent sale or pledge by the party so possessed, divest the owner of his property, or estop him from asserting his right to it."[10]

It was not until Parliament intervened in section 25 of the Sale of Goods Act 1893, and section 8 of the Factors Act 1889, that the concept which was applied to choses in action in *Dearle* v. *Hall*, and which it had been thought in that case was also applicable to goods, was indeed applied to goods, although only in certain circumstances.

Notice of prior assignment

A subsequent assignee who is first to give notice to the customer will lose priority if he knew of the earlier assignment at the time of his own purchase. This was not expressed but was, perhaps, implicit in *Dearle* v. *Hall*. Anyway, it has since become settled law.[11] But knowledge of a prior assignment obtained after the date of the subsequent purchase is immaterial: "it is not a question of what a man knows when he does that which will better or perfect his security, but what he knows at the time when he took his security and paid his money": *Mutual Life Assurance Society* v. *Langley*,[12] per Cotton, L.J.

Notice of a prior assignment need not be actual: constructive notice is sufficient to prevent priority. In *English and Scottish Mercantile Investment Trust* v. *Brunton*,[13] Charles, J. held that:

---

[7] (1836), 2 K. & J. 531; 69 E.R. 893.

[8] (1843), 2 Y. & C. Ch. Cas. 486; 63 E.R. 218.

[9] (1877), 3 C.P.D. 32, C.A.   [10] *Ibid.*, at p. 40.

[11] *Warburton* v. *Hill, Stent* v. *Wickens* (1854), Kay 470; 69 E.R. 199; *Timson* v. *Ramsbottom* (1837), 2 Keen 35; 48 E.R. 541; *Re Hamilton's Windsor Ironworks, Ex parte Pitman and Edwards* (1879), 12 Ch.D. 707, 711; *Newman* v. *Newman* (1885), 28 Ch.D. 674; *Re Holmes* (1885), 29 Ch.D. 786; *Spencer* v. *Clarke* (1878), 9 Ch.D. 137; *Re Weniger's Policy*, [1910] 2 Ch. 291; *Ward* v. *Royal Exchange Shipping Co., Ltd., Ex parte Harrison* (1887), 58 L.T. 174; *Re Ind Coope & Co., Ltd.*, [1911] 2 Ch. 223, at p. 224.

[12] (1886), 32 Ch.D. 460, at p. 468; cf. *McCarthy & Stone* v. *Hodge & Co.*, [1971] 2 All E.R. 973.

[13] [1892] 2 Q.B.D. 1; affd. [1892] 2 Q.B.D. 700, C.A.; see also *Spencer* v. *Clarke* (1878) 9 Ch.D. 137.

". . . notice gives priority, unless the giver of it himself has either actual notice of the prior incumbrance, or else is in such a position and has a degree of knowledge as is in equity equivalent to actual notice."[14]

Floating charges containing a covenant not to assign debts

Knowledge of the existence of a prior floating charge over debts does not of itself affect priorities, for a floating charge allows the company which has given the floating charge to continue to dispose of the assets in the ordinary course of business as the charge crystallises; and there seems little doubt that selling book debts to a financier or factor is in the ordinary course of business,[15] unless ultra vires.[16] However, if the floating charge contains a covenant by the chargor not to assign debts subject to the charge, a subsequent assignee of such debts with knowledge of the covenant at the time of his purchase may lose priority to the chargee. In *English and Scottish Mercantile Investment Trust* v. *Brunton*, above, X company issued debentures secured by a floating charge over all assets, which contained a restriction against giving any charge which would rank in priority to it. It later borrowed from the plaintiff and as security for the loan mortgaged a debt due from an insurance company. The plaintiff, by their solicitor who was informed at the settlement meeting, knew that the debentures existed but did not know in what form. It was established that, by current usage, debentures could be in one of three forms:

(*a*) simply an acknowledgement of debt;
(*b*) an acknowledgement of debt and a charge over the company's property;
(*c*) an acknowledgement of debt, a charge over the company's property and a restriction against giving any charge which would rank in priority to the debentures.

It had previously been established in *Wheatley* v. *Silkstone and Haigh Moor Coal Co.*[17] that the second form of debenture did not preclude giving a subsequent charge with priority. In the present case, Charles, J. held that the plaintiffs ought not to be considered to have constructive notice of the restriction in the debentures because there was "a clear distinction between documents which must necessarily, and those which may, or may not, affect title: see *Jones* v. *Smith* (1841), 1 Hare 43: *Patman* v. *Harland*, (1881), 17 Ch.D. 353. To the latter class the rule [of constructive notice] is not applicable, and it is to this class in my opinion that these debentures belong."[18] In *G. & T. Earle, Ltd.* v.

---

[14] [1892] 2 Q.B.D. 1, at pp. 8, 9.
[15] *Re Hamilton's Windsor Ironworks* (1879), 12 Ch.D. 707; *Govt. Stock Co.* v. *Manila Rail Co.* [1897] A.C. 81, H.L.; *Re Ind, Coope & Co.*, [1911] 2 Ch. 223; *Illingworth* v. *Houldsworth*, [1904] A.C. 355, H.L.
[16] *Re Borax Co, Foster* v. *Borax Co.*, [1899] 2 Ch. 130; [1901] 1 Ch. 326, but note pp. 92–93, *supra*.
[17] (1885), 29 Ch.D. 715.   [18] [1892] 2 Q.B.D. 1, at p. 10.

Hemsworth Rural District Council[19] Wright, J. held that a covenant in a floating charge not to create a mortgage or charge with priority over the floating charge did not affect a subsequent assignee who had no notice of it.

The whole world is deemed to have constructive notice of registered charges.[20] However, a covenant not to assign debts subject to it is not one of the particulars which have to be registered (section 98(1) of the Companies Act 1948). Arguably, a factor should not be regarded as having constructive notice of it even if it appeared on the register as its appearance would not be in accordance with law.[21] By section 95(1) of the Companies Act 1948, a charge is "void against the liquidator and any creditor of the company, unless the prescribed particulars of the charge, together with the instrument, if any, by which the charge is created or evidenced, are delivered to or received by the registrar of companies for registration in manner required by this Act within 21 days after the date of its creation". Only a "liquidator" and "creditor" are referred to. A factor is not a secured lender of money but a purchaser of book debts, and is therefore not a creditor of a client. Thus, it would seem that an unregistered charge is still valid as against a factor. Therefore, a factor who purchased debts with knowledge of a covenant not to sell them in an unregistered charge over the debts, could not plead the invalidity of the charge, because of its non-registration, as a defence to his knowledge of the existence of the covenant.

Apart from the priorities question an assignee's knowledge of a covenant, in a floating charge, against an assignment of debts subject to the charge may make him liable for damages in tort to the chargee for conspiracy to procure breaches of contract and for breaches of contract.[22]

As a matter of practical interest, although contemporary floating charges do commonly prohibit the creation of subsequent charges which will have priority, they often do not prohibit the assignment, sale or factoring of debts subject to the charge. Usually, there is no logic in such an omission.

Notice to customer

In equity, notice to the customer did not have to be in writing. But section 137(3) of the Law of Property Act 1925 says:

> "A notice, otherwise than in writing, given to or received by a trustee after the commencement of this Act as respects any dealing with an equit-

---

[19] (1928), 140 L.T. 69; [1928] All E.R. Rep. 602.
[20] *Wilson* v. *Kelland*, [1910] 2 Ch. 306, at p. 313, *per* Eve, J.
[21] Note the contrary view of Gower, *Modern Company Law* (3rd Edn., 1969) 422–3; and cf. Allen, "Stock in Trade Financing (Australia and New Zealand)" (1967), 2 U. Tas. L.R. 382, at p. 406.
[22] *British Motor Trade Association* v. *Salvadori*, [1949] Ch. 556; [1949] 1 All E.R. 208; *Thomson & Co., Ltd.* v. *Deakin*, [1952] 2 All E.R. 361.

able interest in real or personal property, shall not affect the priority or the competing claims of the purchasers in the equitable interest."

Only a "trustee" is referred to and not a debtor so assignments of debts are excluded from the section and notices of them need not be in writing.

Stop orders

Where a debt has been paid into Court, a stop order constitutes notice of assignment and priorities are determined by the chronological order in which stop orders are obtained. However, if an assignee has given notice of assignment to the customer before the debt is paid into Court his priority cannot be displaced by an assignee who is the first to obtain a stop order. In *Livesey* v. *Harding*[23] X mortgaged his reversionary legacy to A who gave notice of assignment to the trustees. Later, the fund was paid into Court. Then A assigned the legacy to B and B obtained a stop order before A. It was held that A had priority over B. Romilly, M.R. held that:

> "*Brearcliff* v. *Dorrington* (1850), 4 De G. & Sm. 122 proves, that in such a case the order in which the stop orders are obtained does not effect the prior incumbrancer, who has given due notice of his security. I am of the same opinion."[1]

No or simultaneous notices

Where no notices of competing equitable assignments have been given or where the notices are simultaneous priority is determined, in accordance with the general equitable principle, by the chronological order of the assignments, provided the equities are equal. In *Rice* v. *Rice*,[2] Kindersley, V.-C. said:

> "as between persons having only equitable interests if their priorities are in all other respects equal, priority of time gives the better equity or, qui prior est tempore prior est jure. In a contest between persons having only equitable interests priority of time is the ground of preference last resorted to; that is . . . a Court of Equity will not prefer the one to the other on the mere ground of priority of time, until it finds upon a determination of their relative merits that there is no other sufficient ground of preference between them, or, in other words that their equities are in all other respects equal; and that if the one has on other grounds a better equity than the other, priority of time is immaterial. In examining the relative merits (or equities) of two parties having adverse equitable interests, the points to which the Court must direct its attention are obviously these: the nature and condition of their respective equitable interests, the circumstances and manner of their acquisition and the whole conduct of each party with respect thereto

[23] (1856) 23 Beav. 141; 53 E.R. 55; see also Ch.D. C.A. R.S.C. Ord. 50, r. 10.
[1] 53 E.R. 55, at p. 56.   [2] (1854), 2 Drew 73; 61 E.R. 646.

and in examining into these points it must apply the test not of any technical rule or any rule of partial application, but the same broad principles of right and justice which a Court of Equity applies universally in deciding upon contested rights".

Where notice to a customer of competing assignments are simultaneous, priority is determined in order of the chronology of the assignments.[3] It has been said that the law takes notice of parts of days in determining priorities. In *Johnstone* v. *Cox*[4] Bacon, V.-C. held that "there can be no doubt that the law does occasionally take notice of portions of a day and particularly in a case of notice by incumbrancers to a stakeholder". In *Tomlinson* v. *Bullock*[5] Lush, J. decided to the same effect. However, the principle does not appear to have ever been applied. Indeed, notices given at different times on the same day have been held to be simultaneous, and notice delivered to a debtor's business premises after business hours which would not be looked at in the normal course of business until the next day is not considered to be delivered until the next day. In *Calisher* v. *Forbes*[6] there were four successive assignments of the proceeds of sale of an army commission. One assignee delivered a notice to the debtor after business hours which was not opened until 9 a.m. the next morning. Two other assignees also served notice of assignment at 9 a.m. on the same day. The fourth assignee served notice at about 9.30 a.m. James, L.J. held that:

> "there is no substantial question as to the notice which was left at the bank after business hours, as it was contained in a letter which, in the ordinary course of business, would not be opened before the opening of the bank on the morning of the 8th of December. It must be considered, to all intents and purposes, as a notice received at the same time with the other notices, on the morning of the 8th: and we are of the opinion that no priority by notice has been given by anyone, but the incumbrances must take effect according to their dates".[7]

The requirements of notice determining priorities are more stringent than those of notice sufficient to take a debt out of the order and disposition of a bankrupt client. In *Saffron Walden Second Benefit Building Society* v. *Rayner*[8] James, L.J. said:

> "the question what is sufficient notice to prevent a thing from being alleged to be in the order and disposition of an apparent owner with the consent of the true owner stands upon a very different footing from the question what is sufficient notice as regards successive incumbrancers. The Courts have a great inclination to prevent a man losing his property through the fiction that somebody else has been giving credit to the

[3] *Calisher* v. *Forbes* (1871), 7 Ch.App. 109; *Johnstone* v. *Cox* (1880), 16 Ch.D. 571, affd. (1881), 19 Ch. D. 17, C.A.
[4] (1880), 16 Ch.D. 571, affd. (1881), 19 Ch.D. 17, C.A.
[5] (1879), 4 Q.B.D. 230. [6] (1871), 7 Ch.App. 109.
[7] *Ibid.*, at p. 113. [8] (1880), 14 Ch.D. 406, C.A.

bankrupt on the supposition that it was his, which one knows is not the fact in one case out of a hundred."[9]

In *Mutual Life Assurance Society* v. *Langley*[10] Cotton, L.J. said:

> "order and disposition must be with the consent of the true owner, and it may very well be that sufficient has been done to show that the true owner does not consent to the fund remaining as it is, although it would not be sufficient to shew that notice had been given to effectually secure or obtain priority"[11]

Thus, notice to a customers' solicitor may take the debt out of the order and disposition of a client, but it will be insufficient to constitute notice of assignment of that debt in determining priorities unless the solicitor has express or implied authority, as agent, to receive such a notice.[12] Similarly, if part of a debt has been paid into Court, notice to the customer is sufficient to take the whole debt out of the order and disposition of a bankrupt client, but as between competing assignees it is only sufficient to obtain priority to that part of the debt in the hands of the customer and a stop order has to be obtained to obtain priority to the part of the debt which has been paid into Court.[13]

However, the requirements of notice determining priorities are less stringent than the requirements of notice binding a customer to pay the assignor, because, in the latter case, a specific direction to pay the assignor in addition to the notice of assignment would appear to be necessary.[14]

B EQUITABLE ASSIGNEE *v.* STATUTORY ASSIGNEE

A priority competition between an equitable assignee and a statutory assignee is a matter of considerable practical importance because invoice discounting and confidential factoring are conducted on a non-notification basis and because it is the practice of some factors to take assignments in a non-statutory form as a method of avoidance of payment of ad valorem stamp duty (although their factoring agreements almost certainly contain a covenant of further assurance from the client to provide a statutory assignment if required), while other factors take statutory assignments as a matter of course.

The main question is whether, and the extent to which, the priority rule which governs the competition is the general rule of property law that a bona fide purchaser of a legal interest without notice of a prior

---

[9] *Ibid.,* at p. 409; see also *Lloyds Bank* v. *Pearson,* [1901] 1 Ch. 865.

[10] (1886), 32 Ch.D. 460, C.A.   [11] *Ibid.,* at p. 470.

[12] *Saffron Walden Second Benefit Building Society* v. *Rayner, supra.*

[13] *Mutual Life Assurance Society* v. *Langley, supra.*

[14] *Denney Gasquet and Metcalfe* v. *Conklin,* [1913] 3 K.B. 177, at pp. 180–181, *per* Atkin, J.; In Re *Pawson's Settlement, Higgins* v. *Pawson,* [1917] 1 Ch. 541, at p. 544, *per* Sargant, J.

equitable interest has priority over that equitable interest. Henceforth, for the sake of brevity, this will be called the BFP principle.

The BFP principle has had its greatest application in relation to real property, particularly before the Law of Property Act 1925 limited the large number of legal estates which could previously exist in real property to two. The principle has perhaps been no better expressed than by James, L.J. in the real property case of *Pilcher* v. *Rawlins*[15] in reference to a contest between a *cestui que trust* and a subsequent bona fide purchaser of the legal estate in real property without notice of the trust:

> "such a purchaser's plea of purchase for valuable consideration without notice is an absolute, unqualified, unanswerable defence, and an un-answerable plea to the jurisdiction of this Court. Such a purchaser . . . may be interrogated and tested to any extent as to the valuable con-sideration which he has given in order to shew the bona fides or mala fides of his purchase, and also the presence or absence of notice; but when once he has gone through that ordeal, and has satisfied the terms of the plea of purchase for valuable consideration without notice, then, according to my judgement, this Court has no jurisdiction whatever to do anything more than let him depart in possession of that legal estate, that legal right, that legal advantage which he has obtained, whatever it may be. In such a case, a purchaser is entitled to hold that which, without breach of duty, he has had conveyed to him."[16]

As far as personal property is concerned, the BFP principle has been applied to a competition between an equitable interest in after-acquired goods and a legal interest in the goods acquired after they came into existence.[17]

The principle was said to apply to choses in action by the House of Lords in *Performing Right Society, Ltd.* v. *London Theatre of Varieties, Ltd.*[18] The facts of the case were unusual. X was a member of the plain-tiff society. X assigned to the plaintiffs the performing rights of every song afterwards acquired by X. X later acquired songs and the copy-rights and performance rights to them. The defendants, music hall proprieters, permitted one of the songs to be sung in their music hall without the plaintiff's consent. The plaintiffs sought an injunction. Apparently it was very inconvenient for the plaintiffs to obtain statutory assignments of the property from their members after the property came into existence, and they therefore joined issue with the defendants before the House of Lords solely on the question whether it was neces-sary to join the assignor as a party to the action.

The House of Lords held that the assignor had to be joined as a party

---

[15] (1872), 7 Ch. App. 259.   [16] *Ibid.*, at pp. 268, 269.
[17] *Joseph* v. *Lyons* (1884), 15 Q.B.D. 280, C.A.; *Hallas* v. *Robinson* (1885), 15 Q.B.D. 288.
[18] [1924] A.C. 1, H.L.

and analysed the reasons for the rule, which included references to the
BFP principle. On the matter of the BFP principle, Viscount Caves
said that if the assignor did not have to be joined as a party:

> "a defendant after defeating the claim of an equitable claimant might
> have to resist like proceedings by the legal owner, or by persons claim-
> ing under him as assignees for value without notice of any prior equity,
> and proceedings might be indefinitely and oppressively multiplied."[19]

Viscount Finlay said:

> "there may possibly be cases in which a person who has made an equit-
> able assignment might by a subsequent assignment have transferred the
> legal interest in the same work to a purchaser for value without notice,
> whose title would prevail over the merely equitable right, and such a
> possibility is one reason for the rule of making the legal owner a
> party."[20]

Lord Sumner said:

> "the assignor under a legal assignment which does not divide the
> property or the right owned into parts, divests himself of the owner-
> ship of the whole. When the assignment is equitable, he either divests
> himself of the whole, in the sense that equity will compel him to do so
> when called upon, though until then he remains capable of divesting
> himself or of investing a stranger for value without notice, or else he
> divests himself of nothing, but retains the whole 'legal' ownership
> until he is called on to part with it."[1]

Later he added that in the absence of the assignor from the suit, the
defendant has:

> "no means of excluding the possibility that some assignment, other
> than the assignment to the appellants, might rank before it, and in such
> event they would have no answer to proceedings taken by such an
> assignee. If the [assignor] had been joined they might have been
> interrogated on the subject."[2]

A joinder of the assignor obviously does not necessarily reveal the
existence of such a legal assignee, but no doubt it might, particularly if
Lord Sumner's dictum that the assignor can be cross-examined as to
the existence of such an assignee is followed by the parties before the
Court.

Now the *Performing Right*, case was only concerned with an equitable
assignment of a future chose in action. There does not appear to be
any express authority that the BFP principle applies where the equitable
assignment is of an existing chose in action and notice of assignment
has been given. If the BFP principle does apply in the latter situation,

[19] *Ibid.*, at p. 14.
[1] *Ibid.*, at p. 28.
[20] *Ibid.*, at p. 19.
[2] *Ibid.*, at p. 31.

it follows that if a client makes an equitable assignment of an existing debt to A and later statutorily assigns the same debt to B, a bona fide purchaser without notice of A's interest, B would have priority even if notice to the customer of A's assignment is earlier than notice of B's assignment. This result is entirely different from the result under the rule in *Dearle* v. *Hall* where A would have priority as the first to give notice of assignment. It leads to the conclusion that equitable assignments have been imperilled in a manner which was impossible before the Judicature Act 1873.

The difficulty with this conclusion is that it is not easy to reconcile with other authorities nor with the policy of the statutes which created statutory assignments. These authorities say that statutory assignments merely effected procedure and not substantive rights. Thus, in *William Brandts Sons & Co.* v. *Dunlop Rubber Co.*[3] Lord MacNaghten held that the statute "does not forbid or destroy equitable assignments or impair their efficacy in the slightest degree".[4] Similarly, Channell, J. in *Torkington* v. *Magee*[5] said: "This subsection is merely machinery; it enables an action to be brought by the assignee in his own name in cases where previously he would have sued in the assignor's name but only where he could so sue."[6]

It was not the policy of either section 25(3) of the Judicature Act 1873, or of section 136(1)of the Law of Property Act 1925 which replaced it, to imperil equitable interests. In *Brittain* v. *Rossiter*[7] Brett, L.J. said:

> "the true construction of the Judicature Acts is that they confer no new rights; they only confirm the rights which previously were to be found existing in the Courts, either of law or of equity; if they did more they would alter the rights of parties, whereas in truth they only change the procedure."[8]

The guiding policy of the Law of Property Act 1925 was the reduction of the number of legal estates in land and the assimilation of real property law to the law of personalty.[9] It hardly seems consistent with that policy that the danger to equitable interests which Parliament sought to minimise in relation to real property should at the same time be introduced for the first time into the law governing choses in action.

It is submitted that the BFP principle should not be applied to a competition between a competing statutory assignee and an equitable assignee who is first to give notice, because the latter's equitable interest

[3] [1905] A.C. 454, H.L.   [4] *Ibid.*, at p. 461.
[5] [1902] 2 K.B. 427; see also *Tolhurst* v. *Associated Portland Cement Manufacturers (1900), Ltd.*, [1903] A.C. 414, at p. 424, *per* Lord Lindley: It "has not made contracts assignable which were not assignable in equity before, but it has enabled assigns of assignable contracts to sue upon them in their own names without joining the assignor".
[6] [1902] 2 K.B. 427, at p. 435.
[7] (1879), 11 Q.B.D. 123.   [8] *Ibid.*, at p. 129.
[9] Memo prefixed to the Law of Property Bill 1922, Sir L. Scott in 154 H.C. Rep. (5th Sess.) 102, 103.

is so extraordinary. It is quite unlike typical equitable interests. Indeed, it is only thought of as equitable because of the common law's irrational view that a legal chose in action cannot be assigned. Perhaps it is arguable that it should be regarded as a legal interest, or at least as a quasi-legal interest because the rights of an "equitable" assignee against a customer are ultimately dependent on a common law judgement since equity has no jurisdiction over legal choses in action and can do no more that assist the assignee to obtain a common law judgment. Further, it is arguable that the BFP principle is inapplicable because the "equities" to which a statutory assignment is subject under section 136(1) of the Law of Property Act 1925 includes not only a debtor's defences[10] but the claims of a prior equitable assignee.[11]

Instead, it is submitted, the rule in *Dearle* v. *Hall* should be applied to such conflicts because the difference between an absolute equitable assignment, where notice of assignment has been given, and a statutory assignment of an existing chose in action is purely one of form and that hardly seems sufficient reason to apply a different priority rule than would be applied where both assignments are equitable and notice of each assignment has been given. However, in the absence of express authority it is not certain whether the courts would apply the BFP principle or the rule in *Dearle* v. *Hall*.

Where the BFP principle applies, "notice" of an earlier assignment means knowledge of that assignment. It seems that the point in time at which such knowledge of a prior assignment is relevant is the same as under the rule in *Dearle* v. *Hall,* that is, the latest point in time at which such knowledge is relevant to affect the priority of a subsequent assignee in either case is the time that the subsequent assignee takes his assignment and pays his money to the assignor. In *Mutual Life Assurance Society* v. *Langley* a case which was concerned with priorities under the rule in *Dearle* v. *Hall,* Cotton, L.J. said:

> "it is not a question of what a man knows when he does that which will better or perfect his security but what he knows at the time when he took his security and paid his money."[12]

If the BFP principle does govern priority between statutory and equitable assignees of existing debts, it seems to follow that priority rules governing competing equitable interests can be ousted by the simple expedient of converting an equitable assignment into a legal assignment. For example, suppose that a client makes successive equitable assignments of the same debts to factor A and to factor B, a bona fide purchaser for value without notice of A's assignment. A

[10] Pp. 99, 112, *supra.*
[11] See Glenn, Gerrard, "The Assignment of Choses in Action; Rights of Bona Fide Purchaser", 20 Virginia Law Review (1933–34) 621 at 646; *Sutherland* v. *Reeve*, 38 N.E. 130 (1894).
[12] (1866), 32 Ch.D. 460, C.A., at p. 468.

gives notice to the customer before B. Under the rule in *Dearle* v. *Hall,* A has priority. Suppose B discovers A's assignment. If B then takes a statutory assignment from the client he would obtain priority over A under the BFP principle. "The principle has always been this, if a man with ignorance of previous incumbrance takes a mortgage or makes a purchase, when he finds out the truth he may take such steps as he can in order to protect his weak security or his weak purchase": *per* Cotton, L.J. in *Mutual Life Assurance Society* v. *Langley*.[13] In the real property case of *Taylor* v. *Russell*[14] Lord Mac-Naghten said:

> "It is not disputed than an equitable mortgagee who has advanced his money without notice of a prior equitable mortgage may gain priority by getting in the legal estate unless the circumstances are such as to make it inequitable for him to do so, as would be the case for example, if the legal estate were held upon express trusts or, according to recent authorities, if it were vested in a satisfied mortgagee. The mere fact that the subsequent incumbrancer has notice of the prior incumbrance when he gets in the legal estate counts for nothing. 'It is', as Lord Hardwicke says in *Wortley* v. *Birkhead*,[15] 2 Ves. Sen. 574 'the very occasion which shows the necessity of it'."

Furthermore, if an assignee has the right to call in the legal title it seems that he is treated as having it even if he has not called it in[16] but only in a priority competition where the competing equitable assignee has no such rights.[17] Thus, if two competing equitable assignees both have this right by virtue of agreement with the assignor neither gains priority by virtue of that fact. Factoring agreements and other agreements for the assignments of debts generally do give the factor such a right, so in practice few cases are likely to arise where an advantage accrues, as a result of this rule, where the right is not exercised.

C STATUTORY ASSIGNEE *v.* STATUTORY ASSIGNEE

There does not appear to be a case which has dealt with this competition, perhaps because the answer is obvious. It seems clear that a legal assignment strips the assignor of his whole interest in the debt. Thereafter, he has nothing to assign so that the first assignment must have priority over any later legal assignment. This is presumably subject to the general principle that the bona fide purchaser of a legal interest loses priority if he has knowledge of a prior equitable interest at the time of his purchase. Thus, if X assigns to A then to B and B gives notice of assignment before A (both assignments complying with

---

[13] *Ibid.*   [14] [1892] A.C. 244, H.L.
[15] *Ibid.*, at p. 259; see also *Bailey* v. *Barnes*, [1894] 1 Ch. 25, at p. 36, C.A., *per* Lindley. L.J.
[16] *Taylor* v. *London and County Banking Co.*, [1901] 2 Ch. 231, C.A.
[17] *McCarthy and Stone* v. *Hodge & Co.*, [1971] 2 All E.R. 973, at p. 982; see also *Wilkes* v. *Bodington* (1707), 2 Vern. 599; 23 E.R. 991; *Assaf* v. *Fuwa*, [1955] A.C. 215.

section 136(1)), but at the time B bought the debt he knew of A's interest (which at the time was still equitable) A would have priority. But if B did not have such knowledge, B would have priority.

2   Cestuis que Trust

A debt can be the subject of a trust: see *Vandepitte* v. *Preferred Accident Insurance Corporation of New York*.[18] Thus, a client could borrow from A and create a trust of debts in A's favour as security for the loan, then assign the same debts to B, a factor. The formal legal description of A, as beneficiary of the trust, is "cestuis que trust".

The effect of the decision in *Hill* v. *Peters*[19] is that a cestuis que trust has priority over a subsequent assignee who gives notice of assignment to the customer even though no notice of the trust is given to the customer. The facts of the case were as follows. Sydney Gotto assigned as security for a debt his reversionary interest in a share of personalty settled by his father's will expectant on the death of his mother, still living, to solicitors E and H. E and H borrowed money from Peters and executed a declaration of trust declaring themselves trustees of the chose in action for Peters. Later E and H borrowed money from A and assigned the chose in action to A as security. A died and an action was commenced by her executor, Hill, claiming a declaration of priority in respect of the chose over Peters. Eve, J. held that Peters had priority. He endorsed the view of Lord MacNaghten in *Ward* v. *Duncombe*[20] that the rule in *Dearle* v. *Hall* ought not to be extended to new cases, and therefore declined to apply it in a competition between a cestuis que trust and an assignee.

The decision paves the way for a fraud which is hard to detect because if no requirement of notice is imposed on a cestuis que trust, there is no way that third parties can discover the existence of the trust. It is an example of a case where the Court paid too much attention to the form of the instrument which created the security. If the attention had been focused on effect rather than on form, it would have been seen that the object of a trust by way of security is the same as the object of an assignment by way of security. Where the effect of legal instruments is the same, it is submitted that they should be governed by the same priority rules. It can hardly be considered a hardship to require a cestuis que trust to give notice of the trust to a customer. The same anti-fraud argument that supports the rule in *Dearle* v. *Hall* militates for the application of that rule in a competition between a cestuis que trust by way of security and an assignee.

[18] [1933] A.C. 70, at p. 79, P.C.: "a party to a contract can constitute himself a trustee for a third party of a right under the contract and thus confer such rights enforceable in equity on the third party": *per* Lord Wright.
[19] [1918] 2 Ch. 273.   [20] [1893] A.C. 369, H.L.

Although *Hill* v. *Peters* was approved by Lord Reid in the House of Lords in *Lyle, Ltd.* v. *Rosher*,[1] Viscount Kilmuir in the same case said that it was unnecessary to consider whether the opinion of Eve, J. in *Hill* v. *Peters* was correct, that for the purpose of the rule in *Dearle* v. *Hall* there was a distinction between an equitable assignment and a declaration of trust. From this it would seem that he thought that the point was worth further consideration. *Hill* v. *Peters* was only a decision at first instance, and it is to be hoped that it will eventually be overruled and the rule in *Dearle* v. *Hall* applied. This is not to say that the rule in *Dearle* v. *Hall* should be applied in the more usual cases of a trust where the object of the trust is not to effect security for financing. Where the equitable assignment precedes the creation of a trust presumably the general rule should prevail that the earlier equity, if equal, has priority, which in this case would be the earlier equitable assignment.

It is curious that in *Hill* v. *Peters* there is no reference to whether the assignment was statutory or equitable. Presumably it was equitable, for if it was statutory the assignee should have had priority under the BFP principle since the assignee had no notice of the cestuis que trust's equitable interest at the time of his assignment. Thus, in a competition between a cestuis que trust and a later statutory assignee, the latter should have priority under the BFP principle. As between a cestuis que trust and an earlier statutory assignee, the whole interest passes to the latter and he would have priority.

3 Liens

It is thought that credit factors could be involved in priority conflicts with liens of clients' solicitors and agent factors. Before considering these two particular cases, the following general comments on liens may be helpful.

A lien is legal, equitable or statutory. A common law lien depends upon possession of the property. It "is a right in one man to retain that which is in his possession belonging to another till certain demands of him the person in possession are satisfied".[2] It is a passive lien: it cannot be enforced but merely confers a right to withhold possession.[3] However by R.S.C. Ord. 50, r.2, the Court now has a discretion to order a sale for any just or sufficient reason,[4] although a tender regard will be had to the rights of the person in whom the legal title is vested.[5]

An equitable lien is different. It confers a charge upon property until certain claims are satisfied.[6] It exists independently of possession. As

[1] [1958] 3 All E.R. 597.
[2] *Hammonds* v. *Barclay* (1802), 2 East 227, at p. 235; 102 E.R. 356, at p. 359.
[3] *Barratt* v. *Gough-Thomas*, [1951] Ch. 242, at p. 250.
[4] *Larner* v. *Fawcett*, [1950] 2 All E.R. 277.
[5] *Dangar Grant & Co.* v. *Gospel Oak Iron Co.* (1890), 6 T.L.R. 260.
[6] 24 Halsbury's Laws of England (3rd Edn.), para. 2815.

an equitable interest, it will not avail against a bona fide purchaser for value without notice of it nor against a subsequent better equity.[7] It is enforceable by obtaining a judgement and order for sale.[8]

By custom, liens are either general or particular. A general lien extends to all money due from the owner of the property. A particular lien extends to all amounts due from the owner relating to the property the subject of the lien.

A   CLIENT'S SOLICITOR

A client's solicitor may have conducted legal proceedings on the client's behalf to collect a debt which is then factored. The debt may become a judgement debt, or it may be paid into court or to the solicitor If the solicitor claims a lien in respect of amounts due to it from the client, the question arises whether the lien has priority over the factor's assignment. The answer depends on whether the lien and the assignment are, respectively, legal or equitable. Solicitors have three types of lien: legal, equitable, and statutory. They cover taxable costs, charges and expenses (including counsels' fees) but do not extend to loans and advances to the client for other purposes.[9]

A solicitor is not bound to give notice of his lien to an assignee whom he knows is about to take an assignment of the debt.[10] The fact that he is also the assignee's solicitor will not, of itself, cause him to lose priority.[11]

(i) There is a *common law general lien* on property in a solicitor's possession received in his capacity as a solicitor on which he has bestowed his skill and labour.[12] The lien extends to money in his possession.[13] In *Barratt* v. *Gough-Thomas*[14] Evershed, M.R. described it as follows:

> "The nature of a solicitor's general retaining lien has more than once been authoritatively stated. It is a right at common law depending (it has been said) upon implied agreement. It is merely passive and possessory: that is to say, the solicitor has no right of actively enforcing his demand.
>
> It confers upon him merely the right to withhold possession of the documents or other personal property of his client or former client— in the words of Sir E. Sugden, L.C. 'To lock them up in his box, and

---

[7] *Rice* v. *Rice* (1854), 2 Drew 73; 61 E.R. 646.

[8] *Re Stucley, Stucley* v. *Kekewich*, [1906] 1 Ch. 67.

[9] *Re Taylor, Stileman and Underwood*, [1891] 1 Ch. 590, C.A.; *Re Galland* (1885), 31 Ch.D. 296.

[10] *Faithfull* v. *Ewen* (1878), 7 Ch.D. 495.

[11] *Macfarlane* v. *Lister* (1887), 37 Ch.D. 88.

[12] *Re Long, Ex parte Fuller* (1881), 16 Ch.D. 617.

[13] *Loescher* v. *Dean*, [1950] Ch. 491, at p. 496, *per* Harman, J.; applied *Wagg* v. *Law Society*, [1957] Ch. 405; [1957] 2 All E.R. 274.

[14] [1951] Ch. 242.

to put the key in his pocket until his client satisfies the amount of his demand'."[15]

As the lien is legal, it should have priority over a subsequent assignment whether legal or equitable.

(ii) There is an *equitable particular lien* on funds recovered or preserved by a solicitor's exertions. It is not entirely clear whether this is properly classifiable as a lien, or, if so, whether it is equitable or legal. In *Mercer v. Graves*[16] and in *Bibby (James), Ltd.* v. *Woods and Howard*[17] it was said that it was not a lien at all but merely a right to ask the court to charge the property for the amount of the solicitor's costs. In *Re Meter Cabs, Ltd,*[18] Swinfen Eady, J. described it as a common law lien, which is how it is described by Cordery[19] However, in *Mason v. Mason and Cottrell*[20] Lord Henworth, M.R. said "It is merely a right to claim the equitable interference of the court" and in *Haymes v. Cooper*[1] Romilly, M.R. described it as an "equity". Snell[2] views it as an equitable lien and this is probably the best view.

In *Haymes v. Cooper,*[3] Romilly, M.R. stated the following rule to determine competition between an assignment and a solicitors' equitable lien where the debt is represented by a fund in court.

"If a sum of £1,000 were recovered for AB by the exertions of his solicitor, and AB assigned it to CD who obtained a stop order on the fund and gave notice of it to the Accountant-General, then, although CD would have priority over the incumberancers who had not got a stop order, yet he could only claim that which the client could give him, namely, the fund subject to the solicitor's right ... Where a man knows that there is a fund in court, he knows also that it is subject to the solicitor's lien for his costs in recovering it, and that he is entitled to be paid in the first instance. The Act, however, clearly points out that there may be a bona fide purchaser who may have priority."[4]

Similarly, where there is no fund in court but the debt is the subject of a law suit, "notice that the subject matter of the assignment is the subject matter of a suit amounts to notice to the assignee of the existence of the solicitors' right to a lien. Such notice prevents an assignee from being a purchaser for value without notice": *per* Esher, M.R. in *Cole v. Eley*.[5] In that case, a solicitor had acted for the plaintiff in an action which was compromised by the defendant agreeing to pay a sum of

---

[15] *Ibid.*, at p. 242. [16] (1872), L.R. 7 Q.B. 499.
[17] [1949] 2 K.B. 449, at p. 453. [18] [1911] 2 Ch. 557, at p. 559.
[19] Cordery on Solicitors (6th Edn., 1968), p. 416. [20] [1933] P. 199.
[1] (1864), 33 Beav 431, at p. 433; 55 E.R. 435, at p. 436.
[2] Snell's *Principles of Equity* (27th Edn., 1973), p. 438.
[3] *Supra.*
[4] At pp. 433-4. The "Act" to which he referred has now been replaced by the Solicitors Act 1957, discussed below.
[5] [1894] 2 Q.B.D. 350, at p. 351, C.A.

money to the plaintiff by instalments. The plaintiff assigned the money payable to him under the compromise to a witness in the action. The solicitor later obtained a charging order upon the money recovered in an action for his costs. It was held that the solicitor had priority over the assignee. The rule may imply that if the assignee did not have such notice of a solicitor's lien, he would take free from it. Where the assignment is legal, this implication accords with the BFP principle, described earlier. But where the assignment is equitable, it is difficult to understand why the lien, as the earlier equity, should not prevail. Perhaps the rationale is that notice of assignment makes the assignment a better equity than the earlier lien provided the assignee has no notice of the lien. This theory may indicate that the rule in *Dearle* v. *Hall* applies to competitions between solicitors' equitable liens and equitable assignments. Alternatively, perhaps the implication is incorrect: perhaps the rule simply means that the assignee's knowledge of the lien precludes the possibility of the assignment being the better equity, without disrupting the possibility that an assignee without such knowledge would nevertheless lose priority to an earlier lien if the equities were equal.

(iii) A solicitor may convert an equitable particular lien into a *legal charge* under the Solicitors Act 1957, section 72, which says:

> "Any court in which a solicitor has been employed to prosecute or defend any suit, matter or proceeding may at any time declare the solicitor entitled to a charge on the property recovered or preserved through his instrumentality for his taxed costs in reference to that suit, matter or proceeding and may make such orders for the taxation of the said costs and for raising money to pay, or for paying, the said costs out of the said property as they think fit and all conveyances and acts done to defeat, or operating to defeat, that charge shall, except in the case of a conveyance to a bona fide purchaser for value without notice, be void as against the solicitor: Provided that no order shall be made if the right to recover the costs is barred by any statute of limitations."

The "notice" referred to means notice of a right to apply for a charging order.[6]

As stated in the citation from *Haymes* v. *Cooper,* above, the Act points out that there may be a bona fide purchaser who has priority over the charge. There has to be a "conveyance" to the purchaser. This is a real property expression, and may have been used because the section was originally passed mainly to overrule a decision that a solicitor's equitable lien did not extend to real property,[7] although the section by its terms refers to any type of property. The expression is probably apt to include a legal assignment of a debt, but possibly not an equitable assignment.

[6] *Dallow* v. *Garrold* (1884), 14 Q.B.D. 543.
[7] *Shaw* v. *Neale* (1858), 6 H.L. Cas. 581; 10 E.R. 1422.

If so, a subsequent bona fide purchaser who is an equitable assignee would not have priority over the charge. However, a charge is usually declared to be subject to prior subsisting equities.[8]

B CLIENT'S AGENT FACTOR

Suppose a client uses an agent to sell his goods. If the agent is a "factor", in the strict legal sense, he has a general common law lien in respect of debts due to him from the client.[9] In R. v. *Lee*[10] it was held that "by the common law, a factor had the same right to hold goods as security for money advanced on them and in the same manner as a pledge".

The lien extends not only to the goods but to the proceeds of their sale and has priority over an equitable assignment. In *Drinkwater* v. *Goodwin*[11] X sold goods through an agent factor and assigned the resultant debt to Y. Notice of assignment was given to the debtor. X became bankrupt. It was held that the factor had priority to the debt over Y: "a factor has a lien over the price of goods in the hands of the buyer: in this case, though, he had not the actual possession of them, yet as he had a power of giving a good discharge, or bringing an action, he had a right to retain the money in consequence of his lien.[12]

Similarly, in *Webb* v. *Smith*[13] A, an auctioneer, owed X a sum of money arising from the proceeds of sale subject to A's charges in respect of the sale. X charged the debt to B and notice of the charge was given to A. It was held that the charge was subject to the lien and A was therefore entitled to deduct his charges before paying A. Lindley, L.J. said: "The assignor can give no greater right in equity than he himself possesses."

It is not clear whether the agent's right to require the debtor to pay him is a legal or an equitable right. A common law lien is based on possession. Is an agent who has sold goods but who has not yet received the proceeds in "possession" of the debt resulting from the sale? If the lien is legal, it should have priority over a later legal assignment; but if it is equitable, a later legal assignment would presumably prevail under the BFP principle, discussed earlier.

Until 1967 it seemed that there was no doubt that a "factor", in the strict legal sense, meant a mercantile agent entrusted in the normal course of business with the possession of goods or the documents of title thereto for the purpose of sale.[14] However, in that year Denning,

---

[8] *The Paris*, [1896] P. 77.
[9] *Kruger* v. *Wilcox* (1755), Amb. 252; 27 E.R. 168; *Baring* v. *Corrie* (1818), 2 B. & Ald. 137; 106 E.R. 317; 24 Halsbury's Laws of England (3rd Edn.), para. 262.
[10] (1819), 6 Price 369; 146 E.R. 837. [11] (1775), 1 Cowp. 251; 98 E.R. 1070.
[12] At 256. [13] (1885), 30 Ch.D. 192.
[14] 1 Halsbury's Laws of England (3rd Edn.) para. 362 (not reproduced in fourth edition).

M.R. held in *Rolls Razor, Ltd.* v. *Cox*[15] that an additional and essential part of the definition of a factor is that he sells in his own name without disclosing the name of his principal. On this basis, he held that the agent in that case did not have a factor's lien because he did not sell in his own name.

It is respectfully submitted that the two cases which he cited in support of his view do not support it. Indeed, one of the authorities, *Stevens* v. *Biller*[16] seems to directly contradict it. There Chitty, J., at first instance, said: "In *Re Henley, Ex Patre Dixon* (1876), 4 Ch.D. 133, Lord Justice Brett having the question before him with reference to what was a factor, therefore lays down the law thus, that although a factor in the usual course of business sells in his own name, yet he is not necessarily less a factor, because he sells in the name of his principal."[17] Cotton, L.J. on appeal, said "a factor is . . . an agent entrusted with the possession of goods for the purpose of sale. That is the true definition of a factor . . . it is not essential for the purpose of giving him a general lien that he should be free from any restriction as to the name in which he shall sell the goods."[18]

In *Baring* v. *Corrie*,[19] the other case cited by Denning, M.R., it was said that a factor "usually" sells in his own name and where he does a purchaser can off-set a debt due from the factor against the principal. This is manifestly just since the factor has his principal's apparent authority to give the impression that he, the factor, is the principal. However, a factor's lien is a very different question. A factor has a lien because it is usual (or at least it was in the past) for him to make loans to the principal to cover freight, insurance or simply bridging finance during the period of credit allowed to the purchaser. These principles are clearly stated by Holroyd, L.J. in *Baring* v. *Corrie*.[20] The name in which he happens to sell is surely irrelevant to the reason why the law gives him a lien. It is therefore concluded that in principle and on the authorities the view of Denning, M.R. is incorrect and should not be followed.

4 Client's Judgement Creditors

A judgement creditor of the client can obtain rights to debts owing to the client if he either obtains a garnishee order nisi; or issues a writ of sequestration and obtains an injunction to restrain the client from receiving the debt or brings an action to make the sequestration effectual.

Any unconditional debt, whether or not immediately payable, owing or accruing from the customer in his own right beneficially can be

---

[15] [1967] 1 Q.B. 552, at p. 568.   [16] (1883), 25 Ch.D. 31.
[17] *Ibid.*, at p. 34.   [18] *Ibid.*, at p. 38.
[19] (1818), 2 B. & Ald. 137; 106 E.R. 317.   [20] *Ibid.*, at pp. 148, 321.

attached by garnishee proceedings: see R.S.C. Ord. 49; C.C.R. Ord. 2. The judgement creditor will obtain priority to whatever debts the client can honestly deal with at the time the garnishee order nisi is served. Hence, if at that time debts have been previously assigned, even if no notice of assignment has been given, the assignee has priority over the judgement creditor in respect of those debts. In this priority competition, notice of assignment is irrelevant. In Re *General Horticultural Co., Ex parte Whitehouse*,[21] X charged a debt due from Y to A. Notice of assignment was given to Y's liquidator. Later, X also charged the same debt to B and C. No notice was given of these two charges. D recovered judgement against X and gave notice of the judgement to Y's liquidator. D then obtained a garnishee order nisi attaching the debt. It was held that D was postponed to A, B and C, even though B and C had not given notice. Chitty, J. said "the equitable doctrine of notice only comes in as between incumbrancers".[1]

Sequestration is a cumbersome process whereby a judgement creditor, who seeks to enforce a judgement wilfully disobeyed, issues, by leave of the court a writ addressed to at least four sequestrators, nominated by him, directing them to detain the client's property until the disobedience is purged. They have no authority to sell the property except pursuant to an order made on a separate application to the court—a mere writ of sequestration, even if coupled with notice to the customer, cannot defeat a subsequent assignment.

In Re *Hoare, Ex parte Nelson*,[2] A issued a sequestration writ against X, and gave notice of it to B, the executor of a will under which X was entitled to a legacy. X then became bankrupt. It was held that the trustee in bankruptcy had priority over A. Cotton, L.J. said:

> "By virtue of the writ the sequestrators could have seized any property of the defendant upon which they could have laid their hands without committing a breach of the peace, and without legal process. But the fund here in question is a chose in action which could not be recovered without some legal process. Is a charge of a fund in that position created merely by giving notice of a sequestration? In my opinion it would be contrary to all legal principle to hold that it is. In order to create a charge the plaintiff must, in my opinion, either have obtained an injunction to restrain the defendant from receiving the fund, as in *Willock* v. *Ferrell* (1878), 3 Ex. D. 323, or must have brought an action as in *Wilson* v. *Metcalfe* (1823), 1 Beav. 263 to make the sequestration effectual, that is, to do something which the writ itself did not do."[3]

Whether the assignment is statutory or equitable appears to be irrelevant in this context. The above principles apply equally to one type of assignment as to the other.

---

[21] (1886), 32 Ch.D. 512.
[2] (1880), 14 Ch.D. 41, C.A.

[1] *Ibid.*, at p. 515.
[3] *Ibid.*, at p. 47.

5 Clients' General Creditors in Bankruptcy or Winding up

In the bankruptcy of a client who is a sole trader or partnership or in the winding-up of a corporate client, priority conflicts can arise between the client's credit factor and his general creditors represented by the trustee in bankruptcy or the liquidator. Illogically, bankruptcy priority rules are not identical in all respects with winding-up priority rules.

A BANKRUPTCY

(i) *Assignments before the commencement of bankruptcy*

Section 38(a) of the Bankruptcy Act 1914 says that the property of a bankrupt divisible among his creditors includes "all such property as may belong to or be vested in the bankrupt at the commencement of the bankruptcy". Bankruptcy is deemed to commence at the time of the first act of bankruptcy proven to have occurred within three months before presentation of the bankruptcy petition: section 37(1). Thus, the basic rule is that an assignment of debts to a factor prior to the commencement of bankruptcy, which is valid as against the client, is equally valid as against the client's trustee. This rule is subject to the qualifications and elaborations contained in the following paragraphs.

(ii) *Assignments after the commencement of bankruptcy*

By section 45 of the Bankruptcy Act 1914 an assignment of specific debts to a factor for valuable consideration has priority over the trustee provided it takes place before the date of the receiving order and the factor at the time of assignment had no notice of an available act of bankruptcy. The "date" of the receiving order refers back to the earliest moment of that date: thus, if the assignment is on the same day but earlier than the receiving order, the trustee has priority.[4] After adjudication, a debt earned by the client can be acquired by a factor, bona fide and for value, and priority as between the factor and the trustee will go to whichever is the first to give notice of assignment to the customer (debtor).[5] The assignment is not in bad faith merely because the factor knew of the bankruptcy and that the trustee did not know that the client had earned the debt.[6]

---

[4] *Ex parte A.M. Wheeler v. The Trustee in Bankruptcy, Re* Warren, [1938] 1 Ch. 725.
[5] *In re Beall, Ex parte Official Receiver*, [1899] 1 Q.B. 688; *Mercer v. Vans Colina*, [1900] 1 Q.B. 130 n.
[6] *Cohen v. Mitchell* (1890), 25 Q.B.D. 262, at p. 267, C.A.; *Hunt v. Fripp* [1898] 1 Ch. 675; *Re Bennett, Ex parte Official Receiver*, [1907] 1 K.B. 149.

(*iii*)   *Unearned debts*

It has been held that an assignment before the commencement of
bankruptcy of debts which are unearned at the commencement of
bankruptcy is ineffective to pass the title of the debts to the assignee.
In *Re Jones, Ex parte Nichols*,[7] X assigned trade debts, present and
future, to A in trust to secure repayment of advances and to account to
X for the surp s. Notice of assignment was given to the trade debtors.
X then became bankrupt. The trustee in bankruptcy continued the
business and further trade debts arose. It was held as regards the latter
debts that the trustee in bankruptcy had priority over A. Jessel, M.R.
said:

> "... by no assignment or charge can a bankrupt give a good title as
> against his trustee to profits of his business, accruing after the com-
> mencement of the bankruptcy. The bankrupt cannot as against the
> trustee assign these profits; they are not his property."[8]

Thus, debts which are unearned at the commencement of bankruptcy
cannot be assigned before the commencement of bankruptcy. Conse-
questly, a distinction has to be drawn between contracts which are
executed and those which are merely executory. It is up to the trustee
in bankruptcy to elect whether a contract should be completed and if
he does so elect, the resultant debt belongs to him for the benefit of the
general creditors. In *Wilmot* v. *Alton*[9] a trader contracted to supply
dresses to a ballet company and for twelve weeks thereafter while the
show was running to keep up a supply for £40 per week, to provide
wigs as required for £3 per week, and to repair the wigs and dresses as
necessary. The dresses were supplied, and the trader charged the money
payable under the contract to A. Two and a half weeks after the twelve
week period began to run, the trader was adjudicated bankrupt. It was
held that the trustee in bankruptcy was entitled to the money payable
under the contract in priority to A. Rigby, L.J. held that:

> "where a person who has entered into contracts in the course of his
> business ceases to carry on business on account of bankruptcy, there
> is an important distinction, for the present purpose, between cases in
> which, the consideration for the contract having been wholly executed
> by the bankrupt on his part, a sum of money becomes due to him under
> the contract, and cases of executory contracts in which the money
> will not be earned under the contract unless the person contracting
> continues to carry on business and fully performs his part of the con-
> tract which has only been partially performed at the date of the bank-

---

[7] (1883), 22 Ch.D. 782, C.A.   [8] *Ibid.,* at p. 786.   [9] [1897] 1 Q.B. 17, C.A.

ruptcy. In the latter class of cases the bankrupt cannot create greater rights in favour of an assignee from him than he has himself; it rests with the trustee to say whether the business is to be carried on and the contract performed or not, and, if he elects to perform it, he has a right to the consideration for such performance when it becomes due."[10]

A debt which is due but not payable—*debitum in praesenti solvendum in futuro* as Channell, J. described it in *Marchant* v. *Morton Down and Co.*[11]— at the commencement of bankruptcy can be assigned before bankruptcy. In *Re Davis & Co., Ex parte Rawlings*,[12] monies due under a hire agreement were payable in instalments over a period of time. Instalments were assigned to A as security for an advance and notice of assignment was given to the debtor. The assignor later became bankrupt. It was held that A was entitled in priority to the trustee in bankruptcy. Fry, L.J. distinguished *Re Jones, Ex parte Nichols*,[13] above:

> "[It] has no bearing on the present for that which was assigned in the present case was a debt due at the time of the assignment though it was not payable until a future time. In Ex parte Nichols, nothing was due to the bankrupts at the date of the assignment, but they attempted to assign a debt which might become due to the trustee in their bankruptcy at a future time. They had nothing to assign."[14]

By analogy with the foregoing principles, it seems arguable that if after the commencement of bankruptcy and before the date of the receiving order, there is an assignment of debts by the bankrupt which are unearned at the date of the receiving order, and Section 45 of the Bankruptcy Act 1914 is applicable, the trustee will have priority to them over the assignee.

(iv) Reputed ownership doctrine

By section 38(c) of the Bankruptcy Act 1914 debts which are in the "reputed ownership" of the bankrupt, at the commencement of bankruptcy, are regarded as belonging to the trustee in bankruptcy even though they have been assigned. Section 38(c) says that the property of the bankrupt divisible among his creditors includes:

> "all goods being, at the commencement of the bankruptcy, in the possession, order or disposition of the bankrupt. in his trade or business, by the consent and permission of the true owner, under such circumstances that he is the reputed owner thereof; provided that things in

---

[10] *Ibid.*, at p. 22.   [11] [1901] 2 K.B. 829.
[12] (1888), 22 Q.B.D. 193, C.A.   [13] See p. 147, n. 7, *ante*.
[14] (1888), 22 Q.B.D. 193, at p. 199, C.A.

action other than debts due or growing due to the bankrupt in the course of his trade or business shall not be deemed goods within the meaning of this section."

The supposed object of the reputed ownership provision is to prevent a man from obtaining credit on the strength of possession of property which gives the impression of ownership but which he in fact does not own. As regards trade debts, the concept is rather strained because it is not obvious what constitutes "possession" of such intangible property. Nevertheless, it is settled that if notice of the assignment of debts has been given to the debtor at the commencement of bankruptcy, the debts are not in the reputed ownership of the bankrupt and the assignee therefore has priority over the trustee in bankruptcy.[15] Where bankruptcy intervenes between the despatch and delivery of the notice of assignment, the debts are not considered to be in the reputed ownership of the bankrupt and the assignment is effective.[16] The section does not stipulate how trade debts are taken out of the order and disposition of the bankrupt and it may well be that other acts will suffice; for example, by marking the client's books of account and other records in such a way as to indicate that the trade debts have been assigned. The reputed ownership doctrine does not appear to be much favoured by the courts judging by the very liberal attitude which has been adopted towards notice sufficient to avoid the rule,[17] and a sympathetic attitude towards the sufficiency of acts other than notice is probable.[18]

(v)   Fraudulent preferences

By section 44 of the Bankruptcy Act 1914, payment or transfer of property by any person unable to pay his debts as they become due from his own money in favour of any "creditor" with a view of giving such creditor a preference over other creditors is deemed fraduluent and void if the person is adjudged bankrupt on a petition presented within three months after the date of the payment or transfer or a receiving order is made within that period. It is submitted that the section is inapplicable to a factor as a purchaser of debts because such a purchaser owes money to the assignor, and not vice versa, and therefore is not a creditor. However, a loan to a client from a factor repaid by the subsequent assignment of debts would be subject to the section.

---

[15] *Day* v. *Day* (1857), 1 De G. & J. 144; 44 E.R. 678; *Edwards* v. *Martin* (1865), L.R. 1 Eq. 121; *Re Tillett, Ex parte Kingscote* (1889), 60 L.T. 575.
[16] *Belcher* v. *Bellamy* (1848), 2 Exch. 303.   [17] Pp. 131–132 *ante.*
[18] See *Rutter* v. *Everett*, [1895] 2 Ch. 872, at p. 881.

(vi)   General assignments

By section 43 of the Bankruptcy Act 1914, an assignment of existing
or future book debts (or any class thereof), which are unpaid at the
commencement of bankruptcy, by a person engaged in any trade or
business who is subsequently adjudicated bankrupt is void as against
the trustee in bankruptcy unless the assignment has been registered
under the Bills of Sale Act, 1878 as if it were a bill of sale given otherwise than by security for the payment of a sum of money. The section
expressly states that it is inapplicable, inter alia, to the assignment of
existing specified debts or debts growing due under specified contracts. It has been noted earlier[18] that typical factoring agreements are
of two types. One is an "agreement to agree" which contemplates
subsequent agreements for the sale of existing specified debts as they
arise in the future. This type of agreement is not covered by Section 43.
The other type of factoring agreement is an agreement for the sale of
all future debts and contemplates the legal assignment of those debts
as they arise. This type of agreement is registrable under section 43.

B   WINDING-UP

(i)   Assignments before the commencement of winding-up

As with bankruptcies, the basic rule is that an assignment, made
before the commencement of winding-up, which is valid as against the
client, is also valid as against the liquidator. The winding-up of a
company by the court is deemed to commence at the time of the
presentation of a petition for winding-up.[19] A voluntary winding-up
commences at the time of the passing of a resolution to that effect.[20]

(ii)   Assignments after the commencement of winding-up

The assignment by a company of its book debts after the commencement of a winding-up is void unless, in the case of a compulsory
winding-up only, the court otherwise orders.[1] Thus, in the case of a
compulsory winding-up, it is not necessarily unsafe to deal normally
with a company after the commencement of winding-up because the
courts have decided that it is highly likely they will exercise their
discretion under section 227 of the Companies Act 1948 to give the
same legal protection to dealings with companies after the date of the
winding-up petition, but before the date of the winding-up order, as is

---

[19] P. 91, *ante.*   [20] Companies Act 1948, s. 229.   [21] Companies Act 1948, s. 280.
[1] 227, Companies Act 1948, s: "In a winding up by the Court, any disposition of the
    property of the company, including things in action, and any transfer of shares, or
    alteration in the status of the members of the company, made after the commencement
    of the winding up, shall, unless the Court otherwise orders, be void." See also s. 313.

given by section 45 of the Bankruptcy Act 1914 to dealings with bankrupts after the commencement of bankruptcy but before the date of the receiving order. *In Re Répertoire Opera Co.*[2] Vaughan Williams, L.J. said of section 153 of the Companies Act 1862, which has been replaced by section 227 of the Companies Act 1948, that:

> "I have an absolute discretion to validate this transaction or not. If the transaction is one which would be valid under the protective sections of the Bankruptcy Act, that would be a very strong reason for my validating it here. That is what Lord Cairns means in *Ex parte Pearson, In Re Wiltshire Iron Co.* (1868), 3 Ch. 443, 446–7. The cases on section 153 are an adoption by the Court of the principles of the protective sections in bankruptcy. It would be very unfortunate if the principles of administration in bankruptcy and in the winding-up of companies were not as far as possible the same."[3]

Hence transactions, such as the sale of book debts to a factor, which occur after the date of the presentation of a petition but before the winding-up order is made are likely to be validated by the court provided they are bona fide, in the ordinary course of business, and executed by the date of the winding-up order. Lord Cairns, L.C. in *Re Wiltshire Iron Co., Ex parte Pearson,*[4] described the statutory provision and expressed the principle as follows:

> "This is a wholesome and necessary provision, to prevent, during the period which must elapse before a petition can be heard, the improper alienation and dissipation of the property of a company in extremis. But where a company actually trading, which it is in the interests of everyone to preserve, and ultimately to sell, as a going concern, is made the object of a winding-up petition, which may fail or may succeed, if it were to be supposed that transactions in the ordinary course of its current trade, bona fide entered into and completed, would be avoided and would not, in the discretion given to the Court, be maintained, the result would be that the presentation of a petition, groundless or well-founded, would, ipso facto, paralyze the trade of the company, and great injury, without any counter-balance of advantage, would be done to those interested in the assets of the company."[5]

It may be that a broader protection is now given to factors by section 9(4) of the European Communities Act 1972, which states that a company cannot rely against other persons on the making of a winding-up order (or the appointment of a liquidator in a voluntary

[2] (1895), 2 Mans. 314.
[3] *Ibid.,* at p. 316. See also *Re T. W. Constructions, Ltd.,* [1954] 1 All E.R. 744, at p. 746.
[4] (1868), 3 Ch. App. 443.
[5] *Ibid.,* at p. 446. Cf. *Re Park Ward & Co., Ltd.,* [1926] 2 Ch. 828, at p. 831.

winding-up) unless (*a*) official notification has been given of the event and the company can prove that the person heard of the event; or (*b*) fifteen days have elapsed after the date of the official notification (if the last day is a business day it is not counted) unless the third party can prove that he was unavoidably prevented from knowing of the event at that time. "Official notification" means notification in the London or Edinburgh Gazette: section 9(3). This section may have the effect of absolutely protecting assignments before the date of official notification of a winding-up order and therefore may constitute alternative and better protection to a factor than that given by section 227 of the Companies Act 1948.

(*iii*) *Unearned debts*

Again, following the same principle as applies in bankruptcy, an assignment before the commencement of winding-up of a debt which is not earned until after the commencement of winding-up as, for instance, under an executory contract, is void against the liquidator, and the discretion of the court under section 227 of the Companies Act 1948 will not be exercised in favour of the assignee.[6]

(*iv*) *Reputed ownership doctrine*

The reputed ownership doctrine does not apply to the winding-up of companies.[7]

(*v*) *Fraudulent preferences*

The fraudulent preference provision of the Bankruptcy Act 1914 (section 44) is applied to companies by section 320 of the Companies Act 1948. As stated above, it is considered that the fraudulent preference provision is inapplicable to factors as purchasers of debts.

(*vi*) *Floating charges*

A floating charge on debts created within twelve months of winding-up is invalid unless it is proved that the company was solvent immediately after the creation of the charge except to the amount of any cash paid to the company at the time of or subsequent to its creation and in consideration for it together with interest at 5 per cent or as prescribed by the Treasury.[8] The distinction between an assignment and a charge has been explained in Chapter Five, and the section therefore has no direct application to factoring.

---

[6] Re *Wiltshire Iron Co.*, *Ex parte Pearson* (1868), 3 Ch. App. 443; Re *T. W. Construction, Ltd.*, [1954] 1 All E.R. 744.
[7] In Re *Crumlin Viaduct Works Co.* (1879), 11 Ch.D. 755; *Gorringe* v. *Irwell India Rubber and Gutta Percha Works* (1886), 34 Ch.D. 128, C.A.
[8] Companies Act 1948, s. 322.

CHAPTER EIGHT

Recent and Proposed Law Reform

The report of the Crowther Committee[1] contained three major law reform recommendations of significance to factoring: repeal of the Moneylenders Acts 1900-1927; a Consumer Credit Act; and a Lending and Security Act to control some aspects of lending and, more importantly, to revolutionise the law governing security interests in personal property. The first two of these recommendations were implemented in 1974. In this chapter, each of the measures is considered.

1 Repeal of the Moneylenders Acts 1900-1927

The projected repeal of the much criticised[2] Moneylenders Acts 1900-1927 was welcomed by the factoring industry.[3] No single body of law has exercised such a negative influence on factoring. In the first place, there was the ever present fear of drastic consequences, as contained in the provisions of the Acts, if they were held to apply to factoring. Furthermore, ever since the introduction of factoring to England, factors' legal concepts and methods of operation have been carefully moulded so as to reflect factoring as the purchase of assets (i.e. book debts) and to avoid any suggestion that factoring was really lending against the security of book debts and therefore within the scope of the Acts. This often resulted in the employment of some strained concepts in documentation and the use of cumbersome accounting and operational methods, particularly in recourse factoring.

The recourse element is difficult to conceptualise as the purchase of an asset and it is even more difficult to carry out operations on a daily basis so as to faithfully and invariably reflect the concept. However, a further deterrent to changing recourse factoring conceptually to secured lending coupled with services is section 95 of the Companies Act 1948 which would require registration of the agreement, although if the proposed Lending and Security Act becomes law it will be

---

[1] Report of the Committee on Consumer Credit, March 1971, Cmnd. 4596.
[2] For example, see *United Dominions Trust, Ltd.* v. *Kirkwood,* [1966] 2 Q.B. 431; [1966] 1 All E.R. 968, *per* Diplock, L.J.
[3] See the Consumer Credit Act 1974, Sections 192 (3) (b) and (4) and Schedule 5. The repeal remains to be brought into force by statutory instrument.

impossible to avoid public notice filing. Thus, at that time if not sooner, recourse factors may well change the basis of their agreements, or at least their practice, from outright sales to mortgages of book debts. Old-line (i.e. non-recourse) factors are unlikely to make any change in their agreements or practice since their activities are appropriately reflected as outright sales of book debts.

Old habits die hard and the influence of the Acts on factoring documentation and methods is unlikely to disappear overnight. Consequently, it will continue to aid understanding of the concepts and methods of factoring, and will provide a basis for an historical comparison with present and future legislation and legislative proposals, if we briefly examine the moot point of the application of the Acts to factoring and the main provisions of the Acts.

A APPLICATION OF THE ACTS TO CREDIT FACTORING

The original purpose of the Moneylenders Acts 1900–1927 was the protection of private borrowers. Unfortunately, in their terms the Acts are equally as applicable to the business of commercial lending as to the business of consumer lending. They apply regardless of the size of loan.

The Acts contain no definition of a loan. Factors rely on a decision that the purchase of debts at a lump sum discount is not moneylending even where the arrangement is with recourse to the assignor and there is no notification of assignment to the debtor.[4] However, there is uneasiness among factors because that decision was only at first instance, and although it had been approved obiter by the Judicial Committee of the Privy Council,[5] some doubt had been raised as to its strength.[6] Moreover, it is not certain that factors' discount calculated on a day to day basis (as opposed to a lump sum discount calculated in advance), which is the practice of some factors, is a true discount or whether it is in the nature of interest, which postulates the making of a loan.[7]

Furthermore, although the principle upon which a court proceeds in determining the nature of a moneylending agreement is to look at its form and not its object, if evidence is adduced that the transaction as recorded in the agreement is not a true record of the transaction

[4] *Olds Discount Co., Ltd.* v. *John Playfair, Ltd.,* [1938] 3 All E.R. 275, *per* Branson, J.
[5] *Chow Yoong Hong* v. *Choong Fah Rubber Manufactory,* [1962] A.C. 209; [1961] 3 All E.R. 1163. There is also authority that the purchase of bills of exchange at a discount is not moneylending which, by analogy between book debts and bills, is probably also authority: see *Inland Revenue Commissioners* v. *Rowntree,* [1948] 1 All E.R. 482; *Chow Yoong Hong* v. *Choong Fah Rubber Manufactory, supra.*
[6] Cf. *Premier Trading Co., Ltd.* v. *Hillcott* (unreported, 13 February 1969, Newport Mon. County Court), holding that check trading is moneylending.
[7] This doubt was based on the distinction drawn between discount and interest in *Chow Yoong Hong* v. *Choong Fah Rubber Manufactory, supra,* at pp. 217, 1167.

the court will look behind the agreement to matters such as the method of accounting, the description of the transaction in correspondence between the parties, and the methods of operation to determine whether the agreement is a sham and masks the true nature of the transaction.[8] Thus, factors constantly have to be at pains to ensure that not only their agreements but all aspects of their operations faithfully reflect their transactions as true purchases of debts.

Some factors choose to rely on judicial authority and their own sense as to the nature of their activities. Others have obtained exemption orders from the Acts from the Department of Trade and Industry, which, however, are revocable at any time.

B   THE MAIN PROVISIONS OF THE ACTS

A breach of a statutory provision would render a contract void or unenforceable or give rise to criminal sanctions. Where a person carries on the business of moneylending or advertises or holds himself out in any way as carrying on the business of moneylending, he is (unless he falls within certain exempt categories) required to hold an excise licence and to conform to the Acts' various requirements.

Circulars or other documents stating or implying that the money-lender carries on banking business are prohibited; there are severe restrictions on advertising; the employment of agents and canvassers for the purpose of inviting persons to borrow money or enter into transactions involving the borrowing of money is illegal; and no costs, charges or expenses incurred by the moneylender can be charged that are not covered by interest.

A loan and interest are irrecoverable and any security is unenforceable if the loan agreement is not signed personally by the borrower before the loan is made and a copy of the note or memorandum (which has to contain prescribed details) is not delivered to the borrower within seven days of the making of the contract. The borrower is entitled to obtain copies of the contract documents and information showing the state of the account upon payment of one shilling; and it is illegal to charge compound interest or default interest exceeding the contract rate.

The court has wide powers to reopen any transaction in which the interest is excessive or which is harsh or unconscionable or which is otherwise such that a court of equity would grant relief. Interest in excess of 48 per cent per annum is presumed harsh and unconscionable unless the contrary is proved. There is a special limitation period of twelve months for actions by moneylenders.

[8] *Re George Inglefield, Ltd.*, [1933] 1 Ch. 1, at 17; *Chow Yoong Hong* v. *Choong Fah Rubber Manufactory, supra,* at p. 1167.

2   The Consumer Credit Act 1974

The Consumer Credit Act 1974 establishes "for the protection of consumers a new system, administered by the Director General of Fair Trading, of licensing and other control of traders concerned with the provision of credit, or the supply of goods on hire or hire purchase, and their transactions, in place of the present enactments regulating moneylenders, pawnbrokers, and hire purchase traders and their transactions; and for related matters".[9]

A   THE APPLICATION OF THE ACT TO CREDIT FACTORING

Whether the Act applies to factoring is not quite certain; if it does apply it would only be in unusual circumstances; and it is likely that most if not all factors will, with little if any impact on their business, avoid the Act.

The Act defines a "personal credit agreement" as an agreement between an individual ("the debtor") and any person ("the creditor") by which the creditor provides the debtor with credit of any amount.[10] A "consumer credit agreement" is a personal credit agreement by which the creditor provides the debtor with credit not exceeding £5,000.[11] A consumer credit agreement is a "regulated agreement" within the meaning of the Act if it is not an exempt agreement.[12] "Credit" includes "a cash loan and any other form of financial accommodation".

There is authority that the consideration paid for debts purchased at a discount, as in factoring, is not a loan.[13] The question remains whether it is "financial accommodation". Unfortunately, the expression is not defined. However, it would seem that the expression is intended to embrace financing arrangements other than loans and if a discounting arrangement is not covered it is difficult to say what would be. The test of what is "financial accommodation", if commercial reality is any guide, should be the purpose of the arrangement. On this basis advance factoring would involve financial accommodation but not maturity factoring since financing is neither the purpose nor the consequence of maturity factoring.

Assuming that "financial accommodation" does include factoring, or at least advance factoring, the application of the Act to factoring would, in practice, be very limited for two reasons. First, as will be noted from the definitions in section 8, the "debtor" under either a personal or a consumer credit agreement must be an individual, which includes a partnership but not a corporation.[14] In practice, it is rare for factoring

---

[9] Preamble to the Act.   [10] S. 8 (1).
[11] S. 8(2). Note s. 10(3), making special rules as to running-account credit.
[12] S. 8(3). Agreements exempt from the Act are specified in or under s. 16.
[13] See p. 154, *ante*.   [14] S. 189(1).

clients to be other than corporations. Secondly, consumer credit agreements (i.e. regulated agreements), with which the Act is mainly concerned, are at present limited to those where the "credit" does not exceed £5,000. In advance factoring this would mean that a factoring client would probably have to have a turnover of less than £40,000 per annum, and it is rare for factoring clients to be so small: indeed, the practice of most factors is to require the minimum turnover to be very much higher.

The Act also regulates "ancillary credit business" which is defined as "any business so far as it comprises or relates to", inter alia, "debt-collecting".[15] Debt-collecting is defined as "the taking of steps to procure payment of debts due under consumer credit agreements".[16] It would seem that if a factoring client sells to individual customers on credit terms not exceeding £5,000 that the client–customer agreements are consumer credit agreements. If such debts are purchased by a factor, the factor would then be carrying on the ancillary credit business of debt-collecting, unless, perhaps, the purchase of such debts were isolated transactions and there was insufficient system, continuity and repetition as to constitute their purchase a "business".[17]

The application of the Act to factoring may be summarised as follows. The purpose of the Act is to control consumer credit trans-actions and other matters affecting consumers. "Credit" includes "financial accommodation". Maturity factoring does not seem to involve the provision of financial accommodation. It is likely that advance factoring involves the provision of financial accommodation so as to make advance factoring agreements capable of being either personal or consumer credit agreements but the point will not be free from all doubt until clarified judicially. Assuming that advance factoring does involve the provision of financial accommodation, the practice of most factors is such that their activities rarely, if ever, involve entering into personal or consumer credit agreements or the ancillary credit business of debt-collecting, as defined in the Act.

In future, if factors wish to avoid the Act they would be well advised to convert their general practice into a formal policy of:

(i) only factoring corporate clients;
(ii) only entering into advance factoring agreements if the financial accommodation is at least £5,000;
(iii) only factoring debts due from corporate customers.

---

[15] S. 145(1)(d).   [16] S. 145(7). The definition is subject to s. 146(6).
[17] See *Edgelow* v. *MacElwee*, [1918] 1 K.B. 205, at p. 206; *Chow Yoong Hong* v. *Choong Fah Rubber Manufactory*, [1962] A.C. 209; [1961] 3 All E.R. 1163; *Kirkwood* v. *Gadd*, [1910] A.C. 422, at pp. 423, 431; cf. *North Central Wagon Finance Co. Frodoor, Ltd.* v. *Brailsford*, [1962] 1 All E.R. 502, approved in *Wright (Constructions), Ltd.* v. *Frodoor, Ltd.* [1967] 1 All E.R. 433, at p. 450.

B THE MAIN PROVISIONS OF THE ACT

In the credit area the Act is mainly concerned with consumer credit business but it also exercises some control over personal credit business and ancillary credit business.

A licence is required to carry on a consumer credit business.[18] There are two types of licence: "standard" and "group". The former is issued to one person except in the case of a partnership, whereas the latter is issued to more than one person but only if the public interest is better served by doing so.[19] An applicant for a standard licence must satisfy the Director that he is a fit person to engage in activities covered by the licence and that the name or names under which he applies to be licensed is not misleading or otherwise undesirable.[20] Regulations may be made as to the conduct by a licensee of his business.[1] The Director has prescribed powers to vary, suspend or revoke licences.[2] A person who engages in an activity for which a licence is required when he does not have the required licence commits an offence.[3] A regulated agreement made when the creditor was unlicensed is enforceable only if the Director makes an order under Section 40. The licensing provisions of the Act (except Section 40) apply to an ancillary credit business.[4]

An improperly executed regulated agreement is enforceable against the debtor on an order of the Court only.[5] Regulations "shall" be made as to the form and contents of documents embodying regulated agreements[6] and "may" require specified information to be disclosed in the prescribed manner to the debtor before a regulated agreement is made.[7] A regulated agreement is not properly executed unless it complies with such regulations and with other conditions set out in sections 61 to 64. In certain circumstances, a regulated agreement may be cancelled by the debtor within a defined cooling-off period.[8]

There is a duty on the creditor to give information as to the state of the account and other matters to the debtor at the debtor's written request and upon payment of the prescribed fee.[9]

If the Court finds a credit bargain extortionate it may re-open the credit agreement so as to do justice between the parties.[10] This provision applies to any personal credit agreement and not just to consumer credit agreements.[11]

Regulations "shall" be made as to the form and content of advertisements to which Part IV of the Act applies.[12] If an advertisement to which Part IV applies conveys information which in a material respect is false or misleading, the advertiser commits an offence.[13] Part IV

[18] S. 21(1).	[19] S. 22.	[20] S. 25(1).	[1] S. 26.
[2] S. 31 and 32.	[3] S. 39(1).	[4] S. 147.	[5] S. 65(1).
[6] S. 60(1).	[7] S. 55.	[8] S. 67 and 68.	[9] Ss. 77 and 78.
[10] S 137(1).	[11] S. 137(2).	[12] S. 45(4).	[13] S. 46.

applies to any advertisement published for the purpose of the business carried on by the advertiser indicating that he is willing, inter alia, to provide credit[14] unless the advertiser does not carry on a consumer credit business; the advertisement indicates that the credit must exceed £5,000 and that no security is required or the security consists of property other than land; or the credit is available only to a body corporate. The Secretary of State may order that the Part shall not apply to other advertisements.[15]

Some of the advertising provisions (sections 44, 46 and 47) apply to advertisements published for the purposes of a business carried on by the advertiser indicating that he is willing to advise on debtors,[16] unless the advertisement indicates that the advertiser is not willing to act in relation to consumer credit agreements.[17]

Regulations may require a person who carries on a consumer credit business to display prescribed information in the prescribed manner at any business premises where the business is carried on to which the public have access.[18] Regulations may be made as to the form and content of any document (a "quotation") by which a person who carries on a consumer credit business gives prospective customers information about the terms on which he is prepared to do business and requiring a person carrying on such a business to provide quotations to such person and in such circumstances as are prescribed.[19]

If "security" provided in relation to a regulated agreement is not in writing and if a security agreement is not properly executed, the security is enforceable only on the order of the Court.[20] Prescribed information has to be given to the surety at the surety's written request and upon payment of a prescribed fee.[1] There is also a duty on the creditor to give a debtor who requests it in writing and pays the prescribed fee a copy of the security instrument.[2] In both cases, if the creditor defaults the security becomes unenforceable, and if the default continues for one month, the creditor commits an offence.[3]

3 The Proposed Lending and Security Act

The Crowther Committee proposed the adoption of legislation closely modelled on, although not identical with, Article 9 of the American Uniform Commercial Code.[4] The Code was the outcome of many years of intensive research, drafting and analysis and has been adopted by all of the American States except Louisiana, although variations as between the States are common. It has also been success-

---

[14] S. 43(1).   [15] S. 43(5).   [16] S. 151(2).   [17] S. 151(4).
[18] S. 53.   [19] S. 52.   [20] S. 105.   [1] Ss. 107 and 108.
[2] S. 110.   [3] Ss. 109(3) and 110(3).
[4] See report of the Committee on Consumer Credit, Cmnd. 1971 No. 4596, Part Five, pp. 182–230, and Appendix III, pp. 574–580.

fully transplanted into Canada in the form of the Ontario Personal Property Act. In the Crowther Committee's words, "it gave the common law world, for the first time, a comprehensive and rational legal structure for the regulation of security interests in person property".[5]

The proposed legislation would contain relatively few provisions affecting lending but would extensively regulate all personal property security for loans or, to adopt the language of Article 9, security interests in personal property.

A   THE APPLICATION OF THE ACT TO CREDIT FACTORING

The fundamental concept is that transactions should be regulated according to their function and not their form. The law should not be concerned, as at present, with the nature of documents under which the security interest arises but with the nature and intended use of the security itself.

It is consistent with this principle of disregarding the form of transaction in favour of its function that the proposed legislation, although essentially concerned with regulating security interests, should also embrace the outright sale of receivables, following section 9–102(2) of Article 9. Section 9–104(f) excludes from the Article certain transfers of receivables which, by their nature have nothing to do with commercial financing transactions: namely, as part of a sale of the business out of which they arose; for the purpose of collection only; and where the assignee is also to do the performance under the contract.

The Crowther Committee stated, it is submitted rightly, that the distinction between the purchase of receivables and a loan on the security of receivables is particularly fine when the assignor gives recourse for his obligations. It is then barely distinguishable from a direct obligation to repay the sum to be received with interest. The Committee might well have added that the main purpose of receivables financiers and recourse factors constructing their agreements as a sale of receivables rather than as a charge or mortgage of receivables was to avoid the Moneylenders Acts 1900–1927, which will soon be repealed. Subsidiary reasons were avoidance of registration of a charge or mortgage under section 95 of the Companies Act 1948; and, arguably, the better prima facie effect on a client's balance sheet of a sale of receivables compared with a charge or mortgage.

Sales of receivables without recourse are more analogous to the sale of goods but the Committee thought they should still be brought within the proposed legislation for two reasons.[6] First, commercial practice is to obtain warranties from the assignor designed to ensure that the receivables are not only enforceable but likely to be paid and

[5] *Ibid.*, p. 183.   [6] *Ibid.*, p. 576.

a breach of such a warranty entitles the assignee to recover his loss from the assignor. Consequently, the Committee concluded, the distinction between sales with recourse and sales without recourse is not as clear as it might be. It is submitted that the Committee, in its conclusion that the warranties also ensure that the receivables are "likely to be paid", has paid insufficient regard to the crucial feature of a non-recourse factoring agreement that if the customer fails to pay the assigned debt because of financial inability—and not because the debt is invalid or unenforceable (which is usually because the client is in breach of the client-customer contract)—the factor must bear the loss.

However, it is agreed that the Committee's second reason is sufficient to bring non-recourse sales of receivables within the proposed legislation viz., purchasers of receivables need the protection of the filing system since the rule in *Dearle* v. *Hall*[7] is unsuited to their requirements. It is also submitted that there is a further reason: whether a client's debts are being factored is relevant to the investment and credit decisions of the client's existing and prospective shareholders and creditors, but they have no reliable and ready way of knowing that the client is factoring its debts unless they are able to refer to a public registry for the information.

B   THE MAIN PROVISIONS OF THE ACT

Although sales of receivables should be brought within the legislation, the Committee conceded that the normal provisions governing secured transactions should be varied in one respect when applied to the sale of receivables. Since the sale is outright the client should not be entitled to any surplus or liable for any deficiency remaining after the collection of the security unless the agreement so provides.

A factor would be classified by the proposed legislation as a "secured party" which would be defined to include a purchaser of receivables; and a client would be classified as a "debtor" which would be defined to include the seller of receivables. This does not mean that it will be necessary for factors to alter their contracts, brochures or other documentation to adopt such legislative terminology. They would remain perfectly free to use whatever terminology they wished to use. However, there may be confusion if the proposed legislation's terminology was not noted, particularly the term "debtor", since this is an expression which factors often apply to their clients' customers, whereas in the legislation it would refer to the clients.

Two of the important concepts of Article 9 which the Committee proposed adopting were "attachment" and "perfection". Loosely defined, "attachment" means the creation of a security interest effective

---

[7] (1823), 3 Russ. 1; 38 E.R. 475 (Plumer, M.R.); affd. on appeal (1827), 3 Russ. at p. 48; 38 E.R. at p. 492 (Lord Lyndhurst, M.R.); and see pp. 123–127, *ante*.

against the client; and "perfection" means completion of the steps necessary to make the security interest effective against third parties such as subsequent purchasers and encumbrances and the client's liquidator, trustee in bankruptcy and general creditors.

Unless postponed by the security agreement, the security agreement would attach upon fulfilment of the following conditions:

> there is a security agreement.
> value is given.
> the client has rights in the security.
> there is a written memorandum signed by or on behalf of the client which reasonably identifies the security (or, in the case of security other than receivables, the secured party has by the agreement of the debtor taken possession of the security).

A security interest would be perfected by attachment coupled with the filing of a financing statement in a public registry (or in the case of security which is capable of being physically possessed, by possession of the security). The financing statement would be in a short standard form describing the security and containing other prescribed details. Filing would be effective for five years and would be renewable for successive periods of five years.

Filing of financing statement would have two functions: to enable a third party to know what security interest his debtor or prospective debtor had already granted in the debtor's assets; and to protect the secured party by making the filing of notice of his security interest equivalent to public notice so as to preserve the secured party's priority against third parties such as subsequent purchasers, encumbrancers and the debtor's (i.e. the factoring client's) liquidator or trustee in bankruptcy.

The three basic priority rules are contained in section 9–312(5) of Article 9 and apply unless displaced by a special priority rule. They are as follows:

> where both interests are perfected by filing, priority goes to the first to file irrespective of the date of attachment or perfection.
> where one or both of the conflicting interests are perfected otherwise than by filing, priority goes to the first to perfect.
> when neither interest is perfected, priority is determined by the order of attachment.

The Crowther Committee thought that rules (1) and (3) were eminently sensible, but as regards rule (2) they thought the following should be added to the end thereof: "but that where one interest is perfected by filing and the other is perfected otherwise than by filing the latter shall have priority only if perfected before the filing".

Perfection would confer qualified protection in priority situations although it should be effective against the clients' liquidator or trustee in bankruptcy and the general body of creditors. An unperfected security interest would in general be ineffective against third parties while a perfected security interest would bind third parties unless displaced by a special priority rule. The Committee envisaged that there would be a necessity for some special priority rules, displacing the basic rules, to cover special situations such as a conflict between a financier claiming a security interest in personal property as original security and another financier claiming a security interest in the same property as proceeds.

When Article 9 was being mooted in the U.S.A. before its adoption, there was some apprehension expressed by receivables financiers who, of course, operated on a non-notification basis, and also by some factors, that public filing would deter prospective clients from utilising their facilities since the fact that they were using the facilities would become public knowledge. However, experience subsequent to the adoption of Article 9 proved that their volume of business suffered no adverse effect. In any event, disclosure properly serves the interests of existing and prospective shareholders and creditors of clients in that it provides them with information which is relevant to their investment and credit decisions. Furthermore, such legislation is of considerable advantage to factors in terms of improvement in the security of their title to purchased debts as against third parties. Indeed the English factoring industry has indicated that it generally supports the Crowther Committee's proposals for a proposed Lending and Security Act.

Appendices

Non-recourse (Old Line) Factoring Agreement

AN AGREEMENT made the   day of   19   BETWEEN

of

(hereinafter called "the Supplier") of the one part and
FACTORS LIMITED whose registered office is at Plantation House Mincing Lane London E.C.3 (hereinafter called "the Factor") of the other part

WHEREBY IT IS AGREED as follows:—

1. TERM OF AGREEMENT. Subject as hereinafter provided this Agreement shall commence on the date and continue for the period specified in the second schedule hereto. At the expiration of the period of notice specified in the said schedule this Agreement shall cease and determine provided however that any rights or obligations arising out of transactions previously incepted shall not be affected and all terms and conditions and provisions hereof shall continue in full force and effect until such rights or obligations have been fully extinguished.

2. PURCHASE OF RECEIVABLES. The Supplier agrees to sell and the Factor agrees to purchase free from all liens and other encumbrances and upon and subject to the terms and conditions contained herein and to the terms and conditions (hereinafter called the "Standard Conditions") set out in the first schedule hereto and to the Special Conditions (if any) set out in the second schedule hereto all of the book debts, invoice debts, accounts, notes, bills, acceptances and/or other forms of obligation (hereinafter collectively referred to as "receivables") owned by or owing to the Supplier which are in existence at the date of the commencement of this Agreement or which come into existence during the term of this Agreement in respect of transactions entered into by the Supplier for the sale of goods to customers in the United Kingdom, and/or the provision of services for customers in the United Kingdom, in the ordinary course of the Supplier's business, not being customers who are a subsidiary, co-subsidiary, parent or associated company of the Supplier or under the same director or shareholder control as the Supplier.

3. "APPROVED" AND "UNAPPROVED" RECEIVABLES. A receivable which is an approved receivable as defined by Standard Condition 1(a) shall be purchased by the Factor without recourse to the Supplier subject to the provi-

sions of the Standard Conditions. A receivable which is an unapproved receivable as defined by Standard Condition 1(*b*) shall be purchased by the Factor on the basis that the Supplier shall be liable to the Factor for all sums remaining unpaid in respect thereof after they are due to be paid by the relevant customer or otherwise as provided in the Standard Conditions. The purchase of any receivable shall be complete and the rights to such receivable shall vest in the Factor upon the receivable coming into existence.

4. PURCHASE PRICE OF RECEIVABLES. The purchase price payable by the Factor to the Supplier for any receivables purchased pursuant to this Agreement shall be the gross amount payable by the customer for the relative goods and/or services (together with any tax payable thereon) as notified by the Supplier to the Factor in accordance with the Standard Conditions less:—

  (*a*) any discount, commission or other allowances due or allowable to the customer in accordance with the Supplier's normal terms of trade, being terms not more liberal than those set out in second schedule hereto;

  (*b*) a discounting charge calculated in the manner prescribed by Standard Condition 7(*c*);

  (*c*) an administration charge equal to such percentage of the said gross amount as is specified in the second schedule hereto.

5. PAYMENT OF PURCHASE PRICE. Payment of the purchase price for each receivable purchased as aforesaid shall be due and made at the time and in the manner specified in the Standard Conditions, subject to the debits and rights of retention and set-off therein provided.

6. ASSIGNMENT OF RECEIVABLES. The Supplier shall at any time at the request of the Factor and at the expense of the Supplier execute a legal assignment to the Factor of any receivables purchased by it pursuant to this Agreement and of any rights of the Supplier in relation to such receivables of the kind described in Condition 5 of the Standard Conditions and the Supplier hereby irrevocably appoints the Factor its attorney in the name and on behalf of the Supplier to execute any such assignment and to give notice thereof to the customer on behalf of and in the name of the Supplier.

7. COMPLIANCE WITH STANDARD CONDITIONS OF FACTORING. The Supplier hereby acknowledges that all the provisions, conditions, warranties and undertakings expressed in the Standard Conditions and in the Special Conditions (if any) shall be binding on it as if the same were repeated herein in extenso and undertakes to comply therewith at all times.

8. SUBSIDIARIES OF THE SUPPLIER. The Supplier shall at the request of the Factor cause any subsidiary of the Supplier (as defined in section 154 of the Companies Act 1948) to enter into an Agreement with the Factor in terms similar to those contained in this Agreement.

9. NON-ASSIGNABILITY OF AGREEMENT. This Agreement is not assignable by the Supplier without the express consent in writing of the Factor.

10. CHARGES ON RECEIVABLES. The Supplier shall not without the written consent of the Factor grant any fixed or floating charge over any receivables

of the Supplier and shall at the request of the Factor procure the exclusion of receivables from any charge in which any receivables would otherwise be oomprieed.

11. RESTRICTION ON OTHER AGREEMENTS. The Supplier shall not during the currency of this Agreement enter into any Factoring Agreement, or any other Agreement for the charging or discounting of receivables, with any person firm or company other than the Factor. Entry into any such Agreement by any parent, subsidiary or associated company of the Supplier shall be deemed to be a breach of this provision by the Supplier.

12. IMMEDIATE DETERMINATION BY FACTOR. Notwithstanding the provisions of Clause 1 hereof, should the Supplier at any time be in breach of this Agreement or fail to comply with or be in breach of any of the obligations set out in the Standard Conditions or in the Special Conditions (if any) or call any meeting of creditors or have a petition for winding-up presented against it or go into voluntary liquidation or have a receiver of any of its assets appointed or should the Supplier's assets or any part thereof be seized under any execution of legal process or under distress for rent then in any such event the Factor may determine this Agreement forthwith by written notice delivered or posted to the Supplier at the aforesaid address or at the Supplier's registered office or at any other address at which the Supplier carries on business. Such termination shall not affect the Factor's right of retention under Standard Condition 7(*b*) or the running of a discounting charge or allowance under Standard Condition 7(*c*). At any time after termination of the Agreement pursuant to this clause the Factor shall be entitled to reassign to the Supplier any receivables purchased by the Factor and remaining outstanding and upon such reassignment shall debit to the Supplier the amount of such receivables, together with such stamp duty as may be payable on the reassignment.

13. EXCLUSION OF OTHER TERMS. The terms set out in this Agreement represent the whole of the terms agreed between the Factor and the Supplier, to the exclusion of any prior or contemporaneous statements, representations, conditions and warranties on the part of the Factor, whether express or implied and whether oral or in writing.

IN WITNESS whereof the Supplier and the Factor have caused their respective Common Seals to be hereunto affixed the day and year first above written.

THE FIRST SCHEDULE

STANDARD CONDITIONS OF FACTORING

1. DEFINITIONS. Any expression used in these Conditions shall have the same meaning as in the Agreement, and in addition the following definitions shall apply:—

(*a*) A receivable shall rank as an "approved receivable" if
  (i) the Factor shall have notified the Supplier in writing that such receivable is approved in terms of Condition 2(*a*), hereof, or

(ii) the receivable is within any permitted limit established in terms of Condition 2(*b*) hereof or within any permited limit pursuant to Condition 6(*c*) hereof.

provided that a receivable shall not rank as an approved receivable if it is an unapproved receivable under paragraph (*b*) (ii) or (iii) of this Condition.

(*b*) A receivable shall rank as an unapproved receivable if

(i) it does not rank as an approved receivable in terms of paragraph (*a*) (i) or (ii) above or

(ii) it is deemed to be an unapproved receivable under Condition 2(*c*) or

(iii) in relation to the receivable there is any breach by the Supplier of any undertaking, condition or warranty contained in Condition 4.

(*c*) "Date of the insolvency" shall mean:

(i) where the Debtor is a registered company the date of commencement of winding-up of the company (not being a members' voluntary winding-up) or the making of an arrangement or composition (other than for the purposes of reconstruction, amalgamation or merger) with creditors or the appointment of a receiver, whichever is earliest.

(ii) where the Debtors is not a registered company the date of a Receiving Order or the making of any arrangement or composition with creditors whichever is the earlier.

(*d*) "Permitted limit" shall mean a limit established in terms of Condition 2(*b*) by the Factor in relation to any customer of the Supplier, within which the aggregate amount of receivables due from that customer from time to time shall be deemed to be approved.

(*e*) "Goods sold" shall include services provided, "goods agreed to be sold" shall include services agreed to be provided and "goods delivered" shall include services completed.

(*f*) Delivery shall be deemed to be effected when the goods are physically placed in transit to the customer.

2. APPROVALS AND PERMITTED LIMITS.

(*a*) The Supplier may at any time apply for the approval of a receivable which is to arise or which has arisen from any transaction with a customer, and the Factor will notify the Supplier in writing as to whether such receivable is approved.

(*b*) The Supplier may at any time apply for a permitted limit of receivables to be established in relation to a customer or prospective customer and the Factor will notify the Supplier of the amount of the permitted limit established. When making any application under this or the preceding sub-clause the Supplier shall inform the Factor of any fact or matter within the Supplier's knowledge which might influence the decision of the Factor in granting or refusing approval of the receivable or receivables to which the application relates.

(c) Before entering into any contract with a customer under which (i) any payment is to be made by the customer before the delivery of the whole of the goods or performance of the whole of the services to which the contract relates or (ii) delivery of the goods or performance of the services to which the contract relates is to be spread over a period exceeding 60 days. the Supplier shall notify the Factor in writing of the terms of such proposed contract and shall obtain the approval of the Factor thereto. Failing such notification and approval any receivable arising under the contract shall be deemed to be an unapproved receivable notwithstanding that it would otherwise rank as an approved receivable within Condition 1(a)

(d) The grant or refusal of approval as provided by sub-clauses (a) or (c) hereof and the establishment of permitted limits as provided by sub-clause (b) hereof shall be matters within the absolute discretion of the Factor.

3. WITHDRAWAL OF APPROVAL OR PERMITTED LIMITS. Any approval of a prospective receivable may be withdrawn, and any permitted limit established in relation to a customer may be cancelled or varied in its absolute discretion by the Factor who will notify the Supplier of such withdrawal, variation or cancellation, in which event such withdrawal, variation or cancellation shall take effect forthwith except in relation to receivables then in existence and arising from goods delivered before receipt of the said notification by the Supplier or the expiration of 48 hours after the despatch of such notification by the Factor whichever is the earlier.

4. CONDITIONS BINDING ON THE SUPPLIER. The purchase by the Factor of receivables pursuant to this Agreement shall be subject to the following undertakings by and conditions binding upon the Supplier:—

(a) All transactions entered into by the Supplier with its customers shall be governed by English Law and be subject to the terms of trade set out in the second schedule hereto or as the Factor may from time to time approve and to such other terms and conditions of sale or service as may from time to time be approved by the Factor.

(b) The Supplier shall in respect of every receivable (but only after delivery of the relative goods) fully and promptly complete and deliver to the Factor a notification form supplied for such purpose by the Factor and the Factor shall be subject to no obligation in respect of any receivable either under this Agreement or otherwise until a notification form duly completed in relation thereto shall have been received by it. Delivery of such notification form shall constitute a warranty by the Supplier that the said goods have been delivered and that no other person has an interest in the receivable or receivables to which the notification relates.

(c) All receivables sold to the Factor shall be existing and *bona fide* obligations of the Supplier's customers arising out of the sale of goods by the Supplier in the ordinary course of its business.

(d) The Supplier shall immediately after selling any receivable to the

Factor make an appropriate entry in its books of account recording such sale and shall (if so required by the Factor in relation to any receivable) provide evidence to the satisfaction of the Factor of the due delivery of goods.

(*e*) All invoices or other similar documents issued by the Supplier to its customers relating to a receivable purchased by the Factor shall bear a conspicuous notation, in such form as the Factor may from time to time direct, that the receivable has been assigned to the Factor.

(*f*) The Supplier shall promptly supply to the Factor copies of all credit notes issued to customers provided that the Factor shall at all times have an absolute discretion to require that its prior approval be obtained before the issue of any credit note to any customer.

(*g*) In respect of all receivables the Supplier hereby warrants to and undertakes with the Factor that the Supplier has performed all its obligations to its customers and that the customer in each instance will accept the goods sold and the invoice therefore without any dispute or claim whatsoever (whether justifiable or not) including disputes as to price, terms, quantity or quality, set-off or counterclaim or claims of release from liability or inability to pay because of any act of God or public enemy or war or because of the requirements of law or of rules, orders or regulations having the force of law. The Supplier further warrants, that no customer from whom any receivable is due or to become due is a subsidiary, co-subsidiary, parent or associated company of the Supplier or under the same director or shareholder control as the Supplier.

(*h*) The Supplier shall notify the Factor promptly of, and shall at its own cost and expense (including legal fees) settle, all such disputes and/or claims as are referred to in the foregoing paragraph (*g*) provided that if the Factor so elects it shall have the right at all times (and, when appropriate, on the Supplier's behalf) to settle compromise adjust or litigate any such dispute or claim direct with the Supplier's customer or other complainant upon such terms and conditions as the Factor may deem advisable and to apply the proceeds thereof to any indebtedness of the Supplier to the Factor arising pursuant to this Agreement; and anything done by the Factor in terms hereof shall be binding on the Supplier and the Factor shall have no liability whatsoever to the Supplier for any delay, act or omission in relation to any claims to which this Condition relates.

(*i*) In addition to and without prejudice to any other rights to which it shall be entitled the Factor may where there is a dispute between the Supplier and a customer (including any dispute of a kind referred to in paragraph (*g*) hereof), reassign the receivable to the Supplier and thereupon charge the Supplier with the amount of such receivable.

(*j*) The Supplier as trustee for the Factor shall hold as such trustee, and keep separate from the Supplier's other moneys, all remittances which may be received by it in payment of or on account of receivables sold to the Factor and will immediately deliver to the Factor the identical cheques, moneys or other forms of payment received (properly endorsed where required). The Factor shall have the right and is irrevocably authorised to endorse the name of the Supplier on any and all cheques or other form of remittance received where such endorsement is required whether to effect collection or to perfect the Factor's title as a holder in due course or for any other reason.

(*k*) The Factor shall have the right at all reasonable times to inspect verify and check all books, accounts, records, orders and original correspondence and such other papers of the Supplier as the Factor may desire The Supplier will furnish the Factor at the Factor's request with certified statements showing its financial condition and the results of its operations.

(*l*) The Supplier shall throughout the currency of this Agreement disclose to the Factor all facts and matters known to the Supplier which might in any way influence the decision of the Factor in the grant, refusal or withdrawal of approval of any receivable or prospective receivable or of any permitted limit.

5. ACQUISITION OF INTEREST IN GOODS BY FACTOR.

(*a*) On purchase by the Factor of any receivable then any title, property, right or interest of the Supplier in the goods to which such receivable relates (including all such goods that may be rejected or returned by the customers of the Supplier) all the Supplier's rights of lien, stoppage in transitu, demurrage and as unpaid vendor and all other rights of the Supplier under the contract or contracts pursuant to which the receivable comes into existence, shall be deemed to be assigned and transferred to the Factor whether or not the goods shall have been delivered by the Supplier at the time of the said purchase and whether or not the Supplier shall have delivered a notification form pursuant to Condition 4(*b*).

(*b*) Any goods recovered in pursuance of the exercise of any rights referred to in the foregoing paragraph (*a*) shall be treated as returned goods and all returned goods shall be promptly notified to the Factor and shall be set aside marked with the Factor's name and held for the Factor's account as owner. The Factor shall (in addition to and without prejudice to any other rights it may have) have the right to take possession of and to sell or cause to be sold without notice any returned goods at such prices, to such purchasers and upon such terms as it may deem advisable and in the event of any such sale the Supplier shall pay to the Factor on demand (and without asserting any right of set-off):—

    (i) the difference between the amount of the receivable relating to such goods and the amount received by the Factor on any such sale; and

    (ii) any costs and expenses (including legal fees) incurred by the Factor in relation to any such sale.

(*c*) On purchase by the Factor of any receivables then without prejudice to the generality of the provisions of sub-clause (*a*) hereof there shall vest in the Factor the benefit of all guarantees, indemnities, insurances and securities given to or held by the Supplier in respect of such receivables or of goods to which they relate.

6. PROVISIONS AND UNDERTAKINGS APPLICABLE TO UNAPPROVED RECEIVABLES. The following provisions and undertakings shall apply to unapproved receivables:—

(*a*) The Supplier hereby (in addition to and without prejudice to any other rights the Factor may have) unconditionally guarantees the due and punctual payment by the customer to the Factor of all unapproved receivables purchased by the Factor and shall pay to the Factor on demand (and without asserting any right of set-off) the full amount of any unapproved receivable if the customer shall fail for any reason to pay the same on the due date for payment or shall at any time before such due date dispute its liability for payment thereof or make any claim of whatsoever nature in respect of such receivable or the underlying transaction or assert any right of set-off or counterclaim whether against the Supplier or the Factor.

(*b*) In any case where approved and unapproved receivables owing by the same customer shall have been purchased by the Factor and are for the time being outstanding the Factor shall be at liberty (notwithstanding any contrary appropriation by the customer or the Supplier) to appropriate any payment made by such customer or any credit or allowance granted to the customer by the Supplier in or towards satisfaction of any approved receivable so purchased in priority to any unapproved receivable; save that where the customer becomes insolvent the Factor will credit the Supplier with the full amount of any dividend received by the Factor in the bankruptcy or winding-up which is attributable to the unapproved receivable.

(*c*) To the extent that any approved receivable which is within the permitted limit of any customer shall be paid in whole or in part by that customer before withdrawal of the approval or cancellation of the permitted limit pursuant to Condition 3, an unapproved receivable which would, but for the permitted limit, have been an approved receivable, shall, insofar as it remains unpaid and is not overdue, fall within the permitted limit of that customer and be then deemed to be approved. Where there are two or more such unapproved receivables they shall fall within the permitted limit in the order in which they respectively become due for payment and shall in such order be deemed to be approved.

7. RECEIVABLES CREDITED IN FACTOR'S BOOKS; PREPAYMENTS TO THE SUPPLIER; BASE RATE AND DISCOUNTING RATE CHANGE.

(*a*) The Factor shall maintain in its accounts an appropriate record (hereinafter referred to as "the Current Account") to which shall be
    (i) credited
        (A) the purchase price (as defined in Clause 4 of this Agreement but before deducting the discounting charge referred to in that clause and after deducting the administration charge payable

thereunder) of any receivable purchased by the Factor from the Supplier, such purchase price to be credited as soon as a notification form relating thereto has been received from the Supplier pursuant to Condition 4(*b*);

(B) any proceeds received and applied by the Factor under Condition 4(*b*) hereof; and

(C) at the end of each calendar month any discounting allowance that may be payable to the Supplier under Condition 7(*c*) (iii) hereof.

(ii) debited

(A) the amount of any payment made under this Agreement to or on behalf of the Supplier;

(B) the amount of any credit note issued by the Supplier (except in so far as the provisions of Condition 5(*b*) apply);

(C) the amount of any receivable reassigned in terms of Clause 12 or Condition 4(*i*);

(D) the amount of any charge in terms of Condition 5(*b*);

(E) all such other amounts as are chargeable to the Supplier hereunder including any sum payable under Condition 6; and

(F) at the end of each calendar month a discounting charge calculated as hereunder set out.

(*b*) Subject to the provisions hereof at the request of the Supplier the Factor shall remit (and at any time in the Factor's sole discretion it may remit) to the Supplier or to its order any part of the balance for the time being standing to the credit of the Supplier in the Current Account up to the full amount thereof less any amount which the Factor shall in its absolute discretion decide to retain as security for any claims or defences which have arisen or may arise against the Supplier or in the case of any unapproved receivable for any risk of non-payment by the customer. Any balance for the time being standing to the debit of the Supplier in the Current Account shall be payable by the Supplier to the Factor on demand.

(*c*) In addition to the Current Account the Factor will maintain a Discounting Account relating to the Supplier which will be:

(i) credited with every amount to which Condition 7(*d*) hereunder applies and every payment made:

(A) by a customer directly to the Factor in respect of receivables purchased, including any proceeds received and applied by the Factor under Condition 4(*b*);

(B) by the Supplier to the Factor in terms of Conditions 4(*j*), 5(*b*) or 6(*a*);

(C) by any other person to the Factor on any sale in terms of Condition 5(*b*) hereof

all on the fourth day following the date on which the relative cheque or other form of remittance is received by the Factor, and

(ii) debited with

(A) every payment made by the Factor hereunder and every item chargeable to the Supplier on the date on which the relative payment or charge is made,

(B) the amount of any cheque or other instrument credited under paragraph (*c*) (i) of this Condition where such cheque or instrument is dishonoured, the debit being made as at the same time as the cheque or instrument was originally credited,

and the Supplier shall be liable to pay a discounting charge on a day basis on the net daily balance shown on the Discounting Account to be due to the Factor, which charge shall be calculated at the rate specified in the Second Schedule hereto. On any net daily balance shown on the Discounting Account to be due to the Supplier there shall be credited to the Supplier on a day basis a discounting allowance calculated at the rate specified in the Second Schedule.

(*d*) Should any customer of the Supplier become insolvent then the Factor shall credit the Discounting Account with the amount of all approved receivables due from such customer at the date of the insolvency as defined by Condition 1(*c*).

(*e*) Any change in the discounting charge and/or the discounting allowance due to a change in the Base Rate specified in the Second Schedule shall become effective on the first day following such change.

(*f*) Should the general level of interest rates charged by Members of the London Clearing Banks on normal commercial and industrial accounts alter without a corresponding change in the said Base Rate the Factor shall have the right by notice in writing to the Supplier to make a corresponding alteration to the discounting charge mentioned in the Second Schedule hereto to be effective as from the day following the date of posting of such notice.

8. MONTHLY STATEMENT. The Factor will render to the Supplier after the end of each month a statement recording all financial transactions between the Factor and the Supplier during that month in accordance with the terms hereof. Any such statement shall be deemed to be correct and binding upon the Supplier unless the Factor is notified of any error therein within 30 days of the date when the same is rendered.

9. SUPPLIER'S DISCOUNTS, COMMISSIONS OR ALLOWANCES. The Factor shall not be liable to the Supplier for the amount of any discount, commission or allowance wrongfully claimed or deducted by the customer in respect of any receivable unless and until such amount has been received by the Factor.

10. RIGHT OF ENFORCING PAYMENT OF RECEIVABLES. The Factor and its agents or assigns shall have the sole right of collecting and enforcing payment of receivables (other than those reassigned under Clause 12 or Condition 4(*i*) in whatever manner it or they may in their absolute discretion decide, whether or not the Supplier has been debited with the amount of the receivables pursuant to Condition 7, and the Supplier shall upon request co-operate to procure such collection and enforcement and shall for such purpose allow the Factor and/or its assigns to institute and carry on legal

proceedings in the name of the Supplier. All legal costs incurred in collecting and enforcing payment of any unapproved receivables, whether these are the Factor's own costs or those incurred by the Factor to any other person, shall be paid to the Factor by the Supplier.

11. TAX. In the event of a customer failing to pay or satisfy the amount of any receivable arising from the sale of goods and such receivable including any tax then the Supplier undertakes:—

(*a*) that it will use its best endeavours to obtain from the Commissioners of Customs and Excise a remission or refund of any such tax, and

(*b*) that on such tax being remitted or refunded it will account therefor to the Factor.

12. SET-OFF. The Factor shall be entitled to debit the current and discounting accounts of the Supplier with and/or set off against any moneys payable to the Supplier any amount due from the Supplier to the Factor howsoever arising, whether for debt or for damages, whether liquidated or unliquidated and whether payable presently or contingently.

13. REFUND OF AGENT'S COMMISSION. In the event of a customer failing to pay or satisfy the amount of any approved receivable the Supplier shall remit to the Factor, or the Factor shall at its option be entitled to debit to the Supplier, an amount equivalent to any expenses relative to that receivable saved by the Supplier by the non-payment of Agent's commission or otherwise.

14. WAIVERS TO BE IN WRITING. Any delay or failure on the part of the Factor to exercise any right privilege or option herein contained shall in no wise operate as a waiver of such or any other right privilege or option and no waiver shall be valid unless it be in writing signed on behalf of the Factor and then only to the extent therein set forth.

THE SECOND SCHEDULE

1. DATE OF COMMENCEMENT OF AGREEMENT (Clause 1):

2. PERIOD OF AGREEMENT (Clause 1):   months/years (minimum period) and thereafter until determined by not less than months prior written notice to expire not earlier than months after the end of the minimum period.

3. SUPPLIER'S TERMS OF TRADE (Clause 4(*a*) and Standard Condition 4(*a*)):

4. ADMINISTRATION CHARGE (Clause 4(c)):

5. DISCOUNTING CHARGE (Standard Condition 7(*c*)):

6. DISCOUNTING ALLOWANCE (Standard Condition 7(*c*)):

7. BASE RATE (Standard Conditions 7(*e*) and (*f*):

8. SPECIAL CONDITIONS:

THE COMMON SEAL OF

was hereunto affixed in the presence of:—⌡

Director.

Director/Secretary.

The COMMON SEAL of
FACTORS LIMITED was hereunto affixed
in the presence of:—

Director.

Director/Secretary.

Non-recourse (Old-Line) Factoring Agreement

ABC FACTORS LTD.

1 Prudence Lane,
London EC3 1ZZ.

The Directors
(client's name and address)

Dear Sirs,
We herein confirm the terms and conditions upon which we are willing to provide you with a factoring facility. If you are in agreement with these terms and conditions will you please execute under your seal the acknowledgement at the foot of this letter and the enclosed copy and return both to us.
Definitions of expressions appearing in this letter are contained in the Appendix.

1. Offers

(a) You agree to offer to sell to us upon the terms and conditions of this agreement all debts from time to time owing to you by your customer, and to complete and deliver to us at least once during each week (or during such other period as we may from time to time together agree) an offer in such form as we may from time to time require.

(b) Every offer will:
    (i) offer to sell to us every debt not previously offered to us;
    (ii) be accompanied by the original and one copy of each invoice relating to each debt the subject of the offer, together with such evidence as we may require of the delivery of the goods, the carrying out of the work or the performance of the services in respect of which each debt has been incurred;
    (iii) be on the terms and conditions of this agreement;

2. Acceptances

(a) Acceptance of any debt offered to us will be constituted either by our despatching a payment on account of the Purchase Price to you or to your authorised representative or by our not despatching to you a notice of non purchase in relation to the debt within four working days from the first working day after our receipt of your offer, which ever occurs first.

(b) Upon our acceptance of any offer all your interest in the purchased

continued/ . . .

179

debts and all remedies for enforcing the same including without limitation of the foregoing any right of lien, stoppage in transitu or other rights arising in your favour as unpaid seller in relation TO ANY GOODS in respect of which the purchased debts have been contracted shall vest in us.

3. Approved and Unapproved Debts

(*a*) WE WILL HAVE NO RIGHT OF RECOURSE TO YOU in respect of an approved debt or part of a debt if failure of the customer to pay is due to its financial inability, but we will have a right of recourse to you in respect of an unapproved debt or part of a debt if for any reason it is unpaid by its due date of payment or if there is a breach of any other warranty or covenant in paragraph 7 relating to that debt.

(*b*) A debt purchased by us is an approved debt if

    (i) at the time of our acceptance a credit line for the customer owing the debt has been established by us and notified to you in writing, and the debt or part of it comes within such credit line, to the extent that it comes within it; or

    (ii) we give you written notice that we approve the debt or part of it to the extent of the amount approved.

Provided that an approved debt will become an unapproved debt if

    (i) you are in breach of any warranty or covenant in paragraph 8(a) relating to the debt;

    (ii) the customer disputes payment of the debt or any part of it for any reason and you do not promptly issue a credit for the amount in dispute.

    (iii) we withdraw our approval of the debt, which we may do at any time before delivery of the goods or performance of the services to which it relates.

(*c*) If we have not notified you of a credit line for a customer at the time that you receive an order from that customer, you will promptly request us in writing to establish a credit line, or, if it is sufficiently urgent, you may make your request by telephone.

4. Purchase Price of Debts

We shall pay you the Purchase Price of every purchased debt on the Average Maturity Date, except that if you require it we may at our discretion pay you any portion of the Purchase Price, normally to a maximum of 80% thereof, before the Average Maturity Date.

5. Notice of assignment

You agree to endorse on the original and every copy of each invoice relating to a purchased debt a notice in the following form or in such other form as we may from time to time notify you in writing.

"The debt arising under this invoice has been assigned to and is payable only to ABC Factors Ltd., 1 Prudence Lane, London, E.C.3, whose receipt is the only valid discharge. If this invoice is not found to be correct in all respects ABC Factors Ltd. must be notified immediately."

continued/ . . .

6. Collections from Customers

(*a*) We and our assigns will have the sole and exclusive right of collecting and enforcing payment of every debt offered to us by you and you will not, except at our request, be concerned in or attempt the collection of any such debt.

(*b*) You agree, if so requested by us, to co-operate to procure such collection and enforcement, and agree that for such purpose we and/or our assigns may institute and conduct legal proceedings in your name and that we shall have full control of such proceedings.

(*c*) You will immediately notify us of and deliver to us any payment, whether in cash or by cheque or other negotiable instrument, which you receive from a customer in or towards payment of any debt purchased by us and you will not deal with, mark, endorse or otherwise interfere with any such negotiable instrumentl Until so delivered you will hold in trust for us any such payment.

(*d*) If a customer makes either to us or to you a general payment on account of his or its indebtedness, whether or not arising under this agreement, to either or both of us and makes no appropriation of such payment, it will be appropriated first towards approved debts and secondly towards unapproved debts, and if it exceeds the amount so appropriated we will, subject to any deductions which we are entitled to make, immediately pay you the amount of such excess. Any such general payment received by you will immediately be notified to and delivered to us in accordance with the last preceding sub-paragraph.

7. Credits

(*a*) You will give us written notice of any credit which you allow a customer immediately after allowing it and you will issue and attach a copy of the credit note to the notification. We will have the right to require you to obtain our approval before allowing a credit.

(*b*) We will have a right of recourse to you in respect of any such credit which you allow.

8. Warranties and Covenants

(*a*) You warrant and covenant with respect to each debt purchased by us:

(i) that the contract between you and your customer under which the debt arises is valid binding and enforceable according to its terms;

(ii) that you have fully performed your obligations under the agreement giving rise to the debt and that the debt has not been disputed by the customer and is a bona fide obligation of the customer and arises in the ordinary course of your business;

(iii) that the customer has not repudiated, rescinded or claimed damages in respect of the contract under which it arises or made a counterclaim or claimed a right of set-off;

(iv) that we shall obtain and at all times continue to possess a good

continued/ . . .

unencumbered title to the debt with priority over any interest or claim of any other party in or to the debt;

(v) that all information, reports and other papers and data furnished to us (including details of every offer submitted by you under paragraph 1) are accurate and correct in all material respects and complete;

(vi) that you shall not without obtaining our prior written consent waive or modify any terms of the contract which gives rise to the debt except as provided by paragraph 7.

(*b*) You also warrant and covenant with respect to each unapproved debt purchased by us and with respect to the unapproved part of each approved debt purchased by us:

(i) that it will be paid in full by its due date;

(ii) that the customer will at all times be able to pay the debt; and

(iii) that the customer will not commit an act of bankruptcy, commence to be wound up whether voluntarily or otherwise, cease to carry on business, draw a cheque which is dishonoured, call a meeting of or make an arrangement or composition with creditors, or permit a judgment to remain unsatisfied for seven days;

(iv) that no receiver of the assets of the customer shall be appointed nor shall any distress or execution be levied or threatened upon such customer's goods or premises.

9. Minimum Factoring Charge:

(*a*) If in any period of twelve months expiring on the anniversary of the date of this agreement, the total of all factoring charges paid in such period is less than the Minimum Factoring Charge you will pay us a sum equal to the deficiency.

(*b*) If upon termination of this agreement before the expiry of any such twelve month period for any reason other than our default, the total of all factoring charges paid in such period is less than the Minimum Factoring Charge you will pay us a sum equal to the deficiency.

10. Accounts

(*a*) We will maintain such accounts as we may consider appropriate and convenient to record these transactions.

(*b*) Within 15 days after the last day of each month we will send you a statement of account. Unless within a period of 10 days from receipt of any such statement you notify us in writing that you question all or any part of it, that statement will be deemed to be accurate.

(*c*) If any account delivered to you under this paragraph shows a balance due from you to us you will immediately pay that amount to us.

(*d*) We may at any time set off any amount due to us from you against any amount due from us to you.

11. Records, Information and Disclosure

(*a*) You will keep books of account, will permit us or our authorised

continued/ . . .

representative at all reasonable times to inspect such books and any other documents in your possession, custody or control relating to any debt and will deliver to us free of charge all or any of such documents, or copies thereof and copies of all relevant entries in such books when requested to do so by us.

(*b*) Not later than three months after the end of each of your financial years you will cause a proper audit to be completed of books of account of your Company and related companies in relation to that financial year and a copy of the audited accounts, the auditors' and directors' report to shareholders, as required by law, to be forthwith delivered to us.

(*c*) You agree to supply us with monthly, quarterly or interim financial statements relating to your business and the business of any parent subsidiary co-subsidiary or other related business in such form and at such times as we may reasonably require.

(*d*) You will at all times, whether before or after the sale of a debt, disclose to us all matters of fact and opinion known to or held by you or your servants or agents concerning the credit worthiness of customers and the validity of the debt and will assist us in every way to safeguard our interest.

(*e*) You will notify us in writing immediately and, where possible, in advance:

(i) of any change in the terms upon which you usually contract or have contracted for the supply of goods, the carrying out of work or the performance of services; and

(ii) of the happening of any event referred to in paragraph 8 or tending to affect any warranty or covenant in that paragraph.

(*f*) You will immediately upon learning thereof report to us reclaimed, repossessed or returned merchandise, customers' claims and disputes and any other matter affecting debts.

(*g*) You will give us prior written notice of any financial obligation, conditional or otherwise, which you enter into with anyone other than trade creditor.

(*h*) There is no existing charge or other encumbrance on your assets other than whatever you have notified to us in writing, and you will not charge or otherwise encumber your assets in the future without giving us at least one week's prior written notice.

12. Assignments

You will whenever requested by us in writing so to do forthwith at your own cost execute, stamp and deliver to us a deed in a form approved by us assigning to us any purchased debt, together with the benefit of all guarantees or other securities for or in respect of the same and will, if requested by us, forthwith give notice in writing of any such assignment to any customer whose debt is thereby assigned.

13. General

(*a*) We have the sole and exclusive right to factor your debts and while

continued/ . . .

this agreement continues you will not without our prior written consent sell, encumber, assign or transfer any debt to any other person.

(*b*) No forbearance or indulgence granted by us to you or to any customer will in any way discharge you from your liabilities to us under this agreement or establish a precedent.

(*c*) You agree to indemnify and keep us idemnified against any claim of whatsoever nature by a customer against you.

(*d*) All costs paid or payable by us in respect of any claims or proceedings against any customer in respect of any unapproved debt shall be repayable by you to us and in any such claim or proceedings you will render us every assistance.

14. Retention on Termination

If this agreement is terminated by either party hereto under paragraph 15 we may retain any amount received by us in respect of any debt as security for the satisfaction of any financial liability on your part (whether accrued or not) arising under this agreement or under any contract for the purchase of debts by us.

15. Duration

(*a*) This agreement will continue in force unless and until determined by either of us giving to the other not less than three months' written notce to expire at, on or after the expiration of fifteen months from the date hereof.

(*b*) If you commit a breach of any term of this agreement we may terminate this agreement forthwith upon giving you written notice.

(*c*) Termination of this agreement will not affect any rights or obligations of either of us in relation to any debt purchased prior to such termination and the provisions of this agreement will continue to bind both of us so far and so long as may be necessary to give effect to such rights and obligations.

16. Power of Attorney

In consideration of 5p you hereby irrevocably appoint us as your attorney both during and after the termination of this agreement in your name and on your behalf to execute and do all documents and things required in order to give effect to the provisions of this agreement including (but without limiting the generality of the foregoing) the endorsement on your behalf of any negotiable instrument and the execution of a legal assignment or legal assignments of all or any debts which may from time to time be sold by you to us in pursuance of this agreement. We are hereby empowered to appoint and remove at pleasure any substitute or agent for ourselves in respect of all or any of the matters aforesaid.

17. Notices

Any notice of termination given by either of us to the other must either be delivered by hand to the party concerned or its authorised agent or sent by registered post or recorded delivery to such party at its principal place of business or its registered office. At the date hereof our registered office is 1 Prudence Lane, London, E.C.3.

continued/ . . .

18. Resolution of Board of Directors

You confirm that prior to your execution of this agreement your board of directors have passed a resolution that your company enter into this factoring agreement with us and that you may at your discretion agree to amendments hereto from time to time, that this resolution appears in the minutes of the meeting of the Board of Directors, and that you will provide us at the time of execution of this agreement with a copy of such resolution duly certified as true by the secretary or a director of your company.

19. Applicable Law

This agreement is to be governed by and construed in accordance with English Law.

APPENDIX

Definitions

1. "Average Maturity Date" means a date which we will notify to you from time to time calculated by averaging the dates upon which payment is to be received in respect of all debts purchased by us in a particular calendar month based on prior ledger experience.

2. "Customer" means any person, company or partnership to whom you supply goods or for whom you carry out work or perform services, whose principal place of business or registered office is in the United Kingdom, and who is not your parent, subsidiary or associated company.

3. "Debt" means an amount (whether or not presently due), stated on the invoice sent to the customer and notified to us at the time of your offer to sell it to us, which is due to you at the time of your offer for goods supplied, work done, or services performed including any discount which your customer may be entitled to deduct.

4. "Factoring Charge" means   % of a debt.

5. "Factor's Discount" means the sum calculated from day to day at whichever is the higher of   % per annum above XYZ Bank Ltd's base rate and   % per annum upon any Purchase Payments made to you before the average maturity date plus any amount which we lawfully debit to your account less collections, and approved debts which are uncollected on their Average Maturity Dates.

6. "Minimum Factoring Charge" means £   .

7. "Purchase Price" means the debt less the total of the factoring charge and the factor's discount in respect of the debt and any discount taken by the customer to which he is entitled.

Recourse Factoring Agreement

ABC FACTORS LTD.

To: (Client)   19

Dear Sirs,

We confirm the terms and conditions upon which we are willing to provide you with factoring facilities. If you are in agreement with these terms and conditions will you please execute under your seal the acknowledgment and appointment at the foot of this letter and the enclosed copy and return both to us. Definitions of terms appearing in this letter are contained in Appendix 1.

1. Offers

(*a*) You agree to offer to sell to us upon the terms and conditions of this agreement all *debts* from time to time owing to you by your *customers,* and to complete and deliver to us at least once during each week (or during such other period as we may from time to time together agree) an *offer* substantially in the form set out in Appendix II hereto, or in such other form in substitution therefor as we may from time to time reasonably require.

(*b*) Every *offer* will:

- (i) offer to sell to us every *debt* not previously offered to us;
- (ii) be accompanied by the original and one copy of each invoice relating to each *debt* the subject of the *offer*, together with such evidence as we may require of the delivery of the goods, the carrying out of the work or the performance of the services in respect of which each *debt* has been incurred;
- (iii) be accompanied by particulars of credits granted to a *customer* and not previously notified to us and the original and one copy of every credit note issued in respect of those credits;
- (iv) be on the terms and conditions of this agreement;
- (v) remain open for acceptance by us at any time in respect of all or any of the *debts* not already purchased notwithstanding our despatch of a notice of non-purchase in respect thereof.

2. Acceptances

(*a*) In relation to any *debt* offered to us acceptance will be constituted by our despatching a cheque to you on account of the *purchase instalment* or will be deemed to be constituted by our not despatching to you a notice of non-purchase in relation to the *debt* within 8 days from the first working day after our receipt of your *offer*.

(*b*) We may accept an *offer* orally in respect of all or any of the *debts* to which the *offer* relates.

(*c*) Upon our acceptance of any *offer* all your interest in the purchased *debts* and all remedies for enforcing the same, including without limitation of the foregoing any right or lien, stoppage *in transitu* or other rights arising in your favour as unpaid seller in relation to any goods in respect of which the purchased *debts* have been contracted, shall vest in us.

3. Payments to you

We shall pay you the *purchase price* of every purchased *debt* by paying you the relevant *purchase instalment* and *collection instalment* as follows:

(*a*) The *purchase instalment* will be paid to you on the next *remittance day* after your offer provided that it is the subject of an *offer* received not later than 10 a.m. on the previous working day, otherwise on the following *remittance day*; in a case where notice of non-purchase is despatched to you and we decide subsequently to purchase the *debt*, on the next *remittance day* after our decision to purchase.

(*b*) *Collection instalments* will be paid to you on the next *remittance day* after their receipt by us, provided they are received not later than 10 a.m. on the previous working day, otherwise on the following *remittance day*.

4. Notice of assignment

You agree to endorse on the original and every copy of each invoice relating to a purchased *debt* a notice in the following form:

"The debt arising under this invoice has been assigned to and is payable only to ABC Factors Ltd., 1 Prudence Lane, London EC3 1ZZ, whose receipt is the only valid discharge of the debt. If this invoice is not found to be correct in all respects ABC Factors Ltd. must be notified immediately."

5. Collections from customers

(*a*) We and our assigns will have the sole and exclusive right of collecting and enforcing payment of every *debt* offered to us by you and you will not, except at our request, be concerned in or attempt the collection of any such *debt*.

(*b*) You agree, if so requested by us, to co-operate to procure such collection and enforcement, and agree that for such purpose we and/or our assigns may institute and conduct legal proceedings in your name and that we shall have full control of such proceedings.

(*c*) You will not at any time deliver any original or copy invoice, credit note or receipt in relation to any *debt* offered to us direct to a *customer* but you will deliver all such invoices, credit notes and receipts to us.

(*d*) You will immediately deliver to us any payment, whether in cash or by cheque or other negotiable instrument, which you receive from a *customer* in or towards payment of any *debt* offered to us and you will not deal with, mark, endorse or otherwise interfere with any such negotiable instrument. Until so delivered you will hold in trust for us any such payment received in respect of a purchased *debt*.

(*e*) If a *customer* makes either to us or to you a general payment on account of his or its indebtedness, whether or not arising under this letter, to either or both of us and makes no appropriation of such payment it will be appropriated first towards such indebtedness in respect of purchased *debts*, secondly towards the discharge of financial liability (if any) on your part arising from obligations incurred by you under this agreement, and the balance (if any) will be appropriated in such manner as you may determine. Any such general payment will immediately be delivered to us, and if it exceeds the amount so appropriated by us we will immediately pay you the amount of such excess.

(*f*) You will not, without obtaining our prior written consent, waive or modify any of the terms of a contract with a *customer* giving rise to a purchased *debt*, and in particular, but without in any way detracting from the generality of the foregoing, you will not extend the time for payment or give credits or customer discounts. Upon giving our written consent to a credit or customer discount in respect of a purchased *debt* on which the *purchase instalment* has been paid by us, you will reimburse us with   % of the amount of such credit or customer discount.

6. Unpurchased debts

(*a*) In consideration of our agreeing to collect payments due from *customers* in respect of unpurchased *debts*, you will pay us (i) the *factoring charge* in respect of all such *debts*; (ii) such *refactoring charge* (if any) as would be payable under paragraph 10 (b) if the *debt* had been a purchased *debt*.

(*b*) We will remit to you on *remittance days* the net proceeds received by us of any unpurchased *debt* after deduction of the *factoring charge* and any *refactoring charge* payable in respect thereof.

(*c*) The *factoring charges* in respect of unpurchased *debts* will become due to us from you on despatch of our notice of non-purchase.

7. Accounts

(*a*) We will maintain such accounts as we may consider appropriate and convenient to record these transactions.

(*b*) We may at any time set off any amount due to us from you against any amount due from us to you.

(*c*) Within 15 days after the last day of each month we will send you a statement of account. Unless within a period of 10 days from receipt of any such statement you notify us in writing that you question all or any part of it, that statement will be deemed to be accurate.

(*d*) If any account delivered to you under this paragraph shows a balance due from you to us you will immediately pay that amount to us.

8. Records, information and disclosure

(*a*) You will keep books of account, will permit us or our authorised representative at all reasonable times to inspect such books and any other documents in your possession, custody or control relating to any *debt* and will deliver to us free of charge all or any of such documents, or copies thereof, and copies of all relevant entries in such books when requested to do so by us.

(*b*) Not later than three months after the end of each of your financial years you will cause a proper audit to be completed of books of account of your Company and related companies in relation to that financial year and a report thereof to be forthwith rendered to us.

(*c*) You will at all times, whether before or after the sale of a *debt*, disclose to us all matters of fact and opinion known to or held by you or your servants or agents concerning the credit worthiness of *customers* and the validity of the *debt* and will assist us in every way to safeguard our interest.

(*d*) You agree to supply us monthly, quarterly or interim financial statements relating to your business and the business of each subsidiary in such form and at such times as we may reasonably require.

(*e*) You will notify us in writing immediately and, where possible, in advance:—

    (i) of any change in the terms upon which you contract for the supply of goods the carrying out of work or the performance of services; and

    (ii) of the happening of any event
        (a) tending to affect the warranties contained in paragraph 9(*a*); or
        (b) described in paragraph 9(*c*) or paragraph 10.

(*f*) You will immediately upon learning thereof report to us reclaimed, repossessed or returned merchandise, *customers'* claims and disputes and any other matter affecting *debts* whether purchased or unpurchased.

(*g*) You will give us prior written notice of any financial obligation, conditional or otherwise, which you enter into with anyone other than a trade creditor.

(*h*) You will at all times keep us informed of and provide us with specimen signatures of all persons authorised to sign on your behalf *offers* and other documents relating to this agreement.

(*i*) You will disclose to us any existing charge on your assets prior to making an *offer* under paragraph 1 and not permit any further charge to be made on your assets without our prior consent in writing.

9. Warranties, recourse and covenants

(*a*) Every contract arising from our acceptance of any *offer* made by you to sell us any *debt* will be deemed to include the following warranties given by you:

    (i) that the contract between you and your *customer* under which the *debt* arises is valid binding and enforceable according to its terms;

    (ii) that you have fully performed your obligations under any agreement giving rise to the *debt* and that the *debt* has not been disputed by the *customer* and is a *bona fide* obligation of the *customer* to you and arises in the ordinary course of your business;

    (iii) that the amount payable by the *customer* in respect of the *debt* will be not less than the book value of the *debt*;

(iv) that the *customer* is not and will not be entitled to any counter-claim, set-off or defence against you in respect of the *debt* and that you do not know and would not on reasonable enquiry know of any facts likely to lead to any such counter-claim, set-off or defence

(v) that we shall under the contract obtain a good unencumbered title to the *debt*, subject to no prior sale, assignment, transfer or encumbrance;

(vi) that the *customer* from whom the *debt* is owing has not sought to repudiate or rescind the contract;

(vii) that you have not agreed with the *customer* for any extension of the contractual time for payment of the *debt* or for any waiver or modification of the terms of contract except as provided for in this agreement;

(viii) that all information, reports and other papers and data furnished to us (including details in every *offer* submitted by you under paragraph 1) are accurate and correct in all material respects and complete;

(ix) that each *customer* shall pay the full amount payable in respect of each *debt* by the *due date*.

(*b*) If there be any breach of any of the above nine warranties in relation to any purchased *debt* you will reimburse us with the excess of any *purchase instalment* and *collection instalment* paid to you in relation to such *debt* plus the *factoring charge* over the amount paid to us by the *customer*.

(*c*) Covenant:

You covenant and agree in each contract for the sale of a *debt* to us that you will not without our prior written consent at any time sell, assign, transfer or encumber any *debt* purchased under such contract other than to or in favour of us.

10. Repurchase and refactoring charges

(*a*) If:

(i) any *customer* shall dispute the validity of or the amount payable in respect of a purchased *debt*; or

(ii) any *customer* shall institute proceedings to rescind or claim damages for the breach of any contract under which a purchased *debt* arises; or

(iii) any *customer* shall not pay the full amount payable in respect of a purchased *debt* by the *due date*; or

(iv) any *customer* makes a counter-claim or set-off in answer to a claim for a purchased *debt*; or

(v) without obtaining our prior written consent you waive or modify any terms of the contract with the *customer* which gives rise to a purchased *debt*; or

(vi) you commit a breach of any term of the contract with a *customer* under which a purchased *debt* arises; or

(vii) you commit a breach of any term of this agreement or of any contract arising from acceptance of an *offer*; or

(viii) any *customer* who has not fully paid all his *debts* sold to us, enters into liquidation whether compulsory or not, commits any act of bankruptcy, ceases to carry on business, draws a cheque which is dishonoured, calls a meeting of creditors, makes an arrangement or composition with creditors or permits a judgment to remain unsatisfied for seven days; or

(ix) a receiver of any such *customer's* assets shall be appointed; or

(x) any distress or execution is levied or threatened upon any goods or premises of any such *customer*;

we may in our discretion at any time after such event without limitation of other rights available to us hereunder give you written notice requiring you to repurchase our interest in any *debt* owed to us by such *customer* which we have purchased from you and upon receipt of such notice you will be bound to purchase that interest from us and in consideration therefor shall forthwith pay to us the excess of the *purchase instalment* (and *collection instalments* if any) paid to you in relation to such *debt* plus the *factoring charge* over the total amount received by us in or towards settlement of the *debt* together with all other charges due to us under this agreement in respect thereof and upon such payment being made, and upon receipt of your written request, we shall at your expense reassign the *debt* to you.

(*b*) Where any *customer* has not paid to us the book value of a purchased *debt*   calendar months after the *due date* we may, in lieu of exercising our rights under paragraph 10(*a*) and without prejudice to those rights, make a *refactoring charge* in respect of that *debt* or any part thereof until paid. So long as we do not exercise such rights you agree to pay us such *refactoring charge* which will become payable on the first day of each month which next follows the month end in respect of which it is calculated.

11. Factoring charges

(*a*) If in any period of 12 months expiring on the anniversary of the date of your acknowledgment of your agreement with this letter the total of all *factoring charges* payable has not amounted to   you will pay to us a sum equal to the deficiency.

(*b*) If upon termination of this agreement for any reason other than our default the total of all such *factoring charges* either:—

(i) has not amounted to   ; or

(ii) since the latest anniversary of the date of your acknowledgment of this agreement has not amounted to a sum calculated at the rate of   per annum,

whichever is the greater, you will pay to us a sum equal to the deficiency.

12. Assignments

You will whenever requested by us in writing so to do forthwith at your own cost execute, stamp and deliver to us a deed in a form approved by us assigning to us any purchased *debt*, together with the benefit of all guarantees or other securities for or in respect of the same and will if requested by us forthwith give notice in writing of any such assignment to any *customer* whose *debt* is thereby assigned.

13. General

(*a*) Agreement of this letter will grant us the sole and exclusive right to factor your *debts* and while this agreement continues you will not without our prior written consent sell, encumber, assign or transfer any *debt* to any other person.

(*b*) No forbearance or indulgence granted by us to you or to any *customer* will in any way discharge you from your liabilities to us under this agreement or establish a precedent.

(*c*) You will by returning the acknowledgment of this letter agree to idemnify and keep us indemnified against any claim of whatsoever nature by a *customer* against you.

(*d*) You will whenever requested by us in writing so to do forthwith reimburse to us all credit investigation and collection expenses which in our opinion are excessive.

(*e*) All costs paid or payable by us in respect of any proceedings instituted against any *customer* in respect of any *debt* shall on demand be repayable by you to us and in any such proceedings you will render us every assistance.

14. Retention on termination

(*a*) If this agreement is terminated by either party hereto under paragraph 15(*a*) or if we become entitled to terminate this agreement pursuant to paragraph 15(*b*) (whether or not the agreement is so terminated) we may retain any amount received by us in respect of any *debt* (whether such *debt* is a purchased or unpurchased *debt*) as security for the satisfaction of any financial liability on your part (whether accrued or not) arising under this agreement or under any contract for the purchase of *debts* by us.

(*b*) The amounts so retained shall become due and payable by us to you only when and to the extent to which we will by virtue of such contracts have received in the aggregate more than the total of the amounts previously paid by us to you thereunder together with all other amounts due to us from you in respect of those contracts.

15. Duration

(*a*) Subject to paragraph 15(*b*) this agreement will continue in force unless and until determined by either of us giving to the other not less than three months' written notice to expire at, on or after the expiration of fifteen months from the date hereof.

(*b*) We may upon giving you written notice terminate this agreement forthwith upon:

    (i) your doing any of the things mentioned in sub-paragraphs 10(*a*) (v), (vi), (vii) or (viii); or

    (ii) the occurrence to you, your assets, goods or premises of any of the events mentioned in sub-paragraphs 10 (ix) or (x); or

    (iii) our obtaining judgment against you; or

    (iv) your using any payments made by us to you otherwise than in the ordinary course of your business.

(*c*) Termination of this agreement will not affect any rights or obligations of either of us in relation to any *debt* purchased prior to such termination and the provisions of this agreement will continue to bind both of us so far and so long as may be necessary to give effect to such rights and obligations.

16. Power of attorney

In consideration of 1s. (5p) you hereby irrevocably appoint us as your attorney both during and after the termination of this agreement in your name and on your behalf to execute and do all documents and things required in order to give effect to the provisions of this agreement including (but without limiting the generality of the foregoing) the endorsement on your behalf of any negotiable instrument and the execution of a legal assignment or legal assignments of all or any *debts* which may from time to time be sold by you to us in pursuance of this agreement. We are hereby empowered to appoint and remove at pleasure any substitute or agent for ourselves in respect of all or any of the matters aforesaid.

17. Notices

Any notices to be given by either of us to the other must either be delivered by hand to the party concerned or its authorised agent or sent by registered post or recorded delivery to such party at its principal place of business or at its registered office. At the date hereof our registered office is 9, Queen Street, London, E.C.4.

18. Applicable law

This agreement is to be construed and governed in accordance with English law.

Appendix I

Definitions

1. "Collection instalment" means   per cent. of each payment received by us from a *customer* in or towards settlement of a purchased *debt*.

2. "Customer" means any person to whom you supply goods or for whom you carry out work or perform services.

3. "Debt" means an amount (whether or not presently payable) which is due to you at the time of your *offer* for goods supplied, work done or services performed, and in calculating the book value of a *debt* any reduction agreed between you and your *customer* and any discount which your *customer* is entitled to deduct upon prompt payment are excluded.

4. "Due date" means the last day of the month following the month in which a *debt* is incurred (or such other day we as may together agree).

5. "Factoring charge" means   per cent. of the book value of a *debt*.

6. "Factor's discount" means the sum calculated from day to day at whichever is for the time being the greater of   per cent. per annum above XYZ Bank Base Rate and   per cent. per annum upon the excess for the time being of:

the total of the *purchase instalment* and every *collection instalment* paid to you by us in respect of a purchased *debt* plus the *factoring charge*: over

the total amount received by us in or towards settlement of the *debt*. (See also note below.)

7. "Offer" means an offer of *debts* made by you to us in accordance with paragraph 1.

8. "Purchase instalment" means   per cent. of the book value of a purchased *debt* less the *factoring charge*.

9. "Purchase price" in relation to a *debt* means the book value of the *debt* less the total of the *factoring charge* and the *factor's discount* in respect of the *debt*.

10. "Refactoring charge" means a sum calculated from month to month at the rate of   per cent. per month on that part of a *debt* which is unpaid   months after the *due date*.

11. "Remittance day" means the day or days in each week as agreed between us from time to time; or, in any week in which that day is not a business day, the next following business day.

NOTE

We may in our complete discretion and in such manner as may be convenient to us reduce the *factor's discount* in relation to all purchased *debts* by giving at any time an allowance in respect of (*a*) any period between receipt by us of payments in or towards settlement of unpurchased *debts* and payment of such sums to you and (*b*) any period during which payments received by us in or towards settlement of a purchased *debt* exceed the total of the *purchase instalment,* the *factoring charge* and any *collection instalment* paid to you in respect of the *debt*.

APPENDIX II

Offer

ABC FACTORS LIMITED,   (*Date*)
1 Prudence Lane,
LONDON EC3 1ZZ

We hereby offer to sell you on the terms and conditions of our current Factoring Agreement with you the *debts* particularised herein.
Signed for and on behalf of   :

[*Authorised signatory.*]

IN WITNESS whereof this agreement is duly executed the day and year first above written:—

THE COMMON SEAL OF
was hereunto affixed in the presence of:

Director,

Secretary.

THE COMMON SEAL OF ABC FACTORS LIMITED was hereunto affixed in the presence of:

Director.

Secretary.

RESOLUTION

Extract from the Minutes of a meeting of the Board of Directors of

held at

on the   day of   19

It was resolved that the Company enter into a Factoring Agreement with ABC Factors Limited in the form of the print produced to the meeting and that the seal of the Company be affixed thereto.

CERTIFIED THAT THE ABOVE IS A TRUE COPY of the Resolution and that it relates to the within contained agreement.

Director

Secretary.

APPENDIX IV

Credit Approval Request

20 February, 1974.

To: ABC FACTORS LIMITED
From (Client):   JOHN WAYNE (PLASTIC COWBOYS) LIMITED

Re Customer (name): PETER DENNIS (PROMOTIONS) LIMITED
        (address): GREENSTREET GREEN
                FARNHAM, KENT

Order No.	155
Amount of order	£500
Terms	Net monthly
Delivery date	At once
References (or other information)	———

FACTOR ONLY TO WRITE IN THIS SPACE

Subject to the terms of our factoring agreement, we

☐   approve a credit line of £50

☐   approve the above order

☐   approve £   of the above order

☐   decline to approve the above order or a credit line.

Reason:

21 February 1974.   ABC FACTORS LIMITED
                                    By: I. M. A. WISEMAN

Daily Credit Information Sheet

DAILY CREDIT INFORMATION FOR 30.AUG.74

CLIENT	CUSTOMER		CREDIT LIMIT		BALANCE	
0018	034801	MICKEY MOUSE STICKERS LTD.,	10,000	01.12.72	19,328.82	EXCEEDS LIMIT
0018	037219	SNOW WHITE AND COMPANY	0		59.25	EXCEEDS LIMIT (NEW)
0018	038574	JOHN SHAFT ENTERPRISES	0		0.00	NOW WITHIN LIMIT
0018	058230	PONT AND TRAP LTD.,	4,001	30.11.72	25.11	NOT NOW WITHIN 15%

197

Credit Factoring Limited–Statement of Account

Smith House, P.O. Box 50, Elmwood Avenue, FELTHAM, Middlesex TW13 7QD.   Telephone : 01-890 1390

FOR PURCHASES FROM: XYZ CO. LTD.

PAGE No.   1

Statement Address

Invoice Address

R.S.T. LTD
DEAN WORKS
DEAN
SURREY
GU17 0DD

R.S.T. LTD
DEAN WORKS
DEAN
SURREY
GU17 0DD

000

SUPPLIER NUMBER	ACCOUNT NUMBER
000 00060	7362XN18

BRANCH/ORDER NUMBER	TRANSACTION				GOODS/SERVICES AMOUNT
	CODE	NUMBER	DATE	DUE DATE	
	552	27143	25JAN74	28FEB74	2308.00
	552	27145	25JAN74	28FEB74	350.00
	552	27207	31JAN74	28FEB74	204.93
	552	27210	31JAN74	28FEB74	350.00
	552	27214	31JAN74	28FEB74	1442.50
	552	27255	07FEB74	31MAR74	38.28
	552	27263	07FEB74	31MAR74	87.50
	552	27293	08FEB74	31MAR74	1731.00
	552	27295	08FEB74	31MAR74	46.64

CODES 502 CREDIT NOTE   646 CREDIT MEMO   676 UNPAID CHEQUE
       552 INVOICE   670 DEBIT MEMO   677 CASH REFUND
       631 CREDIT ADJUSTMENT   673 DEBIT ADJUSTMENT   679 SHORT PAYMENT
       632 DISCOUNT ALLOWED   674 DISCOUNT DISALLOWED 707 ON ACCOUNT PAYMENT

THIS STATEMENT TAKES ACCOUNT OF ALL PAYMENTS RECEIVED BY US UP TO STATEMENT DATE

Statement of Account

Telex : 22593

DATE   14 FEB 74

NOTICE OF ASSIGNMENT

The indebtedness shown on this statement has been assigned by your Supplier to Credit Factoring Limited. Only we can give a valid discharge for the indebtedness. Any claims or queries must be referred to Credit Factoring Limited quoting your account number.

FOR IMPORTERS

For each imported item exceeding £5,000, please send with your remittance the Exchange Control copy of the Customs Entry.

If this statement is in a currency other than sterling, please note we have authority from the Bank of England under reference C/1067 EC 714/G.4 to accept foreign currency payments from United Kingdom residents in respect of imports provided the foreign currency has been sold to you by an authorised bank in accordance with the terms of Notice EC 53. The relative invoice should be shown to your bank when you request the foreign currency.

Credit Factoring Limited

Smith House, P.O. Box 50, Elmwood Avenue,
FELTHAM, Middlesex TW13 7QD.
Telephone: 01-890 1390   Telex: 22593

PAGE No.   1   DATE   14 FEB 74

PLEASE INDICATE ITEMS YOU ARE
PAYING [✓] AND RETURN THIS
ADVICE WITH YOUR REMITTANCE

SUPPLIER NUMBER	ACCOUNT NUMBER
000 00060	7362XN13

CODE	OTHER CHARGES (NOT SUBJECT TO DISCOUNT)	TOTAL
1	230.80	2538.80
1	35.00	385.00
1	20.49	225.42
1	35.00	385.00
1	144.25	1586.75
1	3.83	42.11
1	8.75	96.25
1	173.10	1904.10
1	4.66	51.30

LINE No.	TRANSACTION NUMBER		TOTAL
1	27143		2538.80
2	27145		385.00
3	27207		225.42
4	27210		385.00
5	27214		1586.75
6	27255		42.11
7	27263		96.25
8	27293		1904.10
9	27295		51.30

1 TAXES
2 POSTAGE/FREIGHT **TOTAL**   7214.73
3 RETURNABLE CONTAINERS
4 MISCELLANEOUS

IF PAYING BY   £   7214.73
CREDIT TRANSFER
PLEASE USE FORM ON REVERSE

Statement

IMPORTANT RETAIN THIS SIDE FOR YOUR RECORDS

SUPPLIER JOHN WAYNE (PLASTIC COWBOYS) LTD,
VAT REGISTRATION NUMBER 233 8022 89

TO MICKEY MOUSE ENTERPRISES
57 SOUTHWARK ROAD,
LONDON N.19

TERMS OF PAYMENT
MONTHLY A/C

PAGE 1

REFERENCE 0016/031084

DATE 18.JUL.73

DATE	INV./REF.	DESCRIPTION	GOODS/SERVICE	VAT	TOTAL	CR
29.05.73	018027	INVOICE	105.89		105.89	
30.05.73	SH/PM1	SHORT PAYMENT	2.50		2.50	
31.05.73	SH/PM2	SHORT PAYMENT	0.59		0.59	
31.05.73	017971	INVOICE	269.99		269.99	
		MAY			378.97	
14.06.73	018236	INVOICE	156.06		156.06	
21.06.73	018376	INVOICE	108.00	10.53	118.53	
		JUNE			274.59	
		TOTAL OUTSTANDING			653.56	

Remittance Advice

Return This Side

ABC Factors Ltd.

Cheques are payable only to

XYZ Bank Ltd 29 Queen Street London EC4P 4DB
Credit transfers to
Sorting Code: 70—09—05
Account No: 000—04210

PAGE 1

REFERENCE 0016/031084

18.JUL.73

Show any allowances claimed
Tick items paid
Use this column for any items in dispute

INV./REF.	AMOUNT	DES	✓
018027	105.89	INV	
SH/PM1	2.50	S/P	
SH/PM2	0.59	S/P	
017971	269.99	INV	
018236	156.06	INV	
018376	108.53	INV	
	653.56		

Remittance Advice
Return This Side

Cheques are payable only to
ABC FACTORS LIMITED, 1 Prudence Lane, London E.C.≡

Credit transfers to
XYZ Bank Ltd. 29 Queen Street, London EC4P 4DB

PAGE 3
0010/015624
09.FEB.73

SORTING CODE 70 - 09 –05
ACCOUNT No. 000 - 042≡0

Show any allowances claimed
Tick items paid

Use this column
for any items
in dispute

INV./REF.	DES	✓	AMOUNT
019230	INV		51.89
019231	INV		15.64
019293	INV		11.18
019294	INV		11.17
019384	INV		37.60
019385	INV		57.76
019386	INV		12.52
FEB 73			197.76
TOTAL			1969.58

Reminder
of Overdue Account

ABC FACTORS LIMITED

SUPPLIER John Wayne (Plastic Cowboys) Ltd.,

PAGE 3

REFERENCE 0010/015624

TO
OLD HILL SEATING CO. LTD.,
WATERFALL LANE, TRADING ESTATE,
CRADLEY HEATH, WARLEY, WORCS.

DATE 09.FEB.73

TERMS OF PAYMENT: MONTHLY A/C

REMINDER

ABC Factors Ltd. wish to draw your attention to the fact that outstanding invoices due on or before the date of the last statement remain unpaid.

We shall be glad therefore if all overdues, details of which are shown opposite, are settled immediately.

Cheques are payable only to ABC Factors Ltd., and should be sent to the above address together with the attached remittance advice.

Please return the remittance advice if payment is made by Credit Transfer.

If there is any reason why payment cannot be made immediately, will you please contact quoting the above reference.

S. R. HAYES

Remittance Advice

Return This Side

Cheques are payable only to
ABC Factors Ltd., Prudence Lane, London E.C.3
Credit transfers to
XYZ Bank Ltd. 29 Queen Street London EC4P 4DB

Sorting Code: 70—09—05
Account No: 000—04210

PAGE 1
0078/012345
20.JUL.73

Show any allowances claimed
Tick items paid
Use this column for any items in dispute

INV./REF	AMOUNT	DES	✓
000737	106.29	INV	
000871	55.66	INV	
001105	37.95	INV	
APR.73	199.90		
001127	796.95	INV	
001145	60.72	INV	
000011	219.45CR	C/N	
MAY.73	638.22		
001187	174.90	INV	
000073	194.33CR	C/N	
000079	18.63CR	C/N	
JUN.73	38.06CR		
TOTAL	800.06		

ABC FACTORS LTD.

SECOND

Reminder
of Overdue Account

PAGE 1

REFERENCE 0078/012345

DATE 20.JUL.73

SUPPLIER JOHN WAYNE (PLASTIC COWBOYS) LTD
VAT REG NO. 456 2894 75

TO
PETER DENNIS (PROMOTIONS) LTD,
GREENSTREET GREEN,
FARNHAM. KENT.

TERMS OF PAYMENT: MONTHLY A/C

SECOND REMINDER

We are concerned to note that invoices due on or before the date of the last statement still remain unpaid.

A reminder letter has been sent to you previously in respect of the invoices giving details of all overdue amounts.

We must ask you to clear these arrears without further delay, or telephone if there is any reason whatsoever for withholding payment. For your convenience we again give details of all overdue items.

When making payment please:

(1) Make cheques payable to and send them to the above address together with the remittance advice, or

(2) if payment is made by Credit Transfer send the remittance advice to us duly completed so that payments can be allocated correctly.

PLEASE GIVE THIS YOUR URGENT ATTENTION

Notice of Dispute

ABC FACTORS LTD.

To: JOHN WAYNE (PLASTIC COWBOYS) LTD.
           WESTERN WAY
           IDAHO
           SUSSEX

Re: PETER DENNIS (PROMOTIONS) LTD.
           GREENSTREET GREEN
           FARNHAM
           KENT

Invoice No: 155   Date: 2 January 1974   Amount: £205

We are advised by your customer that payment of the above invoice is not being made because:

> Contract specifications not met. Customer claims it ordered 1″ plastic cowboys but received 3″ plastic cows.

If customer is correct, please issue credit at once; otherwise, kindly advise on the enclosed duplicate what steps you have taken to adjust dispute.

Very truly yours,
ABC FACTORS LTD.

By: I. M. A. WISEMAN

Recourse Notice

ABC FACTORS LTD.

DO NOT SEND CREDIT MEMO
....

1 March 1974

Charge Back To: John Wayne (Plastic Cowboys) Ltd.
Western Way
Idaho, Sussex

Credit To: Peter Dennis (Promotions) Ltd.
Greenstreet Green
Farnham, Kent

In accordance with our right of recourse to you under our agreement we have today charged the amount detailed below against your account:

Reason: Dispute, credit not issued.

INVOICE	AMOUNT	INVOICE NO.	INVOICE	AMOUNT	INVOICE NO.	DISCOUNT
28 Nov 74	100.00	345				
			TOTAL		£100.00	

ABC Factors Ltd.

By: I. M. A. Wiseman

TO: ABC Factors Ltd.
      Prudence Lane, London E.C.3

SCHEDULE OF ACCOUNTS

FROM: John Wayne (Plastic Cowboys) Ltd.
        Western Lane
        Idaho
        Sussex

1   Client No.   6   13 14

| 0 | 0 | 0 | 0 | 3 | 4 |

Customer NAME		Customer No.					
	7						12
Peter Dennis (Promotions) Ltd., Greenstreet Green, Farnham, Kent.	0	2	8	5	3	6
Ministry of Funny Walks, Funny Walk, London	0	2	8	9	2	5

In accordance with the terms of our agreement, we hereby offer to assign

the above debts to you.

John Wayne (Plastic Cowboys) Ltd.
BY: H. I. LOW

1 2   13 14

| 0 | 0 |

Offer to Assign Debt

```
          27        30
         | 0 | 1 | 0 | 0 |
```

	Invoice Date / Number										
15	Date					Number					26
2	1	0	2	7	4	0	0	0	5	8	1
2	1	2	2	7		0	0	0	5	8	2

Invoice Amount				
31		Amount		38
2	0	0	2	0
2	8	4	9	9

```
  27      30 31      Total      38 39
 | 9 | 9 | 0 | 1 |  |  | 4 | 2 | 9 | 5 | 1 | 9 | D |
```

207

AGE LISTING AS AT 28 FEB. 74

TERMS B 3 IEEI

CLIENT 0034 JOHN WAYNE (PLASTIC COWBOYS) LTD.,

CUSTOMER 028925 MINISTRY OF FUNNY WALKS   CREDIT LIMIT 10,000 REVIEWED 31 DEC. 1973

REFERENCE		DESCRPTN COMMENTS	FEBRUARY	JANUARY	DECEMBER	NOVEMBER	OCTOBER	SEPTEMBER +
29 NOV. 73	000532	INVOICE				94.93		
10 JAN. 74	000554	INVOICE		430.60				
17 JAN. 74	000563	INVOICE		181.16				
31 JAN. 74	000572	INVOICE		184.99				
21 FEB. 74	000582	INVOICE	46.12					
** B 937.80 90+ 94.93 FWD 0.00			46.12	796.75	0.00	94.93	0.00	0.00

CUSTOMER 028536 PETER DENNIS (PROMOTIONS) LTD.,   CREDIT LIMIT 10,000   REVIEWED 31 JAN. 1973

REFERENCE		DESCRPTN COMMENTS	FEBRUARY	JANUARY	DECEMBER	NOVEMBER	OCTOBER	SEPTEMBER +
17 OCT. 73	000496	INVOICE					93.20	
3 NOV. 74	SH/PMI	SH. PMT RETENTION				14.94		
17 NOV. 74	000559	INVOICE				159.16		
21 JAN. 74	CASH	U/A CASH NO R/ADVICE		100.20				
24 FEB. 74	CASH	U/A CASH	27.40					

Age Listing

TERMS B 3 IEEI

SUMMARY OF DEBTORS AS AT 13 JAN. 74

CLIENT 0010 PETER PAN (TOURS) LTD.

		90+	FWD	JANUARY	DECEMBER	NOVEMBER	OCTOBER	SEPTEMBER	AUBUST +
GROSS RECEIVABLES	B 244062.58	29051.40	215.19	107641.61	68700.22	38454.16	14494.39	7048.01	7509.00
		11.90%	0.08%	44.10%	28.14%	15.75%	5.93%	2.88%	3.07%
NON INVESTMENT ITEMS	B 1006..26	8741.71	0.00	0.00	206.49	1113.06	1618.93	3463.37	3659.41
		3.58%	0.00%	0.00%	0.08%	0.45%	0.66%	1.41%	1.49%
NET INVESTMENT	B 234001.32	20309.69	215.19	107641.61	46493.73	37341.10	12875.46	3584.64	3849.59
		8.32%	0.08%	44.10%	28.06%	15.29%	5.27%	1.46%	1.57%

209

Credit Factoring Limited–Summary of Debts Purchased

CLIENT No.	CLIENT NAME AND ADDRESS	ACCOUNT	MONTH ENDED
00-00060	XYZ PRODUCTS LIMITED BEST ADDRESS LANE EVERYWHERE SURREY	(A) DEBTS PURCHASED £ STERLING	14 FEB 74
		VAT REGISTRATION No.	DOCUMENT No./PAGE
		222-4520-09 VAT RATE 10.000%	0001372/01

ENTRY DATE	DUE DATE	CODE	TRANSACTION ITEM	REF. No.	AMOUNT DEBIT	AMOUNT CREDIT
26NOV73	03FEB74	553	MATURED DEBTS	00001827	8107.82	8107.82
17DEC73	14FEB74	553	MATURED DEBTS	00001828	34543.16	34543.16
18DEC73	17FEB74	552	SCHEDULE OF OFFER	00001829		3215.87
18DEC73	25FEB74	552	SCHEDULE OF OFFER	00001830		6368.18
28DEC73	07MAR74	552	SCHEDULE OF OFFER	00001831		10305.31
08JAN74	19MAR74	552	SCHEDULE OF OFFER	00001832		4532.63
15JAN74	25MAR74	552	SCHEDULE OF OFFER	00001833		6820.58
22JAN74	01APR74	552	SCHEDULE OF OFFER	00001834		9657.64
26JAN74	05APR74	552	SCHEDULE OF OFFER	00001835		9089.75
05FEB74	15APR74	552	SCHEDULE OF OFFER	00001836		8126.35
12FEB74	22APR74	552	SCHEDULE OF OFFER	00001837		6704.34
			TOTAL		42650.98	107471.63
			NET BALANCE			64820.65

SMITH HOUSE, P.O. BOX 50, ELMWOOD AVENUE, FELTHAM, MIDDLESEX, TW13 7QD. REGISTRATION NUMBER 662221. ENGLAND

Credit Factoring Limited–Client Account

CLIENT No.	CLIENT NAME AND ADDRESS		ACCOUNT	MONTH ENDED
00-00060	XYZ PRODUCTS LIMITED BEST ADDRESS LANE EVERYWHERE SURREY		(B) CLIENT ACCOUNT £ STERLING	14 FEB 74
			VAT REGISTRATION No.	DOCUMENT No./PAGE
			222-4520-09 VAT RATE 10.000%	0001373/01

ENTRY DATE	DUE DATE	CODE	ITEM	REF. No.	DEBIT	CREDIT
31JAN74		000	BROUGHT FORWARD	00000000	64002.89	
03FEB74		553	MATURED DEBTS	00001827		8107.81
05FEB74		103	SERVICE CHARGE	00001836	138.15	
05FEB74		102	DISCOUNT CHARGE	00001836	241.56	
05FEB74		190	VAT CHARGE	00001836	13.82	
05FEB74		101	PAYMENT TO CLIENT	00001313	3200.00	
05FEB74		502	CREDIT NOTE LISTING	00008214	53.35	
07FEB74		101	PAYMENT TO CLIENT	00001343	5000.00	
08FEB74		675	FACTOR'S CREDIT NOTE	00000733		43.62
12FEB74		103	SERVICE CHARGE	00001837	113.97	
12FEB74		102	DISCOUNT CHARGE	00001837	199.29	
12FEB74		190	VAT CHARGE	00001837	11.40	
13FEB74		101	PAYMENT TO CLIENT	00001051	4600.00	
14FEB74		553	MATURED DEBTS	00001828		34543.16
			TOTAL		77574.43	42694.60
			NET BALANCE		34879.83	
			TOTAL SERVICE CHARGE		252.12DR	
			TOTAL VAT CHARGE		25.22DR	
			TOTAL DISCOUNT CHARGE		440.85DR	
			INTEREST CREDIT		0.00DR	
			INTEREST ADJUSTMENT		0.00DR	
			TOTAL CASH DISCOUNTS		0.00DR	

THIS STATEMENT WILL BE ACCEPTED BY H.M. CUSTOMS AND EXCISE AS A TAX INVOICE FOR THE SALE OF OUR FACTORING SERVICES TO YOU

SMITH HOUSE, P.O. BOX 50, ELMWOOD AVENUE, FELTHAM, MIDDLESEX, TW13 7QD. REGISTRATION NUMBER 662221. ENGLAND

Index

A

ACCOUNTANCY,
practice compared with financial analysis, 47
valuation of assets, reliability, 53

ACCOUNTING METHODS,
agreement specimen, clauses in, 174–175, 182, 188
client accounting procedures, 82–83
customer accounting procedures, 81
set-off clauses in agreements, 182, 188

ACID TEST RATIO, 56

ADVANCE,
definitions and usage, 8

ADVANCE FACTORING,
balance sheet of client, effect on, 17
benefit assessment, table, 23
financial accommodation in, 156
financial strength of client, importance, 46–47
guarantees etc., effect of availability, 63
payment practices, 7–8
percentage paid to client, 14

ADVANCE PAYMENTS,
in confidential factoring, 11
in supplier guarantee factoring, 10

ADVERTISING,
by moneylenders, 155
consumer credit business, 158–159

AGED ANALYSIS OF DEBTS,
balance sheet liabilities examination, 53
client provided with, 22–23
customer accounting procedure, 81–82, 208

AGENT,
authority, apparent and usual, 94
client as—
  in confidential factoring, 11
  in invoice discounting, 25
customer's solicitor as, 132
factoring agreement execution, 93
law of agency applied to factors, 93
mercantile. *See* MERCANTILE AGENT
of client, status, 93–94
usual authority, 94

AGENT FACTOR,
bill of exchange, use of, 31
colonial America, in, 33
colonial trade, role in, 32
credit factoring origins, in, 34
English factors abroad, 32
English history of, 30–33
historic origins, 30
lien of, 143
McKinley tariff, effect of, 34
mediaeval cloth industry, in, 31

AMERICA,
North. See NORTH AMERICA

AMERICAN UNIFORM COMMERCIAL CODE, 159

APPROVAL OF DEBTS,
standard conditions clauses, 170–171

APPROVAL OF ORDERS,
client's shipment without, 75
credit man's functions, 76
factor's procedures, 73–76
withdrawal, factor's right, 41, 75

ASSETS,
balance sheet, presentation in, 48
current—
  definition, 48
  items included as, 48
  prepaid costs as, 48
fixed—
  depreciation, 52
  items included, 52
  replacement cost, 52
intangible—
  construction, 53
  valuation treatment, 53
life insurance on business officers, 51
liquid, definition, 56
marketable investments, 49

ASSIGNABILITY, 109

ASSIGNEE,
legal proceedings powers, 135
mortgagee, as, 123
priority determination—
  competition between several, 137
  mortgage, assignee as, 123

Printed by Billing & Sons Limited,
Guildford and London